FRIENDS OF A KIND

A Circle of Acquaintances
Who Defined
How We Remember
the Great War

MATTHEW MILLS STEVENSON was born in New York City and grew up on Long Island. His university degrees are from Bucknell and Columbia universities, and he spent a year abroad with the Institute of European Studies in London and Vienna. He moved to Geneva, Switzerland, in 1991. He is a contributing editor to *Harper's Magazine* and has worked professionally in finance and investing. His essays and reporting have been published in many magazines, including, most recently, in *CounterPunch*. He is the author of many  books, including *Reading the Rails*, *Appalachia Spring*, *The Revolution as a Dinner Party* (about China throughout its turbulent twentieth century), and *Biking with Bismarck*, about the Franco-Prussian wars and the Treaty of Versailles. His recent books are *The View From Churchill*, an introduction to Churchill's extraordinary life, and *Our Man in Iran*, an account of travels across the Islamic Republic.

Why is he known as the Cycling Historian? As this extract shows, he gains his inspiration to write by visiting, often on this folding Brompton bicycle, the places where the men and women he writes about have made history. Here he writes:

"Every time I thought I was near to a stopping point, I unearthed another piece of the literary puzzle that sent me scurrying toward a village in France (Festubert comes to mind) or somewhere in the English Midlands (such as where Wilfred Owen's father worked in Shrewsbury when the poet was in his teens). I went about four times with my bicycle to the Western Front in France, and each time after I left I discovered that I had missed some important piece of the interlocking story."

His email address is matthewstevenson@sunrise.ch

His website is: www.matthewmstevenson.com

FRIENDS OF A KIND

A Circle of Acquaintances
Who Defined
How We Remember
the Great War

A winding journey by bicycle and train across
England, Ireland, Scotland, France, and the Hejaz
in search of T. E. Lawrence, Siegfried Sassoon,
Robert Graves, John Buchan, Joseph Conrad,
Erskine Childers, Winston Churchill, Raymond
Asquith, Wilfred Owen, Lady Ottoline Morrell,
Edward Marsh, and Rupert Brooke.

MATTHEW MILLS STEVENSON

Marble Hill London

First published in 2025 by Marble Hill Publishers
Flat 58 Macready House
75 Crawford Street
London W1H 5LP
www.marblehillpublishers.co.uk

© Matthew Mills Stevenson 2025

Matthew Mills Stevenson has asserted his right to be identified as the author of this work in accordance with the Copyright, Designs and Patents Act 1988.

All rights reserved.

No part of this book may be reproduced or transmitted in any form or by any means, electronic, mechanical, recording or otherwise, without prior written permission of the copyright owners.

A CIP catalogue record for this book is available from the British Library.

ISBN: 9781738497089
E-ISBN: 9781068360800

Typeset in Adobe Caslon Pro
Printed and bound by IngramSpark
Copy editor: David Aretha
Text and cover design by Paul Harpin

CONTENTS

Preface   xi

I. T. E. Lawrence (of Arabia)   1
   Wool, England: On the road
   Clouds Hill: At home with Aircraftman Shaw   4
   Bovington: Lawrence's last ride   7
   Moreton: Across Thomas Hardy's Egdon Heath   9
   Lawrence: A prince of our disorder   11
   To Arabia: The young Lawrence   14
   Seven Pillars of Hollywood   20
   Wessex Tales on the Bike   25
   Hardy's Dorchester: The return of the outsider 28

II. Siegfried Sassoon Rides to the Guns   33
   The Train to Frome
   Mells: The great war in modern memory   35
   Weirleigh and the Weald of Kent: To the hounds 37
   The Unquiet Western Front: Siegfried's journey 42
   Heytesbury's Sassoon: A country gentleman   46
   Sassoon and Lawrence: Postwar friends   48
   Warminster: Trainspotting memoirs   51

III. Robert Graves: Hello to All That   57
   With Siegfried Sassoon
   Graves at Charterhouse   61
   Graves, Lawrence, and Rory Stewart   64

IV. Across the Lawrence Desert in Saudi Arabia   69
   The Legend Grows in Aqaba
   A Theoretical Route into Saudi Arabia   75
   The Wadi Rum Stage Set   77
   A Frozen Desert Border   79
   The Hejaz City of Tabuk   81
   The Closely-Watched Bus to Medina   84
   A High-Speed Haj   87
   Seaside Jeddah on the Red Sea   89
   A Lawrence Cruise to Yenbo   91
   The 1921 Cairo Conference Imagines Lines in the Sand 94

CONTENTS

V. The John Buchan Way — **101**
    Oxford: Unravelling Lord Tweedsmuir
    Buchan After the Great War — 106
    Elsfield Manor, Oxford: At home with the novelist — 109
    Peebles, Scotland: Tramping with Richard Hannay — 112
    Buchan and John F. Kennedy: Kindred spirits — 116

VI. Heart of Joseph Conrad — **121**
    Along the River Thames
    Sailing Toward Poland — 124
    Canterbury Tales — 128
    Conrad and Lawrence: Confluent shipwrecks — 131

VII. The Riddles of Erskine Childers — **137**
    Dublin
    England at Sea: Childers issues a warning — 140
    Childers and Lawrence: The making of Irish rebels — 142

VIII. Winston Churchill in the Trenches — **151**
    Plugstreet
    The 1914 Christmas Truce — 159
    Messines: Ireland on the Western Front — 162

IX. Graves and Sassoon Go To War — **165**
    Some Desperate Glory
    Lions Led by Donkeys — 168
    The Black Hole of Loos — 174
    Arras: A forlorn plan of attack — 177
    Craiglockhart War Hospital: The battle for Sassoon's soul — 183
    The Man Who Shot Sassoon — 189
    Belfast on the Somme — 192
    The Somme's Thiepval Monument: Site of mourning — 195
    Graves and Sassoon: Once More to Mametz Wood — 199
    Albert and the Road to Corbie — 204

X. Wilfred Owen's Long Road — **209**
    Coming of Age Near Liverpool
    Owen's Childhood: Woodside, Birkenhead, Shrewsbury — 211

CONTENTS

    The Making of the Modern Poet   213
    Owen Enlists   215

XI. Raymond Asquith: Friend to Many   219
    Echoes of War in Amiens Cathedral
    The British High Command at Château Querrieu   222
    The Red Baron Falls to Earth   225
    Sassoon's War Opera Box: Bois Français above the Somme   227
    The Death of Raymond Asquith   230
    A Dark Ride Toward the Hindenburg Line   234

XII. Wilfred Owen: The Last Footsteps   236
    The American Cut Grass at Bellicourt
    Joncourt: Owen's Military Cross   239
    Beaurevoir to the Maison Forestière Owen   242
    The Long Shadows Over the Sambre-Oise Canal   246
    An Owen Farewell   248

XIII. Rupert Brooke, Lady Ottoline Morrell, Sir Edward Marsh   253
    Defining the War
    On the Road to Birmingham and Coventry   255
    Remembering Rupert Brooke   257
    At Rugby School   260
    Back to Oxford and Garsington Manor   261
    Lady Ottoline Morrell's Drawing Rooms   263
    Sir Edward Marsh's Many Degrees of Connection   267
    Grantchester: Byronic summer days   271
    Gallipoli and the Distant Echoes of Troy   275

XIV. The Last Post   278
    War's End on Skyros

Acknowledgements   282
Copyright Permissions   287
The Cycling Historian   288
About the Bicycle   290
In Search of the Great War and its Writers   292
Index   294

LIST OF MAPS

The Home Fronts in England, Scotland, Wales and Ireland   viii
Writers at War in France   xi
Near East Battles   xiii

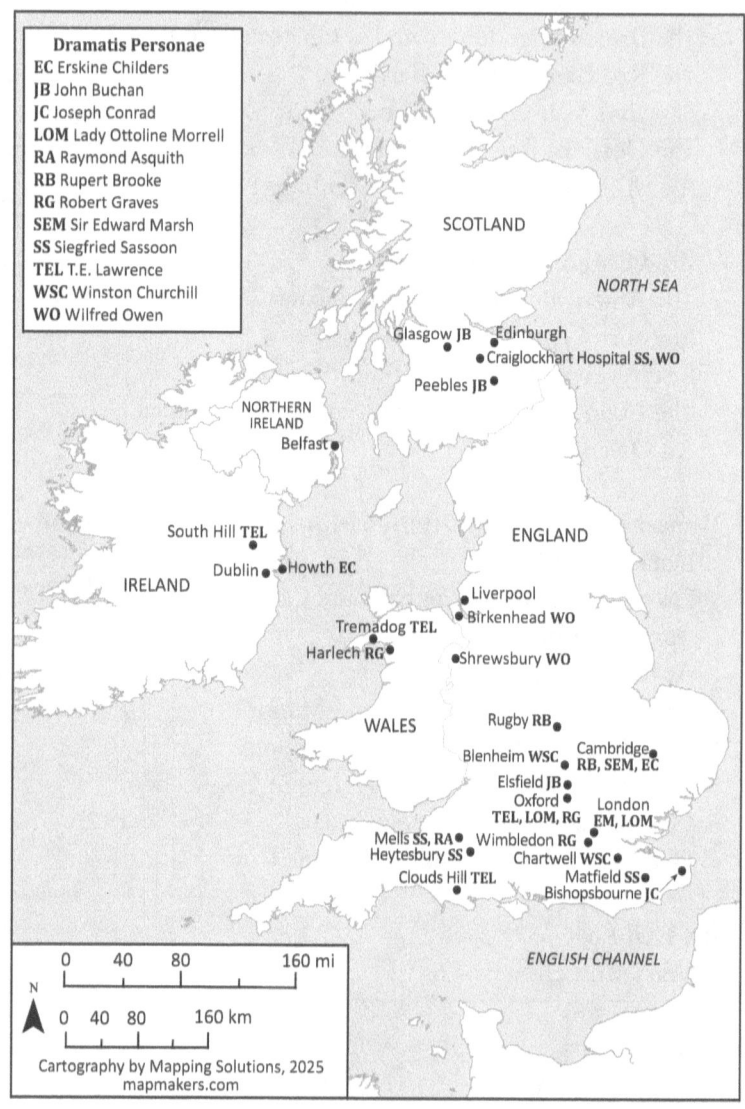

The Home Fronts in England, Scotland, Wales and Ireland

PREFACE

ONE WINTER BEFORE the Great Pandemic, I spent much of my time reading and thinking about a collection of mostly British writers and political figures, many of whom had endured battle at its worst in the Great War. In the corner of my home office, books about T. E. Lawrence (of Arabia), Siegfried Sassoon (*Memoirs of an Infantry Officer*), Robert Graves (*Good-Bye to All That*), John Buchan (*The Thirty-Nine Steps* and many others), and Erskine Childers (*The Riddle of the Sands*, an early spy novel) formed a growing pile.

With Lawrence, for example, I read not just several biographies of his life but also made it through his epic narrative, *Seven Pillars of Wisdom*, his account of desert warfare across the Hejaz and Palestine in World War I. In those books, I came across many Lawrences—the young, inquisitive archaeologist tramping across Syria; the celebrated guerrilla warrior of the desert; and finally the tortured soul who enlists, under several assumed names, as a private in the air force, to escape his celebrity.

So, too, did I come across a myriad of Siegfried Sassoons, who served with valour as a British infantry officer on the Western Front, including at the Somme, but then in 1917 denounced the war in poems, essays, and a well-circulated statement. There is the Sassoon of his poetry, the Sassoon of his many memoirs, and then the Sassoon of his personal life, which was yet another cabaret of the dissolute 1920s.

I found many of the same contradictions in the life of Erskine Childers, an Englishman who wrote eloquently, before World War I, about the potential threat of German militarism but who later was executed, for treason, for supporting the violent cause of Irish independence. Was it the war that changed all of these men or did each of them have a predisposition toward some kind of fatal eccentricity?

As I progressed with my reading—most of it done by the fireplace in the darkness of a Swiss winter—I discovered that many of these writers had been friends. I knew that Sassoon and Graves served in the same Welch regiment, but I learned that the connections overlapped in many other directions. After the war, for example, T. E. Lawrence got to know the decorated anti-war poet, Siegfried Sassoon, who when he first met the Arab officer was amazed that someone so young could have risen to the rank of colonel. (Although Sassoon fought in the Palestine campaign, he had not heard of Lawrence or his legend.) Both men later shared friendship with the novelist and poet Thomas Hardy. Likewise, both Lawrence and Sassoon had an association with Winston Churchill, who took Lawrence with him to the 1921 Cairo Conference and who memorised several of Sassoon's poems about the trenches. Sassoon, himself, remained leery about Winston and what he perceived as his militarism.

Churchill was well acquainted with Erskine Childers, both his warnings about the Germans (which at the time Churchill thought were overblown) and later his fifth-column activism for Irish independence (Churchill did nothing to keep Childers from facing a firing squad). And it turned out that John Buchan, who wrote many thrillers, including *Greenmantle*, about Arab nationalism and the Middle East, very much admired Lawrence, about whom he said: "I am not a very tractable person or much of a hero-worshipper, but I could have followed Lawrence over the edge of the world. I loved him for himself, and also because there seemed to be reborn in him all the lost friends of my youth."

When spring came and I tired of my fireside reading, I decided that these men would only come alive for me if I were to visit a few of the places in their lives—a house where they had lived or perhaps a battlefield on which they had fought. Already, in my travels, I had seen a number of places that were easy to associate with one man or another. In 2000, I had taken several members of my family to the British battlefields on the River Somme in northern France, and there had tracked down the town of Mametz, which is described at length in Sassoon's *Memoirs of an Infantry Officer*. I had also searched, at the British cemetery on Guillemont Road, for the headstone marking the grave of Raymond Asquith, the son of the then British prime minister, Herbert Asquith, and someone Buchan writes about at length in his memoirs, *Pilgrim's Way*. (I was interested in him as he was also the grandfather and namesake of my friend, Raymond Asquith, who is now the 3rd Earl of Oxford and Asquith.)

Similarly, on travels in the Middle East, beginning in 1985, I had—al-

PREFACE

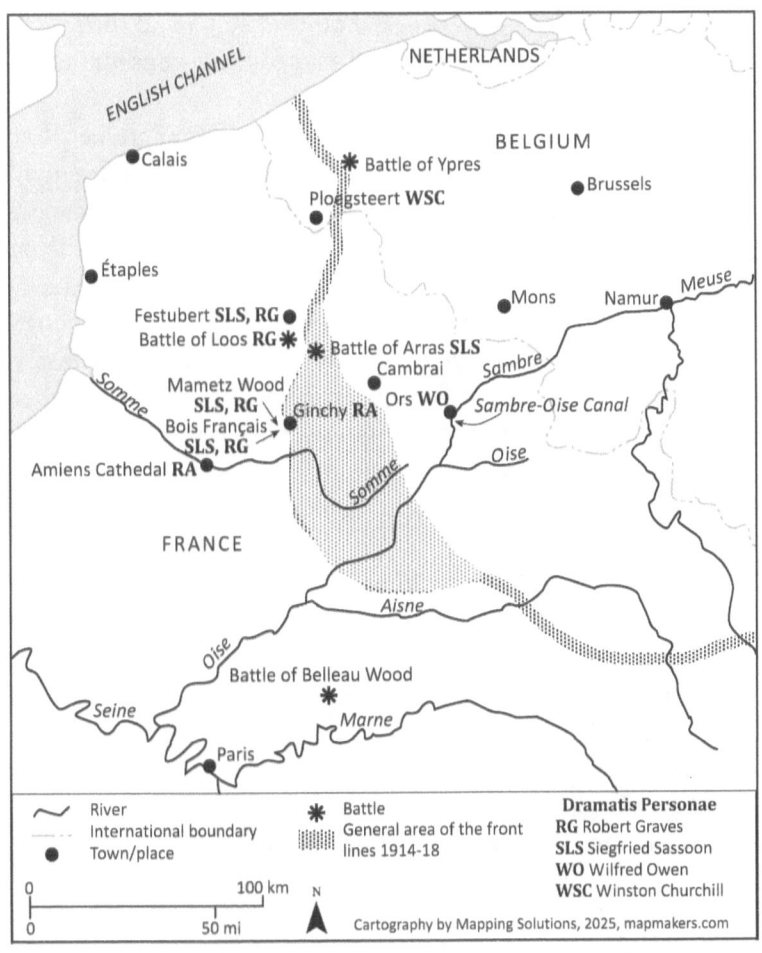

Writers at War in France

though in a casual manner—been to many of the places that are associated with Lawrence of Arabia. In 1985, my wife and I drove from Amman to Petra—where much of the action in *Seven Pillars* takes place—and in 2010 my son Charles and I retraced the steps that Lawrence took in 1909, when he walked across Syria to explore Crusader castles. But as I read about Lawrence, Childers, Buchan, and others I still found their presence remote and decided that I would try, as best I could, to connect more concrete dots from their hectic lives.

Using my collected books, several atlases, and the internet, I spent many evenings at my Geneva desk calculating how I might stitch together a trip that would make the lives of these writers more immediate. I began by plotting the coordinates of Clouds Hill, the cottage that was Lawrence's only home in the postwar years. I was drawn to the idea that someone as famous as Lawrence of Arabia had lived in a small bungalow cottage in Dorset, in what was essentially Thomas Hardy's Wessex, the setting for so many of his novels. Lawrence bought the cottage when he was serving in the air force (one of his bases was nearby), and he used the house for vacations and to entertain his friends, even though the house lacked a kitchen and a toilet (for that, there were the woods out the front door).

From Moreton—the village where Lawrence lived and is also buried—I figured out that I could easily take in Heytesbury, the manor house where Sassoon lived after his ill-fated marriage to Hester Gatty, and then (by train and bicycle) track down Sassoon's grave in the churchyard at Mells, a village twenty miles away. Finally, I decided that I could end up in Dublin, where *Asgard*, the gun-running yacht that belonged to Erskine Childers, is on display in the national museum.

I regretted that it would be impossible to detour to Peebles, the Scottish village where Buchan set so many of his stories along the River Tweed. But with luck I might develop a greater appreciation for Thomas Hardy, as Dorchester (Casterbridge in his fiction) would be on my route.

Once I had decided where I wanted to go, there remained the question of how to get there. As always, I first thought of trains and my bicycle. There is a Channel ferry from Cherbourg to Poole, near the Lawrence cottage. But that would have meant several days of travel just to get there,

PREFACE

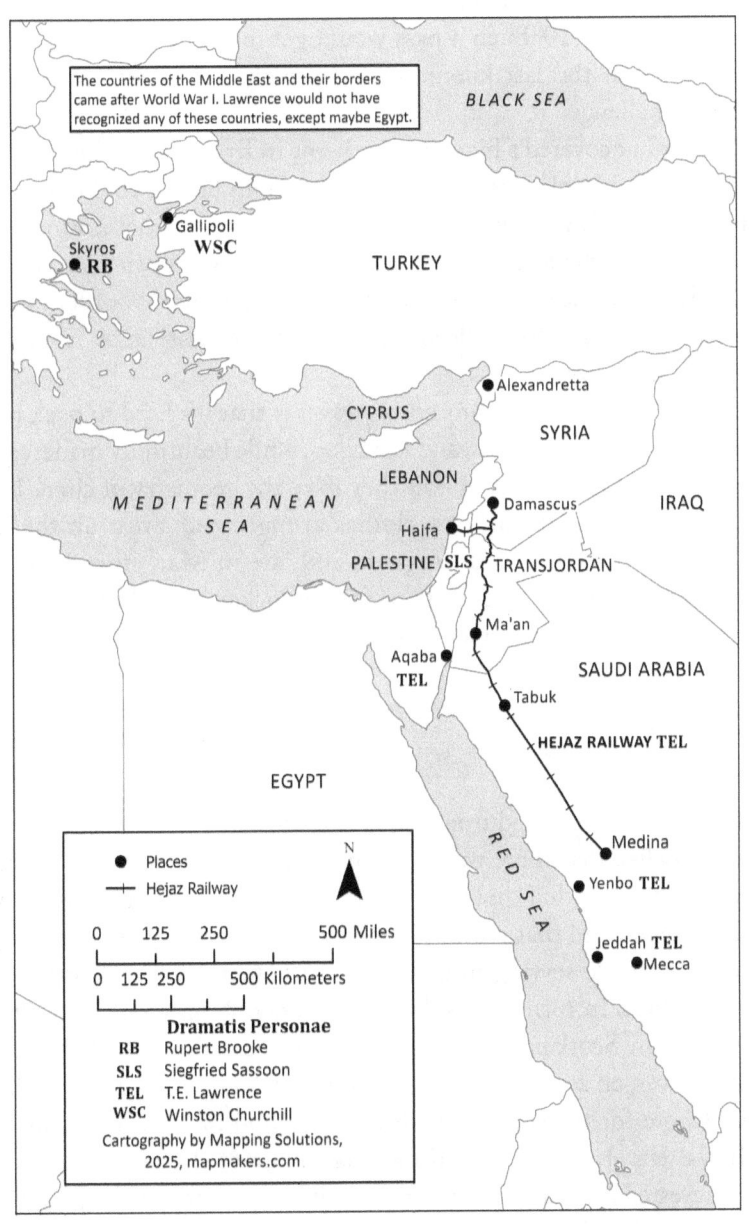

Near East Battles

and then my bicycle would have been stranded in England when I went to Dublin, either by plane or on the train ferry. Next I discovered that British rail offers what it calls a Southwest Pass, unlimited travel on regional trains for about £110. Such a pass would get me close to Clouds Hill or Mells, although the last kilometre—to use the broadband phrase—remained a challenge.

Finally I uncovered a bike rental scheme in Britain that hires out folding Brompton bicycles for £5 a day. With one in hand I could board any train in the Southwest (even the high-speed expresses that normally ban bikes) and from the local stations, I could bike to wherever I chose. Thus, Clouds Hill became a short ride (seven miles) from the Wool station, and I figured I could get to Mells and the Sassoon headstone by riding over some hills from Frome.

The only downside of Brompton travel is that it's hard to pack much more than a change of socks, and the bikes, while beautifully made, can be a challenge in the hills, given that they have the geometry of circus bikes. Figuring that I could wash my clothes at night and sweat up the hills, I enrolled in the Brompton program, and late in May, after flying into Gatwick, I retrieved a folding bike from a locker in Redhill and set off with my rail pass in the direction of Lawrence of Arabia, Thomas Hardy, and Siegfried Sassoon.

Only when I returned from the first of my rail-pass-and-bicycle travels did I realize that there was much more that I wanted to see. Visiting Sassoon's grave in Mells made me more curious about his friendship with Robert Graves, and that prompted me to investigate where the two writers had met while serving in the British Army on the Western Front of the Great War. In turn, that led me to wonder about Craiglockhart, the sanatorium in Scotland where Sassoon was treated for shell shock and where Graves, on a weekend visit, was introduced to the war poet Wilfred Owen (there for the same treatment as Sassoon). And it was only after my initial travels that I figured out that many of the poets and writers who interested me had something in common, not just to T. E. Lawrence and Thomas Hardy, but also to Winston Churchill and Joseph Conrad. Those associations pushed me to buy more biographies, and download more maps and timetables, so that I could make the connections between

PREFACE

Churchill and Sassoon or Lawrence and Conrad. I never saw this as a group of friends who would have gotten together for a meal or a long weekend in the country. At the same time I was surprised that so much of the literature closely associated with the Great War came from a circle of men who never had more than one degree of separation.

There were many sites still to see after my first exploration of the frontlines of World War I literature. On that initial trip to England and Ireland, I had missed, for example, where Robert Graves lived in Wimbledon or where he went to school at Charterhouse. Likewise, when I went to Oxford I had not known that John Buchan's home in Elsfield was just down the road from where Lawrence grew up on Polestead Road. On subsequent trips, I retraced many of my first steps and added to them with further travels around England, Ireland, Scotland, and northern France.

On most of these subsequent trips, instead of relying on rental bikes, I toted along my own folding Brompton bicycle, which is a great pleasure of the road (it gets me everywhere). And on my Kindle, I brought with me various literary guides and biographies. I cannot say that each stop was always a resounding success. When I finally rolled up to Craiglockhart, the front door was locked (it's now part of Edinburgh Napier University), and there seemed no way to get inside, until a hardworking student coming out of the building held the door open and pointed me in the direction of the War Poets Collection Exhibition, an excellent museum and library that has many first editions by World War I writers and poets. And only by an awkward alliance of trains, buses, and taxis was I able to find the suburban house where Joseph Conrad lived his last years in Bishopsbourne, a village outside Canterbury. There I discovered that he was close to Lady Ottoline Morrell, who was instrumental in persuading Sassoon to go public with his denunciations of the Great War. Likewise, on a visit to Magdalen College, Oxford, to look at T. E. Lawrence artefacts, I came across his friendship with (and biography by) Robert Graves, something that had escaped my attention on earlier travels.

Toward the end of my wanderings, I found the hardest challenge was figuring out where the road ended. Every time I thought I was near a stopping point, I unearthed another piece of the literary puzzle that sent me scurrying toward a village in France (Festubert comes to mind) or somewhere in the English Midlands (such as where Wilfred Owen's father worked in Shrewsbury when the poet was in his teens). I went about four times with my bicycle to the Western Front in France, and each time after I left I discovered that I had missed some important piece of the interlocking story.

The first time I went to Fricourt, on the Somme in France, I looked up at the Bois Français but missed where Sassoon had witnessed the first day of the battle (as if from the box seats at a violent opera). Then it took me two tries to find the spot between Ginchy and Lesbœufs where Raymond Asquith was killed in September 1916. (Asquith was close, in particular, to both John Buchan and Winston Churchill.) I felt as if my puzzle had neither a fixed number of pieces nor a picture on the box.

It did not help that many of the roads down which I was headed came to a dead end in the pandemic, which made it almost impossible, for more than a year, to go anywhere in Europe. For those months I was reduced to armchair traveling, but I have to confess that it provided many rewards and helped to get me through the shutdowns. On dark nights of the virus, I studied flights to places such as Liverpool and Manchester or train connections to Amiens and Ors (the nearest station is Le Cateau).

After dinner in front of the fireplace, I would endlessly flip from my computer to my maps and then back to my timetables, trying to work out all the connections; for example, to the world of Wilfred Owen. I could be lost in these travels for hours. I would study road gradients for biking; train connections to Paris or London; hotels that worked both for history and cycling; and books that I might read along the way. I know that the pandemic was a time of anxiety and sadness for many, but on the nights when I took to my imaginary roads, I found as much pleasure as I do from actual traveling. No matter how bleak were the headlines or dire the newscasts, whenever I was lost in my planning or reading, I had a clear view of distant horizons, and they gave me hope.

Only after I was done with most of the writing did I decide to end the book with one more visit to England and then another on the island of Skyros, where the poet Rupert Brooke is buried. He died there in 1915, when he was part of the Allied invasion fleet that was headed toward the fateful landing at Gallipoli. I decided to get to Skyros in a round-

PREFACE

about manner: by way of Brooke's schools in Rugby (where he grew up) and Cambridge (where he went to university). I also made brief stops at Garsington Manor, which is outside Oxford and which was the country retreat of Lady Ottoline Morrell, and at some of the London addresses of Sir Edward Marsh, who would have known most, if not all, the figures in this story. By day Marsh was Winston Churchill's private secretary; off hours, he was a patron of the arts and many poets, and he loved nothing more than to introduce his prized writers to each other.

For a long while I didn't think Rupert Brooke belonged in this story, as he did not overlap with many of the other characters. He never met Robert Graves, and only through Marsh was he introduced briefly to Sassoon at a large social function. (This was before the war and before Sassoon had found his voice as a poet.) Nor did Brooke ever meet T. E. Lawrence, and although he was once in the company of Thomas Hardy, they did not speak.

The more I thought about Brooke and his poetry, the more I came to believe that his work inspired a coming generation of poets and writers to record their impressions of the war. Even if he was not personally acquainted with some of the figures here, they were all well aware that his poetry had inspired their own writing (even if few of them wrote so sentimentally about the fighting). I began to think of Brooke as a transitional figure, without whom there might never have been the literary record that we have of the Great War.

Had she been French, Lady Ottoline Morrell would have been described as a *salonnière* for her social gatherings in London and at Garsington Manor. These attracted any number of writers, poets, artists, actors, and politicians. More important to this story is that it was at Garsington Manor that Sassoon reviewed his protest statement and decided to publicly denounce the war in summer 1917, an act that could have delivered him to a firing squad, had not Churchill's secretary, Sir Edward Marsh, intervened with his boss. By then Churchill himself was back from the trenches and understood the horrors an officer such as Sassoon had endured, and he (among others) arranged for Sassoon to be treated for shell shock in Scotland rather than shot at dawn.

For all of Marsh's contributions to the worlds of politics and the arts (he donated hundred of paintings to British art galleries all around the country), there's really no place to go in England to take stock of his life. In London, I managed to find some of his former addresses, but Marsh lived modestly, even if he did cover his apartments with original works of art that today, if still in his hands, would be worth millions.

At one point in my travels I figured out that a portrait of Sir Edward Marsh was hanging near Manchester at the Huddersfield Art Gallery. I wrote an email to the museum, asking for more details and to arrange a visit. The director kindly wrote back: "The gallery is currently closed for refurbishment and our collection (including this work) is in deep storage; unfortunately there is no public access to the collection at the moment (and for the foreseeable future). I have attached a high resolution version of the painting for you." So for Marsh, I largely had to make do with an internet photo.

If there is an unsung hero in this story, it is Sir Edward Marsh. He encouraged Graves (while still a schoolboy at Charterhouse) to carry on with his poetry, and it was Marsh who introduced Sassoon to Lawrence, and it was Marsh who knew Erskine Childers well from Cambridge and introduced him to both Sassoon and Churchill. Marsh corresponded with John Buchan. He also wrote an early biography (1922) of Rupert Brooke and was close to Raymond Asquith's sister. Beginning in 1905, Marsh worked with Churchill for years, in good times and bad. (He was not with him, however, in the trenches.) In this account he is the man for all seasons, who lived for his friends and for his country. Had he been along with me on these rides (I am not sure he was a cyclist), he would have known everyone at each stop and he would not have been surprised that all of them managed to convert their wartime hardships into art that has shaped our understanding of the Great War.

To my grandson

Raymond McArdle Stevenson

I hope you grow up loving some of the

things that I love:

trains, bicycles, and European history.

And to

Cole Harrop

Friend across two continents and many decades.

AFTER GRADUATION FROM Oxford University in 1910, **Thomas Edward Lawrence** ("of Arabia") worked on an archaeological dig at Carchemish, on what is now the Turkish-Syrian border, and there perfected his Arabic and developed an uncanny ability to relate to diverse Arab tribes, who he befriended on his overland walks across the Syrian desert. With the outbreak of war in 1914, his knowledge of the Arab world proved invaluable to British intelligence in Cairo. After 1916, as a liaison officer to the house of Saud, he led raiding parties against the crumbling Ottoman army and managed to capture Aqaba from the land side, mostly with irregular troops. *Seven Pillars of Wisdom* is both his memoir of the fighting (much of it raids against the Hejaz Railway) and a meditation on the politics of the Middle East.

Section I
T. E. LAWRENCE (OF ARABIA)

Wool, England: *On the road*

REDHILL IS AN industrial suburb of London, not far from Gatwick, which has been made over with Costa cafés and glass-faced office buildings. I was there long enough to retrieve the Brompton bicycle, mail a package, have morning coffee with my daughter (who was working there for an Asian and African development company), and catch a local train to Guildford that ran along the tracks of the Great Western Railway. The train was crowded, and I had to wedge the Brompton, which folds to the size of a suitcase, in between several bags and sit with my saddlebag propped in my lap. At Guildford, I changed to a train that was heading to Woking, where, after a wait, I caught another train headed southwest. It all took time and I didn't arrive in Wool until well into the afternoon.

At Wool station—little more than a country platform—I found a taxi parked out front and asked the driver if he would take me and the folded bike to Clouds Hill. His taxi was a minivan, with one woman and her small dog in the back seat. Instead of taking both of us to our destinations, the driver gave me a lecture about taxi etiquette, the upshot of which was that, if I was going to make it to the Lawrence homestead, I would have do so on the bicycle. At least I had printed out maps from the station to the house, and on the train I had memorized many of the crossroads, fearing that I might have to leg it to Clouds Hill.

Unfortunately, as I set out in the direction of the armor base at Bovington (it figures in many Lawrence biographies, related to his postwar service), it began to rain, and I lost precious time off the bike kitting myself out for the bad weather. I put on gloves, a jacket, and a rain hat the size of a fireman's helmet, and then continued to pedal with conviction, what in the Tour de France is called "pushing the big gear."

Brompton folding bikes are not racers, so I had time, despite my huffing, to take in Bovington, which as best as I could tell from the road is a camp set up to train tank crewmen and other armored vehicle servicemen. (Even as a private in ranks, Lawrence was a prescient militarist, and he believed in the future of the tank, as well as in aircraft.) I passed barracks and saw soldiers making their rounds on the base, which is behind a loose wire fence but otherwise open to the community.

Bovington had more the feeling of a boys' summer camp than the home of an armored division. Pedaling along the perimeter it was easy for me to imagine the days before and after D-Day in 1944 when it would have been a staging area for thousands of Allied soldiers heading to France. The Channel is so close I could smell the salt air and hear seagulls when at the right angle to the strong wind.

I knew that Clouds Hill was up the road from the Bovington base, but I stopped and asked another cyclist, just to be sure. He pointed to a crest in the road and said, "It's just after that." I wondered if perhaps that was the hill where Lawrence had his fatal motorcycle accident in 1935. (In the film *Lawrence of Arabia*, he is shown, in the first scene, crashing his bike on a narrow gravel lane, but this road was straight and paved.) Over the small hill and behind a hedgerow, I found Clouds Hill and pulled up to the small gift shop where they sold admission tickets.

The time was 4:56 p.m., and I explained to the staff on duty that while I knew the house closed at 5 p.m., I would be happy if all I could do was have a quick look around. (After all, the cottage is essentially two rooms.) Instead of allowing me a quick look, however, the guides on duty reverted to what George Orwell might call civilservantspeak, which involved a long story about how the Lawrence house closes at 5 p.m., how the work there is a grinding hell, and how the staff needed to go home and rest. I answered by explaining that I had left my home in Switzerland at 5 a.m., rented the Brompton in Redhill, and come here by train and bike via Portsmouth, all with the intention of writing something about Clouds Hill in a book. All that prompted was more whinging and the suggestion that I come back tomorrow.

By now, we had spent more time debating closing time than it would have taken for them to open the front door at Clouds Hill and show me the sitting room where Lawrence played records, entertained friends (including the Thomas Hardys), and corrected the proofs for *Seven Pillars of Wisdom*. But I gave up and, in frustration, took my bike helmet and threw it against a grassy embankment, as if I had just struck out in Little

League baseball. All I was allowed to do was have a quick look at the garden, which is nothing more than scattered woods. (Lawrence wasn't a gardener, and since the house had no toilet, he used the woods for other things.)

From the outside, Clouds Hill was slightly larger than I had expected. The walls were painted brick. I had thought it might look like a Maine seaside cottage; instead it is a featureless, square box of a house, set behind the hedges along the side of the road on which I had biked. The British National Trust has converted several outbuildings into a small exhibition center and a gift shop. Otherwise, the house is as Lawrence left it when in 1935 he went for his last ride.

While I was inspecting the woodshed and trying to figure out how I could ride twenty miles back and forth to the hotel to see the house the next day, a woman approached me, introduced herself as a member of the Lawrence family who was on the board of his foundation, and offered to show me around Clouds Hill once the overworked staff had departed. I didn't exactly catch her connection to Lawrence, but I came away with the impression that my savior was the granddaughter of a Lawrence stepsister (his father had another family of daughters before he ran off with the babysitter, who became T. E. Lawrence's mother). Lawrence himself was one of five boys (all by his father's second "wife"), but none of them had children. At that point, however, I wasn't listening carefully and was simply grateful that my guardian angel came with a key to the front door.

FRIENDS OF A KIND

Clouds Hill: *At home with Aircraftman Shaw*

TO SAY THAT I went on a "house tour" would be to exaggerate, as Clouds Hill only has a few rooms. Inside it does have the feel of a seaside cottage with a collection of old furniture, some worn art (including a portrait of Feisal, the Saudi prince of *Seven Pillars*), lots of books, and several fireplaces.

We started upstairs in the living room, which has the largest gramophone I have ever seen—its horn speaker could amplify a state fair. Apparently the record player was a gift to Lawrence from Mrs. George Bernard Shaw (Charlotte Frances Payne-Townshend), who had it shipped to Pakistan in 1928 when Aircraftman Shaw (a.k.a. Lawrence) was on duty in the subcontinent. From his letters she thought he needed some cheering up. Otherwise, the sitting room has high windows, old sofas and chairs, and the sense that Lawrence and his friends would have spent many hours here, perhaps on rainy days, reading books, listening to records, poking at the fire, and sipping tea.

Downstairs is Lawrence's bedroom. I was a bit surprised that he had a double bed. I had pegged him as someone who might have slept on an army cot, as many times in *Seven Pillars* he falls asleep on rocky desert or a station floor. The large bed takes up most of the room. All around on the walls are bookshelves filled with those small leather-bound volumes for which British publishing is famous. I had known that Lawrence studied history at Oxford and had worked in Syria as an archaeologist before the war, but I had not realized (although it should have been obvious from his writing) that he read so extensively. I recognized on the shelves many of the editions of his own writing, which I also have, although in his lifetime *Seven Pillars* had a limited distribution.

One thing that I found missing in the house was a writer's desk or typewriter. Nor was there even a corner of the bedroom or in the sitting room that he had walled off to do his writing. Clearly Lawrence was one of those writers who could compose wherever he happened to be, including on trains or in hotel rooms. For example, much of *Seven Pillars*, at least the first draft, was written while he was attending the Paris Peace Conference in 1919, although that manuscript was lost in the Reading railway station, when his briefcase was stolen or misplaced.

Lawrence took over the leasehold on Clouds Hill in 1923, and he lived there, on and off, while in the service until 1935. After that, he lived in the cottage full-time until his death several months later. When money came his way (usually from the sale of books or articles), he used it for home-improvement projects, the most notable being a boiler for hot water and a bathtub, which remains in an alcove near the front door. (If a toilet was later installed, I never saw one, and when I asked about such luxuries, the niece said Lawrence "used the woods" and made a shoveling gesture with her hand, which also implied that Beduoin habits die slowly.) The "kitchen" was the fireplace in Lawrence's bedroom, where it was easy to imagine guests toasting crumpets with those long, cast-iron forks that sit beside so many English fireplaces.

The best description of life at Clouds Hill comes from a Lawrence letter that Jeremy Wilson, his authorized biographer, unearthed while researching his life. It reads, with some of Wilson's notes:

> '...the cottage is alone in a dip in the moor, very quiet, very lonely, very bare... Furnished with a bed, a bicycle, three chairs, 100 books, a gramophone of parts, a table. Many windows, oak trees, an ilex, birch, firs, rhododendron, laurels, heather. Dorsetshire to look at. No food, except what a grocer and the camp shops and canteens provide. Milk. Wood fuel for the picking up. I don't sleep here, but come out at 4.30 p.m. till 9 p.m. nearly every evening, and dream, or write or read by the fire, or play Beethoven or Mozart to myself on the box. Sometimes one or two Tank-Corps-slaves arrive and listen with me...but few of them care for abstract things. If you came you would be very much alone all day....' 'Entry is made through the bathroom window on the ground floor at the back'. The cottage 'has no kitchen. You can boil tea and boil eggs, if you collect fuel... Food is bread: butter: jam: honey: reinforced by potted things: and things in tins. Beastly I call it.' The accommodation was basic: 'a bed with blankets and a mattress and sheets... Cottage consists of a sitting room and a bedroom (very small): and builders' men

are whitewashing an adjoining kitchen [now the bunk room], making it smell and reek and splash awfully.'

Finally, the 'Weather is Dorset weather: wind and rain: rain and wind: wind: rain: and so on.'

Leaving the house and walking with the niece to her car, we talked at length about the lack of a proper Lawrence library and memorial. I began the conversation by asking her if such a place existed, and she said no, although she mentioned that the Lawrence family home in Oxford at 2 Polestead Road was probably for sale and that the large townhouse not far from the university would make an ideal location for such a center. That reference led us to a discussion about the money needed for the venture, and she mentioned £4 million as the required amount to buy the house and to create a foundation that would run the museum and organize Lawrence conferences and the like.

Standing in the parking of Clouds Hill (all the outbuildings were now closed and the staff had scattered, no doubt happy to be done with me), I suggested that the family approach all the nations in the Middle East that Lawrence had a hand in creating, notably Jordan and Iraq (Syria and Lebanon came more from the watch of Messrs. Sykes and Picot). Certainly if any countries owed a debt to one man, Lawrence, it would be those. As he writes toward the end of *Seven Pillars*:

> There remained historical ambition, insubstantial as a motive by itself. I had dreamed, at the city school in Oxford, of hustling into form, while I lived, the new Asia which time was inexorably bringing upon us. Mecca was to lead to Damascus; Damascus to Anatolia, and afterwards to Bagdad; and then there was Yemen. Fantasies, these will seem, to such as are able to call my beginning an ordinary effort.

But I cannot see them stumping up for a Lawrence Centre. For the time being, they have their oil-producing countries, and Lawrence's heirs have a cottage.

T. E. LAWRENCE

Bovington: *Lawrence's last ride*

LEAVING THE PARKING lot at Clouds Hill, I was heading in the direction of Moreton and the village church where Lawrence is buried. But first I decided to retrace the skid marks of his fatal accident, as the niece said there was a marker in the woods indicating the place where he had crashed his motorcycle. She also said that Lawrence owned eight motorcycles in his lifetime and that the National Trust and Clouds Hill were trying to buy one of the few remaining bikes, to have it on display. It is owned by a local man, who sympathizes with the museum's interest in acquiring the bike. At the same time, she also mentioned that the American TV personality Jay Leno (of *Tonight Show* fame) had spent over $2 million to acquire other Lawrence motorcycles and likely he would get his hands on this one. I felt sad to think of the motorcycle, on which Lawrence might have died, locked up in a Hollywood garage so that stars could exclaim over it at garden parties, as opposed to having it on display in the wooden outbuilding at Clouds Hill, where it belongs.

As if a claims adjuster for a car insurance company, I spent more time than I should have trying to figure out how Lawrence had died. In the popular imagination (from the film and many biographies) he was returning to Clouds Hill from Bovington (along the road on which I had biked) and after cresting a small hill, he came upon two local boys on their bicycles in the road. They were not riding along single file but riding abreast and doing tricks on their bikes, as small boys are wont to do.

To spare them from an accident, Lawrence steered his bike into the woods lining the road. He did not die instantly but lingered for six days—at one point he seemed to be pulling out of his coma. When he died, he caused grief not just to his friends and family, but much of Britain. Winston Churchill was among those who wept when he was buried in Moreton.

The problem with the popular theory of Lawrence's fatal accident is that it makes no sense. The stretch of road where he crashed is on a straightaway, and, unless they bolted from the woods at the last minute, he would have seen the playing boys from a long distance. The hillock, which might have obscured the boys, is farther down the road, closer to Clouds Hill, but that's not where Lawrence crashed. So to me, his fatal accident

FRIENDS OF A KIND

is a mystery.[1] Maybe he was accelerating (he did love speed) on the flat stretch to push the bike to its limits? Maybe a tire blew at an inopportune moment? Maybe he was daydreaming on his way home and skidded? After all, he did write famously in *Seven Pillars*:

> All men dream: but not equally. Those who dream by night in the dusty recesses of their minds wake in the day to find that it was vanity: but the dreamers of the day are dangerous men, for they may act their dream with open eyes, to make it possible. This I did. I meant to make a new nation, to restore a lost influence, to give twenty millions of Semites the foundations on which to build an inspired dream-palace of their national thoughts. So high an aim called out the inherent nobility of their minds, and made them play a generous part in events: but when we won, it was charged against me that the British petrol royalties in Mesopotamia were become dubious, and French Colonial policy ruined in the Levant.

Lawrence was a dreamer "of the day."

---

[1] Several reporters and biographers have speculated that Lawrence was assassinated, perhaps for his emerging right-wing sympathies with Sir Oswald Mosley, leader of the British Union of Fascists. Some witnesses to his fatal accident spoke of a mysterious black car that was present and could well have run Lawrence off the road. I have no further evidence to any plots, but from the scene of the accident, a killing makes more sense than does the accepted story of the playing boys and a road accident.

T. E. LAWRENCE

Moreton: *Across Thomas Hardy's Egdon Heath*

I HAD TO use the compass on my phone to head in the right direction to Moreton, which is about three miles from Clouds Hill. At one point I picked up a walking trail sign for the village and decided to follow it, even though it led along a dirt road that was thick with mud and rainwater. I knew I could have stayed on the paved road, but I felt nervous riding in traffic with such a heavy mist on the ground. On a backroad, I felt I might get a firsthand impression of Egdon Heath, the bleak landscape that opens Thomas Hardy's equally depressing novel, *The Return of the Native*. He writes: "A Saturday afternoon in November was approaching the time of twilight, and the vast tract of unenclosed wild known as Egdon Heath embrowned itself moment by moment." (Monty Python used the same passage in a sketch called "Novel Writing from Dorset," to satirize cricket commentary.) In my case, I found what felt like a seaside pine forest that occasionally gave way to bogs and streams, and it was easy for me to imagine the time when the British Army used such a "vast track" to teach tankers how to maneuver around the simulated mud of trench warfare or the forests of the Rhineland.

Close to the village, I asked directions from a woman walking a dog, and she said I needed to turn left when I came upon a teahouse. I followed her instructions and shortly pulled up in front of an old stone church that was surrounded with headstones, many at odd angles that reflected the age of the marker, if not the moist soil.

Looking for Lawrence's grave, I hunted around the cemetery without success. Nor did I come across any tourist sign postings. The Moreton church might well be unchanged since Hardy wrote in *Far from the Madding Crowd*: "God was palpably present in the country, and the devil had gone with the world to town."

Tired of playing hide-and-seek with grave markers, I dug into my saddlebag and retrieved an article that explained Lawrence had been buried in Moreton but in a new cemetery, down the road from the old church. I made a few loops of the neighborhood on my bike and shortly found the right graveyard, which has a distinctly modern look to it.

Lawrence is buried at the back of the small walled cemetery, under a great slab of marble that takes note of his name and dates, and that he was a fellow at All Souls College, Oxford. His mother insisted that this be the only reference, so there is no mention "of Arabia" or any of his writings. Besides Churchill, Mrs. Thomas Hardy, and E. M. Forster, another mourner at his burial was the poet Siegfried Sassoon, whose contribution to the day was later to write a poem ("this legend mask of stone") about Lawrence; he also shooed away the press photographers who had followed the processional from the church to the graveyard.

Standing over the extensive slab of marble, I noticed that I was there on the eighty-first anniversary of his death, May 19, 1935. The coincidence explained why there were fresh flowers leaning against the marker and some handwritten messages. Otherwise, I was alone in the cemetery, encased in a fine mist and my own thoughts, when I recalled a passage in Robert Graves' *Good-Bye to All That*, which describes a meeting at All Souls when Lawrence was a fellow there. Later I looked it up, and it reads as follows:

> Lawrence's rooms were dark and oak-panelled, with a large table and a desk as the principal furniture. There were also two heavy leather chairs, simply acquired. An American oil-financier had come in suddenly one day when I was there and said: 'I am here from the States, Colonel Lawrence, to ask a single question. You are the only one who will answer it honestly. Do Middle-Eastern conditions justify my putting any money in South Arabian oil?'
>
> Lawrence, without rising, quietly answered: 'No.'
>
> 'That's all I wanted to know; it was worth coming for. Thank you, and good day!' In his brief glance about the room he missed something and, on his way home through London, chose the chairs and had them sent to Lawrence with his card.

Clearly Lawrence never studied business at All Souls.

T. E. LAWRENCE

Lawrence: *A prince of our disorder*

I HOPED THAT my visit to Clouds Hill and the Moreton cemetery would help me make more sense of Lawrence's guarded personality, and perhaps clarify some of the many contradictions that surround the "of Arabia" legend. Depending on what you read or who you ask, Lawrence was—in no particular order—an archaeologist or a British spy, the liberator of the Arabs or their betrayer, someone painfully shy or the engaging political friend of Winston Churchill, and a closet homosexual or someone who had no romantic life at all. He is remembered as the godfather of many Arabic nations—notably Jordan and Iraq—and in addition to his war record in the desert, he served on Churchill's staff at the 1921 Cairo Conference.

Yet for the last thirteen years of his life, he lived in anonymity between Clouds Hill and his service as an army private in the tank and air corps, all under an assumed name. Such reclusion might make sense as a reaction to the stress of the World War I years, except that as he hid from the limelight, he also published several bestselling books, appeared often in the newspapers, and befriended many literary giants, including Hardy and Graves. On any given day, Lawrence was that very British riddle wrapped inside an enigma.

Most of the biographies that I have read about Lawrence's formative years make much of his illegitimacy and the fact that his mother was a consuming, often combustible, presence in the life of her five boys. Technically, Lawrence was born in Tremadog, Wales, along the Irish Sea, the son of Thomas and Sarah Lawrence, who were posing as a newlywed couple. In fact, his father was Thomas Chapman, an Englishman with Irish estates and an ample income, who left his wife, Edith (known locally as "the Vinegar Queen"), and their four daughters, to run off with the babysitter, Sarah Lawrence, whom he never did officially marry. She would bear him five sons, including Thomas Edward "Ned" Lawrence, but for a long time, until settling down on Polestead Road in Oxford, they lived as fugitives between England and France, dreading that someone would recognize Thomas as the deadbeat dad from South Hill, Delvin, Co Westmeath, Ireland.

Whether Ned Lawrence knew for sure he was illegitimate or just sensed it from household conversations is not clear, but many biographers believe it explains why he grew up in the fantasies of medieval Europe—dreaming of knights errant, chevaliers, and fog-encased fortresses—more than he did in his local grammar schools. He wrote: "I also read nearly every manual of chivalry. Remember that my period was the Middle Ages, always." His psycho-biographer, John Mack, writes in *A Prince of Our Disorder*: "Lawrence's devotion to Sir Thomas Malory and to the Arthurian legends which, like himself, were born in Wales and developed in France, epitomized his medievalism." He quotes George Bernard Shaw on Lawrence's arrested development:

> Lawrence had, in my opinion, no real adolescence at all, his energies remaining in many respects those of a lively and lively-minded schoolboy. "His great abilities and interests," as George Bernard Shaw wrote, "were those of a highly gifted boy."

While much of his childhood was spent in solitary pursuits—collecting pottery fragments for Oxford's Ashmolean Museum or cycling long distances in England to come back with brass rubbings—personally I think it is a stretch to think that his parents' common-law marriage (otherwise, they were very conventional) drove him to a life of eccentricity. Nor do I subscribe to the theory, popular among many biographers, that Sarah Lawrence left her son an emotional cripple, at least when it came to relations with women. Lawrence liked to say: "I always felt that she was laying siege to me, and would conquer, if I left a chink unguarded." Much later, he wrote: "One of the real reasons (there are three or four) why I am in the service [as a private] is so that I may live by myself. She has given me a terror of families and inquisitions."

To be sure Lawrence was a solitary child, given to grown-up pastimes (pottery collecting), and later never married or showed much interest in cultivating the affections of a woman. (As a young man, he did make a half-hearted marriage proposal to a family friend, Janet Laurie, and later he was emotionally close to two married women, Charlotte Shaw, the wife of the playwright Bernard, and Clare Smith, married to an RAF officer.) But for Sarah Lawrence to get all of his emotional baggage delivered to her Polestead Road door strikes me as an exaggeration. Mack writes that she "was a remarkable woman, possessing unusual energy, great charm and prodigious will and determination." It could also be said that she endowed Lawrence with self-sufficiency, courage, an ability with languages, eloquence as a writer, and modesty, none of which strike me as fatal characteristics.

From all accounts, Lawrence had the gift of friendship, and his leadership in the Arab world, first evident while on his archaeological dig at Carchemish, evolved from his remarkable ability, despite a stiff English upbringing, to empathize with the men in his work groups and to bond emotionally not just with individual Arabs, but with entire villages and tribes. His particular friend, the young Arab Dahoum, who assisted him at Carchemish, explained his leadership this way:

> 'You ask why we love Lawrence? And who can help loving him? He is our brother, our friend and leader. He is one of us, there is nothing we do he cannot do, and he then excels us in doing it. He takes such an interest in us and cares for our welfare. We respect him and greatly admire his courage and bravery: we love him because he loves us.'

How could an emotionally smothering mother produce such a compassionate son?

FRIENDS OF A KIND

To Arabia: *The young Lawrence*

PART OF THE reason Lawrence is so hard to figure out is that his life can be divided into many discrete phases. After grammar school in Oxford, he read history at Jesus College, Oxford. His undergraduate thesis, even then, became something of a legend, as in researching the influence of Crusader fortifications on Western castles, he rode his bike some two thousand kilometers around France and then, in another summer off from university, tramped across Syria to inspect its fortresses. Clearly Lawrence was someone who learned by seeing, but he also wrote well (if in a style that can occasionally read like a bad imitation of a knight at the roundtable) and read extensively in his field.

After university, because he was known at the Ashmolean for his pottery excavations around Oxford, he was signed on, for no pay, at an archaeological dig in Carchemish, which is now on the Turkish-Syrian border northeast of Aleppo, but was then a remote Ottoman province. There he distinguished himself for his ability to speak many dialects of Arabic and for his ability to integrate into the local population. He also had a rigorous sense of classification and detail about the archaeological finds. Toward the end of his several years at the site, he may have also provided useful assistance to British intelligence on the geopolitical landscape of Palestine.

That Lawrence went from archaeology to the military wasn't quite the leap of faith that it seems to some historians. At the time the British footprint in the Middle East, which operated from Cairo, was a small world of diplomats and military advisors. In such a cloistered world, the eccentric Lawrence (he often walked from Beirut to Carchemish) would have been discussed both for his oddities and his perseverance, so it makes sense that, come World War I in August 1914, he would have found his way back to Cairo as a military intelligence and liaison officer. He drew maps and contributed scholarly papers on tribal politics until 1916, when he went on a mission to Jeddah in the Hejaz, in what is now Saudi Arabia, to investigate the possibility that an Arab rising against the Ottoman Turks might assist the Allied cause.

From that scouting mission came his role as an aide-de-camp to Feisal's slightly ragtag army and his participation in the taking of Aqaba— the Red Sea port guarded by a Turkish garrison—from the north. (The

Turks had their guns and eyes turned to the sea in the south.) In the film *Lawrence of Arabia*, Lawrence practically takes it single-handedly at the head of a camel charge. In his two-year campaigning in the desert it was his one victory in what might be called a set-piece battle. (Tafileh might be the second.) Usually he fought in guerrilla skirmishes, although they could be equally deadly, on a smaller scale. Mentioned less often than the fall of Aqaba is the take-no-prisoners massacre of the Turkish garrison, carried out by Arab irregulars, that followed the victory. I have often thought much of Lawrence's guilt from the war years might be associated with the lack of control that British officers had over Arab bloodlust. (Another famous massacre took place near Damascus at Tafas, where the Turks had first massacred Arab civilians.)

After the war ended in November 1918, Lawrence's affinity with Arabic, his knowledge of tribal affairs, and his friendship with Feisal and many other Arab leaders saw him posted to the Paris Peace Conference at Versailles. By then he had learned that the Sykes-Picot fix was in for the subdivision of Arabia between British and French spheres of influence.

Campaigning in the desert, Lawrence had promised many tribal elders that they were fighting for the liberation of Arabia from Ottoman oppression. Instead he delivered his tribal allies to colonial subservience under either a French or British flag. No wonder Paris filled him with disgust and gave him ample time to work on his memoirs of the campaigns, which became, after a number of drafts, *Seven Pillars of Wisdom*. In it he writes:

> Rumours of the fraud reached Arab ears, from Turkey. In the East persons were more trusted than institutions. So the Arabs, having tested my friendliness and sincerity under fire, asked me, as a free agent, to endorse the promises of the British Government. I had had no previous or inner knowledge of the McMahon pledges and the Sykes-Picot treaty, which were both framed by war-time branches of the Foreign Office. But, not being a perfect fool, I could see that if we won the war the promises to the Arabs were dead paper. Had I been an honourable adviser I would have sent my men home, and not let them risk their lives for such stuff. Yet the Arab inspiration was our main tool in winning the

Eastern war. So I assured them that England kept her word in letter and spirit. In this comfort they performed their fine things: but, of course, instead of being proud of what we did together, I was continually and bitterly ashamed.

After the war, Winston Churchill became an admirer of Lawrence, and he took him to Cairo and its conference in 1921, along with the Arabist Gertrude Bell, with the goal of establishing Britain's colonial structure in the Middle East, notably in Iraq, which had been unsuccessfully cobbled together from the outlines of Mesopotamia. That assignment could well have positioned Lawrence for a postwar career as a senior civil servant in foreign affairs, with no limit on how high he might rise based on his stellar war record and well-placed friendships. Instead Lawrence decided to become the modern equivalent of a monk (with or without the vow of chastity; it's not clear). He joined the air forces as a private, using an assumed name upon his enlistment, J. H. Ross. When that cover was blown, he served briefly in the army and later back in the Royal Air Force as T. E. Shaw.

By Lawrence's own account, he found contentment after enlisting as a private in the armed forces. He was spared a bourgeois family life and the daily routines of cooking and cleaning, and he found comfort in living sparely in an all-male community, as he had most of his life. His biographer Mack writes: "To friends who wondered aloud how he could endure the company of the barrack-room and its bareness T. E. might retort, almost fiercely, that he had gone back to his boyhood class and was at home." Service life also left him with enough time to work on his books and writing, and to carry on with his far-flung literary friendships.

The peacetime army was a casual affair. At Clouds Hill, he could also recreate the bungalow that his parents had built for him behind the Oxford house on Polestead Road (he lived there while studying at Jesus College and writing his thesis). In my mind, life as Aircraftman Ross and Tank Crewman Shaw allowed Lawrence to live eternally as a nineteen-year-old undergraduate, forever writing his thesis about Crusaders and their fortresses, of whatever era.

In parsing the many Lawrences, most biographers cannot help speculating about his sexuality, the historiography of which often surpasses analyses of his desert campaign. Was he homosexual or just asexual? Did he even have an erotic life? Mack, for example, suggests that he was terrified of women, writing: "Although I am in substantial agreement with Janet Hallsmith [aka Hall-Smith, née Laurie] and other women who have maintained that it is nonsense to say that Lawrence hated women—he had, after all, a number of social relationships with them that were mutually gratifying—because of his deeply ambivalent attitude toward women as sexual beings, and the intense sexual inhibitions related to this attitude, he never, to my knowledge, ever again attempted to form a serious love bond with a woman."

Elsewhere, Mack implies that Lawrence was a forty-year-old virgin when he died. He also writes at length about Lawrence's devotion, which borders on love, for a young Arab boy, Dahoum, to whom he later dedicated *Seven Pillars*, after the boy either died of cholera or vanished into the desert. Depending on who you read, Lawrence was either his father figure, brother, or unrequited lover. In explaining his conduct in the desert campaign, he writes: "I liked a particular Arab very much, and I thought that freedom for the race would be an acceptable present."

The reason Lawrence's sexuality is so mixed up with the legend is because of what happened to him in Dera'a, a city now in southern Syria (where the present civil war began). Dressed as an Arab, Lawrence had gone into the city during the desert campaigns to assess the Turkish garrison. He was fond of such solo reconnaissance missions. This time, however, Turkish soldiers arrested him, although they didn't know that this man was T. E. Lawrence, on whose head the Ottoman authorities had placed a bounty. Instead they delivered him up to the bestial base commander, who liked the idea of "having his way" with a blond and blue-eyed young Arab man, identifying himself as Circassian. For refusing the commander's tender advances, Lawrence was severely beaten and probably sodomized, something that at once horrified him, but also strangely may have given him pleasure and brought him to climax.

For the record of what happened and what he felt, we only have Lawrence's account of the incident in *Seven Pillars*, which he rewrote and edited more than any other section in the book. He writes:

> At last when I was completely broken they seemed
> satisfied. Somehow I found myself off the bench, lying

> on my back on the dirty floor, where I snuggled down, dazed, panting for breath, but vaguely comfortable. I had strung myself to learn all pain until I died, and no longer actor, but spectator, thought not to care how my body jerked and squealed. Yet I knew or imagined what passed about me.... Their consideration (rendered at once, as if we had deserved men's homage) momently stayed me to carry the burden, whose certainty the passing days confirmed: how in Deraa that night the citadel of my integrity had been irrevocably lost.

Mack concludes: "I have little doubt that Lawrence underwent a painful, humiliating assault at Dera'a at the hands of the Turkish commander and his soldiers, and the element of sexual pleasure he experienced in the midst of such indignity, pain and degradation was particularly intolerable and shameful to him."

Unfortunately, the Dera'a story does not end when the Turkish pederasts throw him into the street, unaware that they were releasing from their grasps the man they most feared in the desert. For Lawrence the indignities that he suffered were always on his mind, to such an extent that, in the 1920s at Clouds Hill, he set about to purge his soul of its impurities. Like some medieval saint given to self-flagellation, Lawrence hired a local Scotsman named John "Jock" Bruce to come around to the cottage and lash him with a leather belt, birch, or something similar. Presumably, Lawrence would have laid on his bed in the cottage when getting whipped (something that crossed my mind when the niece was showing me around, but I didn't drop a reference into our conversation).

Whether the beatings helped Lawrence come to terms with his past or clarified his sexual orientation in the future, I don't know. Looked at in a modern context, I see more post-traumatic stress disorder in trying to hurt himself and less of a kinky turn-on, at the hands of a dour village laborer. To me Mack comes closest to explaining his postwar cocoon and self-styled isolation when he writes about the conflicts, pain, and guilt that were with Lawrence after the war. Mack writes:

> The horrors he observed and took part in during 1917 and 1918 following the deaths of his two brothers; the

political conflict; the disillusionment with the behavior of the Arabs; the multiple bouts of febrile illness; the death of Dahoum; and, above all, the traumatic assault at Der'a and the loss of control at Tafas, brought about profound changes in Lawrence's mental state and personality.

Keep in mind that Lawrence's conception of justice and fairness came from medieval heralds and poetry, not from the random and brutal violence of modern warfare. He writes in *Seven Pillars*:

> When combats came to the physical, bare hand against hand, I was finished. The disgust of being touched revolted me more than the thought of death and defeat: perhaps because one such terrible struggle in my youth had given me an enduring fear of contact: or because I so reverenced my wits and despised my body that I would not be beholden to the second for the life of the first.

FRIENDS OF A KIND

Seven Pillars of Hollywood

WHAT EXPLAINS MY lifetime fascination with Lawrence? Much of it must have to do with the film, *Lawrence of Arabia*, to which my mother took me when I was about eight years old. That morning, a dentist had pulled out four of my baby teeth (they were slow to fall out), and in the afternoon I was taken to the movies and watched Peter O'Toole liberate Arabia. I have watched the movie since and what strikes me now is how painfully slow the direction is, including the first four minutes, which feature a blackened screen while the music plays.

After college, I knew that *Seven Pillars of Wisdom* must hold some clues to the current problems in the Middle East, but the book eluded me. In 1980 I did read the abridged version, *Revolt in the Desert*, which prompted me, five years later, to go with my wife to Jordan, where we retraced many of Lawrence's camel tracks between Amman and the Red Sea, including to the "rose-red" Nabatean city of Petra. On that trip I carried with me a Penguin edition of *Seven Pillars*, but either the type was too small or the writing too dense for me to make much headway.

After our travels in Jordan, I would, on occasion, read some of the new biographies that were published frequently about Lawrence. I read Jeremy Wilson's authorized biography when it was published in 1990, and that book got me interested in Clouds Hill, even though it took me another twenty-six years to get there.

In 2002, I read Lowell Thomas' biography, *With Lawrence in Arabia*, which came out in 1924 and which helped to initiate the Lawrence legends. (More than anything else, that book was the template for the O'Toole film, although it also is based extensively on the Robert Graves biography, *Lawrence and the Arabs* and Lawrence's *Revolt in the Desert*.) Then in 2010, my youngest son, Charles, and I tramped on trains and buses from Istanbul to Damascus. During several days we retraced Lawrence's footsteps from the summer 1909, visiting a number of Crusader castles in Syria, including Crac des Chevaliers (he called it "the finest castle in the world: certainly the most picturesque I have seen—quite marvelous"). We stayed in Baron's Hotel in Aleppo, where one of Lawrence's hotel bills was preserved in a dusty cabinet off the main lobby. We also fell in love with Aleppo, which Lawrence describes this way:

> Aleppo was a great city in Syria, but not of it, nor of Anatolia, nor of Mesopotamia. There the races, creeds, and tongues of the Ottoman Empire met and knew one another in a spirit of compromise. The clash of characteristics, which made its streets a kaleidoscope, imbued the Aleppine with a lewd thoughtfulness which corrected in him what was blatant in the Damascene. Aleppo had shared in all the civilizations which turned about it: the result seemed to be a lack of zest in its people's belief. Even so, they surpassed the rest of Syria. They fought and traded more; were more fanatical and vicious; and made most beautiful things: but all with a dearth of conviction which rendered barren their multitudinous strength.

Our bonds with Aleppo and Lawrence's presence there grew stronger, when several months after we left Syria on a night train, the civil war began in earnest, with the first embers igniting, appropriately or not, in Dera'a.

Only in winter 2016 did I finish reading the unabridged *Seven Pillars*, which spoke to me not only as a World War I memoir—it's the peer of Graves' *Good-Bye to All That* and Sassoon's *Memoirs of an Infantry Officer*—but as a primer in Middle Eastern tribal politics and as a handbook in guerrilla warfare. (In the 1960s, why were all those Green Berets reading Mao's banal *Little Red Book* when the same libraries had copies of *Seven Pillars*?) And more than any psycho-biography that speculates about Lawrence's relationship with his mother, the memoir is the best insight we shall get into the workings of his fine mind. (Lawrence writes: "The Arab war was geographical, and the Turkish Army an accident. Our aim was to seek the enemy's weakest material link and bear only on that till time made their whole length fail. Our largest resources, the Beduin on whom our war must be built, were unused to formal operations, but had assets of mobility, toughness, self-assurance, knowledge of the country, intelligent courage. With them dispersal was strength.")

In my mind, the *Seven Pillars* can also be read as a companion volume to the *Confessions of St. Augustine*, as much of what Lawrence recounts is his disillusionment with a modern political world that tempted the Arabs with the ideals of independence only for them to end up in colonial shackles. He writes: "I had had no concern with the Arab Revolt in the beginning. In the end I was responsible for its being an embarrassment to the inventors. Where exactly in the interim my guilt passed from accessory to principal, upon what headings I should be condemned, were not for me to say. Suffice it that since the march to Akaba I bitterly repented my entanglement in the movement, with a bitterness sufficient to corrode my inactive hours, but insufficient to make me cut myself clear of it. Hence the wobbling of my will, and endless, vapid complainings."

To be sure, Lawrence led the Arabs into war against the Turks, and was the liaison officer who secured substantial British aid for the guerrilla campaigns, and he did not knowingly deceive them. But he was also serving two masters who had differing goals (one was fighting for independence, the other colonialism), and as the war dragged on, Lawrence fell into the darkness of that divide, from which he would never return. He writes at length:

> Among the Arabs I was the disillusioned, the sceptic, who envied their cheap belief. The unperceived sham looked so well-fitting and becoming a dress for shoddy man. The ignorant, the superficial, the deceived were the happy among us. By our swindle they were glorified. We paid for them our self-respect, and they gained the deepest feeling of their lives. The more we condemned and despised ourselves, the more we could cynically take pride in them, our creatures. It was so easy to overcredit others: so impossible to write down their motives to the level of our own uncharitable truth. They were our dupes, wholeheartedly fighting the enemy. They blew before our intentions like chaff, being not chaff, but the bravest, simplest and merriest of men. Credo quia sum? But did not the being believed by many make for a distorted righteousness? The mounting together of the devoted hopes of years from near-sighted multitudes, might endow even an unwilling idol with Godhead, and strengthen It whenever men prayed silently to Him.

Ironically, I found the memoir least interesting in its descriptions of desert warfare. ("The Arab Movement had lived as a wild-man show, with its means as small as its duties and prospects.") There was a sameness in the writing about yet another trek across the arid plains or the destruction of yet more track on the Hejaz Railway. (In Damascus, Charles and I met the director of its museum and historical society, who proposed we look at his pictures of the line, and then confessed that they numbered seventeen thousand.)

In my mind Lawrence shines in his analysis of the fractured nature of Middle Eastern politics. Even though he was writing in the 1920s, about travels and fighting that took place in the 1910s, his insights into the region's divides could easily illuminate contemporary war planning in Washington or London. For example, here is his description of Syria's tribal structure:

> Mixed among the Ansariyeh were colonies of Syrian Christians; and in the bend of the Orontes had been some firm blocks of Armenians, inimical to Turkey. Inland, near Harim were Druses, Arabic in origin; and some Circassians from the Caucasus. These had their hand against all. North-east of them were Kurds, settlers of some generations back, who were marrying Arabs and adopting their politics. They hated native Christians most; and, after them, they hated Turks and Europeans. Just beyond the Kurds existed a few Yezidis, Arabic-speaking, but in thought affected by the dualism of Iran, and prone to placate the spirit of evil. Christians, Mohammedans, and Jews, peoples who placed revelation before reason, united to spit upon Yezid. Inland of them stood Aleppo, a town of two hundred thousand people, an epitome of all Turkey's races and religions. Eastward of Aleppo, for sixty miles, were settled Arabs whose colour and manner became more and more tribal as they neared the fringe of cultivation where the semi-nomad ended and the Bedawi began.

It could well be an extract from a white paper on the rise of ISIS, as when he writes:

The tale of Syria was not ended in this count of odd races and religions. Apart from the country-folk, the six great towns—Jerusalem, Beyrout, Damascus, Horns, Hama, and Aleppo—were entities, each with its character, direction, and opinion. The southernmost, Jerusalem, was a squalid town, which every Semitic religion had made holy. Christians and Mohammedans came there on pilgrimage to the shrines of its past, and some Jews looked to it for the political future of their race. These united forces of the past and the future were so strong that the city almost failed to have a present. Its people, with rare exceptions, were characterless as hotel servants, living on the crowd of visitors passing through. Ideals of Arab nationality were far from them, though familiarity with the differences of Christians at their moment of most poignant sentience had led the classes of Jerusalem to despise us all.

The idea that Lawrence's political movement could have led to a hundred-years war across much of the Middle East might not have surprised him, but it would have filled him with even more gloom.

T. E. LAWRENCE

Wessex Tales on the Bike

BIKING AWAY FROM the cemetery in Moreton and Lawrence's grave, I wondered why I was spending so much energy on the details of his complicated life. For this part of the excursion, I had long sought and finally acquired Anthony Sattin's *The Young T. E. Lawrence* (which covers the time up to World War I), much as, on earlier trips to New York and the Strand bookstore, I had wandered the stacks looking for David Fromkin's *A Peace to End All Peace* (he finds Lawrence something of a poseur, writing: "Lawrence possessed many virtues but honesty was not among them; he passed off his fantasies as the truth.")

Hunting for the right road to Dorchester, my next stop, I came to the conclusion that what most interested me about Lawrence was that his many enthusiasms had helped shape my own life. I might be indifferent to the desert warrior or the mysteries of his sexuality, but I have always warmed to the story that he researched his college thesis by biking hundreds of miles in France and traveling across Syria (both of which I did also, if in different ways).

I appreciate—even if it is a film chock full of Hollywood clichés—that *Lawrence of Arabia* opened my eight-year-old eyes to the politics of the Middle East, which may explain why, as an adult, I have been trying to visit and write about all of the countries in the region. (Surprisingly for an Arabist, Lawrence believed that Jewish immigration was the key to success in the Middle East, writing: "The sooner the Jews farm it the better: their colonies are bright spots in a desert.")

I also have sympathy for Lawrence's conflict between his promises of Arab independence and the power politics that were codified in the Sykes-Picot Agreement, having myself worked abroad for much of my adult life and tried to reconcile American corporatism with local realities. Finally, I admire Lawrence's simplicity—his walk across Syria with little more than a change of underwear or his Clouds Hill home that values books, reading, music, bicycles, and friendship more than the appliances of a modern kitchen. I feel badly that the war years so haunted his dreams, but at the same time I can easily imagine a contented man, in his parlor at Clouds Hill, pouring over the galley proofs of *Seven Pillars* while sipping tea and listening to Mozart. Worse lives can be imagined.

How do I imagine Lawrence? Unlike the calm presence of Peter

O'Toole in the film, I see Lawrence, when engaged with a project, always on the go. (One acquaintance compared his movement to that of a hopping bird.) To his friends, I am sure there was no better companion, someone who would listen to their stories and empathize with their frustrations. To those that bored him, I can imagine that he simply stared off into space or walked away.

I can also easily imagine Lawrence spending hours alone with his own thoughts, crouched in a hunched position while admiring the sunset or lost in reveries while on a bicycle or motorcycle. (My guess for his fatal accident is that he was dreaming—by day.) I am sure he had a developed, if odd, sense of humor, and part of the reason he did so well in the tribal worlds of Arabia is that people warmed to his easy laughter and his ability to adapt to any local situation without a moment's hesitation.

In the war years I imagine someone perfectly suited to the desert campaigns. He would have been indifferent, if not happy, with the privations, and he would have seen himself, mounted on a camel, as a knight errant doing battle with heathens. I am sure, too, that Lawrence's personal courage was an inspiration to many of those around him, even if the form that it took was more that of optimism and confidence than fiery speeches about the enemy. Finally, I see someone governed by his many passions—archaeology, medievalism, the Arabic language, history, military tactics, diplomacy, writing, and literature. Whatever he did, he did with fire.

I regret that Lawrence might have seen his life as a failure. His father and two brothers were dead, and he had yet to reconcile his feelings about his domineering mother. The war years had closed off his promising career as an archaeologist, perhaps his greatest passion. In the fighting, he felt that he duped those Arab leaders he had most respected and left them in the grip of colonial masters. At Cairo, he had been unable to prevent Churchill and British imperial interests from reasserting control over the artificial construct that was modern Iraq.

After a short-lived career as a senior diplomat, he turned to writing, and even though *Seven Pillars* became recognized as a masterpiece of World War I literature, he was so uncomfortable telling his own story that he banned publication of the book for much of his lifetime. With the book written, he decided to live underground as an army private, which he said offered him much fulfillment and reward, although I find it hard to believe that someone who thought of becoming an army general by age thirty would have loved cleaning latrines in Bovington—as a form of penance, maybe, but not for a dreamer of the day. Nor can I believe, whatever his sexual orientation, that occasional lashings restored much equilibrium to his tortured emotional life. Maybe the essence of Lawrence's humanity was that he was a hero to everyone except himself?

FRIENDS OF A KIND

Hardy's Dorchester: *The return of the outsider*

WHEN I EMERGED from the woods around Moreton, I found myself heading toward Dorchester on Route 2 of the British national cycle network. Every so often there would be a small arrow or sign to indicate a turn. It meant that I didn't have to think or look at maps while riding through Hardy's Wessex ("a merely realistic dream country"), which here, instead of heath, was rolling farmland broken by the occasional stand of trees.

At one point I passed a sign indicating a turn toward Hardy's birthplace. I thought of making the detour, but all I would have seen was the outside of a thatched cottage, and a misty rain had begun to fall. Instead, I decided a bike ride through his fictional Wessex at twilight would have to suit me to acquire a sense of his life.

My acquaintance with Hardy, besides the many references to him as a good friend to T. E. Lawrence, among others, dates to the late 1980s, when on a series of summer vacations in Maine I read a handful of Wessex novels, beginning with *The Mayor of Casterbridge*. That book was a holdover from my summer reading lists in junior high school, when I found the idea abhorrent to spend a summer afternoon with a nineteenth-century grain merchant from what is now Dorchester. To my seventh-grade self, Hardy was a variation on Charles Dickens and his *Hard Times*.

In my late thirties, however, Hardy's novels about crooked preachers, innocent women "heavy with child," fraudulent last wills and testaments, and scheming husbands felt like a Victorian soap opera, and I could not wait for the latest installment. In rapid succession I went through *Tess of the D'Urbervilles* and her fall from grace, *Jude the Obscure*, and *The Return of the Native*, and I grew to admire the modernism of Hardy's characters, even those with such medieval names as Clym Yeobright. They might trudge on foot or take ox carts between Wessex villages, or spend their evenings in conversation with a parson, but their greed, vulnerability, selfishness, and quiet dreams make many of the characters seem distinctly contemporary. For example, Hardy writes about Tess:

> She might have seen that what had bowed her head
> so profoundly—the thought of the world's concern at

her situation—was founded on illusion. She was not an existence, an experience, a passion, a structure of sensations, to anybody but herself. To all humankind besides, Tess was only a passing thought.

For most of my Wessex ride, I passed very few cars. Only nearer to Dorchester did I begin to mix with traffic, although the cycle path routed me around intersections and through many back alleys. In Dorchester, I came upon a huge manor house, locked behind a gate. For a moment I thought it might be a small hospital or a school for boys. The house had turrets and many chimneys, not to mention spacious grounds.

Only when I saw a sign on a portico did I realize that this was Max Gate, Thomas Hardy's home for much of his adult life. From here he had bicycled over to see Lawrence at Clouds Hill, and here he had entertained many other writers who figure in this story, including Siegfried Sassoon and Robert Graves. I had assumed that Hardy's adult home had been something similar to the Dorset cottage where he was born. (He once wrote: "I was born bad, and I have lived bad, and I shall die bad in all probability.") Instead, Max Gate suggested a portrait of the artist as a well-paid media celebrity.

Near one of the main intersections in town, I found Hardy's statue. He is cast in bronze and seated reflectively near a traffic light. I wondered as I waded into the street to take a picture of the author if many Dorchester residents remember Hardy or can quote some of his more memorable passages. In *Jude the Obscure* he writes gloomily: "Sometimes a woman's love of being loved gets the better of her conscience, and though she is agonized at the thought of treating a man cruelly, she encourages him to love her while she doesn't love him at all. Then, when she sees him suffering, her remorse sets in, and she does what she can to repair the wrong." No wonder his first wife said he was "a great writer, but not a great man."

My hotel for the night was outside Dorchester. I had booked it because it showed up on a list of "bike-friendly" accommodations, but when it began raining harder, I decided to get to the hotel on a regional bus. To find the correct stop in town meant many questions and several loops around the downtown, which looked mournful in the mist. When I crowded in the right bus shelter to wait for the X51 bus to Bridport, I had to share the close quarters with two drunk teenagers, who were sprawled on the pavement to protect themselves from the rain. The bus arrived on time and fifteen minutes later it dropped me at White Chase Alley, where I found my hotel and, more importantly, a lovely pub next door where I could dry my rain jacket on a radiator and eat lasagna for dinner. I am sure Lawrence would have engaged the publican in a conversation about his tribe, but I was too tired from my early departure to do more than study the map for the next day.

Siegfried Sassoon survived the Great War, despite his aggressive style as an infantry officer. Sassoon was known for his solo attacks on German trenches, especially in action along the river Somme in 1916. The men under his command admired his fortitude and courage. His poetry and prose, including *Memoirs of an Infantry Officer*, remain some of the finest descriptions of those battles. While on home leave recovering from wounds in 1917, he published an open letter denouncing the war, writing: "I am making this statement as an act of wilful defiance of military authority, because I believe that the War is being deliberately prolonged by those who have the power to end it."

Section II

SIEGFRIED SASSOON RIDES TO THE GUNS

The Train to Frome

THE NEXT MORNING, after an early breakfast at a hard-luck café in Dorchester, I caught a train to Frome, about an hour to the north. For being a large market town, Dorchester has an insignificant railway station, and the train that arrived ten minutes late was a sorry, two-car affair, which meant everyone was packed together in the small seats. I had looked forward to a morning coffee and leisurely train ride through what in London is called "the West Country." Instead I was jammed into the British equivalent of a New York City subway car, having to apologize ("sorry…") for bringing along a folding bike. I was reminded of Hardy's aside: "Some folk want their luck buttered." I was one of them.

I went to Frome simply because it was the closest rail station to Mells, where the writer and poet Siegfried Sassoon is buried in the churchyard of St. Andrew's Church. By my calculations, the bike ride to Mells was only about four miles. What I had not counted on was bad directions (a station clerk sent me out of town on the wrong road) and gear-snapping hills. Sweating up one such hill reminded me that Bromptons were invented more for city commuting than for country explorations, and more than a few times the grades were so steep that I was forced to walk and push the bike up a long hill. In the language of the Tour de France, this is known as "putting your foot on the ground," and the phrase is meant to evoke shame and embarrassment, which is what I felt when cars passed me on the narrow, steep inclines.

The village of Mells, as elegant as any in England, is at the bottom of several hills, nestled in a dale. As I descended toward the general store in town, I came across several cyclists, one of whom had a detailed map of the area. We were all happy to meet each other. I told them about the hills between Mells and Frome, and they showed me on their map how, later that day, I could bike to Heytesbury, where Sassoon owned a large manor house. Our lively discussion in front of the village store prompted a few onlookers to intervene, and one of them directed me toward St Andrew's churchyard. Like Charles Ryder, the protagonist in Evelyn Waugh's *Brideshead Revisited*, and like Waugh himself, Sassoon converted to Catholicism late in life. The minister at Mells was among his confessors, which explains his burial in a village where he never lived.

In planning my trip, I had written to my friend Raymond Asquith, great-grandson of the World War I prime minister Herbert Asquith, because he and his wife Clare live on the family estate in Mells. Unfortunately, they were traveling to London on the day I was to roll through town. Missing them was a shame, as his grandfather, Raymond Asquith, who was killed in the Battle of the Somme, knew many of the people I am writing about in this book. In his memoirs, *Pilgrim's Way*, John Buchan writes: "For the chosen few, like Raymond, there is no disillusionment. They march on into life with a boyish grace, and their high noon keeps all the freshness of the morning." Buchan knew Asquith at Oxford, and this passage in particular resonated with Lieutenant (junior grade) John F. Kennedy, who talked about the memoir while on PT duty in the Solomon Islands. And my Raymond Asquith, growing up in the 1950s and '60s, had personally known Sassoon (through his parents) and remembers playing cricket with the poet in the garden, when Sassoon was in his seventies.

SIEGFRIED SASSOON

Mells: *The great war in modern memory*

FOLLOWING THE DIRECTIONS I was given in front of the general store, I biked to the churchyard of St Andrew's and began hunting for Sassoon's headstone, which, however, eluded me. The man who gave me the directions said that the churchyard had a guide "to the famous markers," but I could find neither the map nor the grave. Finally, as I had done at earlier crossroads, I went back to my saddlebags and fished out a photograph that I had printed from the internet, showing Sassoon's grave. Then I walked around the ancient burial ground until the spot where I was standing matched the coordinates of the photograph. Sure enough, there was a simple headstone that had the name Siegfried Sassoon.

Standing in front of the grave, it occurred to me that I had been thinking about Sassoon since 1977, when I met my then girlfriend, now wife, and she insisted that I read Paul Fussell's *The Great War and Modern Memory*. I read it immediately, and I too came under its spell. The book is a literary history of World War I told through the poetry and memoirs of those who served in the trenches. Mostly Fussell writes about English soldier-authors—Robert Graves, Wilfred Owen, Edmund Blunt, and Siegfried Sassoon—but the study includes mentions of German writer Erich Remarque (*All Quiet on the Western Front*) and American novelist William March, who wrote *Company K*, the most singularly depressing war book I have ever read (and I have read a lot of them).

Fussell's thesis, sometimes expressed in stiff academic jargon, is that the modernist sense of irony is a legacy of World War I memoirs. Even though World War I's soldier-authors saw the war at its worst, they remembered in language that detached them from the horrors, enabling them both to carry on as soldiers and later to express the reality to their readers. Fussell writes: "The irony which memory associates with the events, little as well as great, of the First World War has become as an inseparable element of the general vision of war in our time." Later memoirs of World War II took it for granted that war was an absurd practice, best remembered with derision and satire; but that's only because the ground was broken with the poetry, fiction, and memoirs that emerged from the Western Front of

World War I. Fussell concludes: "And that new dimension is capable of revealing for the first time that full obscenity of the Great War."

Fussell's book also introduced me to Siegfried Sassoon and his *Memoirs of an Infantry Officer*. It turned out that this book is the middle volume of a trilogy, *The Memoirs of George Sherston*, which Sassoon wrote after the war. Ostensibly the books are fiction; in reality Sherston's memoirs are those of Sassoon. He came to the trenches from a pastoral life of fox hunting and cricket in the Weald of Kent, and won a Military Cross for his daring trench raids, but then denounced the fighting in a published anti-war statement, which almost led to him being court-martialed and executed.

About the time I discovered Fussell's book, I was hired as an assistant editor at *Harper's Magazine*, and Fussell was among the writers with whom I worked. Then he was an English professor at Rutgers University in New Brunswick, New Jersey, but also a contributor to many magazines. When he came to my office, we would spend time talking about Sassoon, his poetry and memoirs, and I recall Fussell proudly showing me the galleys of his forthcoming book, *Siegfried Sassoon's Long Journey*, which Oxford University Press published in 1983. On another occasion, when I told him that my girlfriend and I were planning a bicycle trip along the Western Front in France, he kindly brought me some of his maps and brochures of Verdun, which I have to this day. He and I enjoyed each other's company, and it is because of him that I was now poking around a graveyard in Mells.

SIEGFRIED SASSOON

Weirleigh and the Weald of Kent:
To the hounds

LIKE LAWRENCE, SASSOON was a child of Victorian England. He grew up south of London in Kent in the presence of a strong-willed mother and attended Oxford University. Again like Lawrence, he came of age in a pampered, isolated world and filled in the loneliness of his childhood with heroic fantasies. The respected biographer, Max Egremont, writes in *Siegfried Sassoon: A Life*: "He read Longfellow, Shelley and Tennyson secretly, thrilled by Tennyson's 'many towered Camelot.'"

Sassoon got his first horse at age twelve and thereafter rode to the hounds; hence the first volume of the Sherston trilogy is called *Memoirs of a Fox-Hunting Man*, and it evokes rural England as a variation on Arcadia. It begins with this sentence: "My childhood was a queer and not altogether happy one…. It is no use pretending that I was anything else than a dreaming and unpractical boy." It was only on another journey that I finally made it to Weirleigh, the house in which Sassoon grew up and in which he set the first volume of his memoirs. With a car, the house would have been easy to find—halfway between Paddock Wood (in Kent) and Royal Tunbridge Wells, the larger and more prosperous market town. But as I was still traveling by train when I went in search of Weirleigh, getting there proved something of an adventure. And on this occasion, I did not even have a bike to travel the last kilometers.

From the station in Paddock Wood, about two miles from the Sassoon house, I tried dialing up Uber, as there were no taxis waiting at the train station. But that deep into the Weald of Kent, no Uber drivers were answering my online siren call, so I ended up walking along the busy main street to Whyte's Corner, where I found a bus stop and timetables for several buses (mostly the number 6) that passed over Gedges Hill, on which Weirleigh sits close to the top.

Waiting at the bus stop proved a lively affair, with several older women pulling market trolleys engaging me in a long discussion about which bus would pass closest to the house. (One of the women at the stop even said that her husband had grown up in the house, although she knew nothing about Siegfried Sassoon or about any of his books set in the surrounding fields.)

FRIENDS OF A KIND

Once the double-decker bus arrived, the driver joined in the ongoing conversation about my interest in Weirleigh. What concerned the driver was that the road that passed in front of the house was narrow, winding, and lined with thick vegetation. He didn't like the idea of me walking along the side of the road, even if it was in the cause of literary adventurism.

In the end a compromise was reached: I was stationed in the top forward seat of the double-decker bus, and the driver agreed to slow down as we approached the house, so that I could film the exterior and the surrounding gardens. Earlier in our conversation, he had said that the house was under renovation, so it would be pointless, in any case, to try knocking on the front door. The driver added, as well, that Sassoon was little more than a ghost on the property, which he passed each day on the bus and which had in the last thirty years been subdivided into something of a suburban development. Yes, I heard him say, Weirleigh was still standing, but the house I was looking for probably only existed in the pages of Sassoon's memoirs.

I appreciated that the driver of a public bus took such a passionate interest in my research, and true to his word he slowed the bus down to a crawl as we snaked up Gedges Hill and went past Weirleigh, which was surrounded by fencing and construction equipment. The house itself might well be that of Nathaniel Hawthorne's *Seven Gables*, given that my first impression was of chimneys and sloping rooflines all converging on top of a rambling, red brick house. I did feel a warm sense of accomplishment to have finally seen it, if only from a passing bus, as in many ways the house (along with the trenches of the Western Front in World War I) explains so much about Sassoon's development as a writer.

When I was later at home and seated in front of my own fireplace, I finished reading the *Memoirs of a Fox-Hunting Man*, although for the longest time I had put off picking it up, fearful that I would find the writing stilted and the subject unpleasant. I find the idea of fox hunting cruel and inhumane, and as much as I had liked and admired Sassoon's descriptions of the Great War, I thought I would get nowhere with his recollections of the Kent countryside and weekends riding to the hounds. But I read the first volume of the memoirs with near endless pleasure, as it offered me a glimpse into a world as vanished as Leo Tolstoy's Russia or Harper Lee's Georgia—one that the trench warfare of the Western Front 1914-18 swept into oblivion.

In the memoir Sassoon describes himself as "dreaming and

unpractical," and the literary persona of Sherston as a "fox-hunting man" is that of a country gentleman, in his early twenties, who in many ways is as aimless as Benjamin Braddock, played by Dustin Hoffman in *The Graduate*. Sherston/Sassoon attends Oxford but does not graduate, preferring to drift back into the world of a country gentleman. He is done with schooling, has time on his hands, is still living at home, and has no idea what he wants from life. He says, with insight into his drift: "The mental condition of an active young man who asks nothing more of life than twelve hundred a year and four days a week with the Packlestone is perhaps not easy to defend. It looks rather paltry on paper. That, however, was my own mental position, and I saw nothing strange in it…"

Sassoon managed to preserve in print not just a slice of aristocratic life (fox hunting) but a picture of what it was like, in the prewar years, to live on the Weald of Kent in the embrace of a loving aunt (Sherston's parents are dead—although Sassoon's mother was very much alive when he was there) and her devoted staff (Dixon is the stable manager who fills the barn with ponies and horses).

The memoir is the story of Sassoon's innocence projected onto a landscape that many consider to be among the finest in England. He writes: "When I was twelve years old I hadn't been to London half a dozen times in my life and the ten sleepy miles to the county town, whither the village carrier's van went three times a week, were a road to romance…. How little I knew of the enormous world beyond that valley and those low green hills."

For Sassoon, fox hunting is his ticket out of his cloistered childhood. He traveled around Kent for meets, learned to ride, made friends, attended dinners, and jumped fences and overcame obstacles, many of which arose from his isolation as an only child. As someone squeamish over the idea of dead foxes, I was also happy that Sassoon was more attracted to country manners than to the idea of a pelt on a barn door. He writes:

> I lay stress on these facts because it is my firm belief that the majority of fox-hunting riders never enjoy a really "quick thing" while it is in progress. Their enjoyment, therefore, mainly consists in talking about it afterwards and congratulating themselves on their rashness or their discretion, according to their temperaments. One

man remembers how he followed the first whip over
an awkward stile, while another thinks how cleverly he
made use of a lucky lane or a line of gates....

Memories within memories; those red and black
and brown coated riders return to me now without
any beckoning, bringing along with them the wintry
smelling freshness of the woods and fields.

The memoir drifts toward war, although most of the time that Sassoon is riding to the hounds he is living in the same splendid isolation that engulfed the rest of England. (He writes: "Europe was nothing but a name to me. I couldn't even bring myself to read about it in the daily paper.") Nor does he have any inkling that military service, let alone heroism or poetry in trenches, lies in his future. He writes: "Officers at the barracks were only an ornament; war had become an impossibility. I had sometimes thought with horror of the countries where they had conscription and young men like myself were forced to serve two years in the army whether they liked it or not."

Before the declaration of war, he enlisted in the Yeomanry, although he points out, come August 1914: "For me, so far, the War had been a mounted infantry picnic in perfect weather." Later, he reflects, as if he has passed through an invisible door: "Everything was behind us, and the First Battalion was in front of us."

The memoir ends on the Western Front, with Sherston/Sassoon trying desperately to recall his prewar idyls in the Weald of Kent. He writes of a letter he has received from his aunt's groom, the male presence in his life after his father died:

> Dixon's letter sent me off into pleasant imaginings;
> to have him near me would make all the difference,
> I thought. Everything I had known before the War
> seemed to be withering away and falling to pieces...but
> with Dixon to talk to I should still feel that the past was
> holding its own with the War; and I wanted the past to
> survive and to begin again; the idea was like daylight
> on the other side of this bad weather in which life and
> death had come so close to one another.

Soon, he learns that his beloved horse, the groom Dixon, and many of his fox-hunting friends will not be coming home from the war, except in his memories. He reflects: "The War seemed to have made up its mind to obliterate all those early adventures of mine."

FRIENDS OF A KIND

The Unquiet Western Front:
Siegfried's journey

AFTER A PERIOD of training, Sassoon was commissioned as an infantry officer in the Royal Welch Fusiliers. Late in 1915, he was sent to France, and for the next three years—what with wounds, illness, and leave—he was back and forth between the front lines and England, much the way in his writing he contrasts pastoral Britain with death in the mud. In his poem "Suicide in the Trenches," he writes:

> *You smug-faced crowds with kindling eye*
> *Who cheer when soldier lads march by,*
> *Sneak home and pray you'll never know*
> *The hell where youth and laughter go.*

Although initially Sassoon served as the battalion transport officer, he made his name as a platoon and company commander who was fearless when leading raiding parties into German trenches. (He writes in the *Memoirs*: "I also stated that as for me, I more or less made up my mind to die because in the circumstances there didn't seem anything else to be done.") He gave death its best shot when, after dark, he would crawl on his belly into no-man's-land and throw grenades into German positions. Late in his life, as quoted in Egremont, Sassoon told a fellow soldier how "he had found commanding a company 'very tiring' and preferred 'doing stunts' in no-man's land." That said, he, like T. E. Lawrence, enjoyed the deep respect of the men he commanded, who never felt he was above carrying out the same orders that he gave to those serving under him.

What changed the war for Sassoon was the death of several fellow officers (notably his friend David Thomas on the Somme in 1916), after which, to use an expression of World War II, he might have "gone native" and sought out every opportunity to take revenge on the Germans. Egremont quotes him:

> 'I want to get a good name in the Battalion, for the sake of poetry and poets, whom I represent,' he wrote. But since David Thomas's death, there was another motive:

'hate' and 'the lust to kill'.... 'I definitely wanted to kill someone at close quarters.' Overcoming the individual tragedies of his comrades' deaths, a thrill seized him: addictive, heroically solitary, without introspection or regret.

Such bloodletting led to his Military Cross but perhaps also to his disillusionment with the war in general.

Although the British Empire suffered more than a million casualties in World War I, the dividing line between fox-hunting England and postwar disillusionment took place on July 1, 1916, when some 57,000 British and Commonwealth soldiers were killed and wounded in the first waves of the attacks along the banks of the River Somme. Sassoon's battalion was in reserve that day, near the village of Mametz, just outside Albert.

In 2000, after a family wedding in Paris, I drove north in search of Mametz Wood, in part to retrace Sassoon's footsteps on that fateful day. All I saw were several monuments, an open agricultural field, and a distant forest, from which no doubt the Germans poured fire against the attacking British (who walked in the direction of German guns, with a few kicking soccer balls). Although Sassoon was to fight hard in the Battle of the Somme, on that first morning, according to Egremont, he was a spectator at the perch near the Bois Français:

> Eating oranges, Sassoon saw a lark, heard the cry of birds as the explosions died out and imagined 'a sunlit picture of hell'. The Manchesters walked out of their trench, and news came through in the evening that Montauban and Mametz had been taken.

Some weeks later, while the fighting raged, he fell ill and a kindly doctor, at a dressing station, seeing the Military Cross on his tunic, decided that he had "done enough for a while" and sent him back to England to recuperate. That leave and a subsequent one led to his denunciation of the war in print, in a statement that was drafted with the assistance of philosopher and anti-war protester Bertrand Russell and his lover, Lady Ottoline Morrell.

In his midlife memoir, *Siegfried's Journey*, Sassoon writes of this period:

> I could no longer indulge in fine feelings about being a hero, for although my period of active service had given me confidence in myself as a front-line officer I was ceasing to believe in the War itself. Like most of the infantry, I had expected too much of the Battle of the Somme. We had been told that it would be 'the Great Advance'. It was now obvious that it had been nothing of the kind, and disillusionment was inevitable....
>
> My mutual behaviour had become a typical case for the student of war psychology, made more interesting, perhaps, by the fact that disillusionment was combined with determination to employ my discontents as a subject for literary expression.

Sassoon's letter was published on June 15, 1917 in the newspapers and discussed in Parliament. That the author was a decorated officer from the trenches made it harder to dismiss. Sassoon expected either to be court-martialed or dispatched on the next troop train to the front. (He wrote: "The idea of being martyrised appealed to me emotionally as a form of 'heroism.'") What saved him from a court-martial was his friendship with Eddie Marsh, who was the private secretary to Winston Churchill, back in government from his own exile to the front after the Gallipoli disaster. Churchill later boasted at a dinner party that he had intervened with the war department to keep Sassoon from a firing squad. Instead, Sassoon was deemed to be suffering from shell shock (why else would he denounce the war?) and was bundled off to Craiglockhart, an Edinburgh sanatorium, where he was placed under the care of Dr. William Rivers. Egremont writes:

> Rivers became not the ideal friend but an ideal father, discovering someone shocked by war—as [Sassoon's] dreams showed—and gripped by two fears: of returning to the trenches and of failing the test of manliness, an anxiety since a boyhood suffused with sexual doubt and romantic notions of chivalry.

Since then, their relationship has been the subject of novels, biographies, and even a television mini-series, as both men were eloquent, and the bond that they formed exemplified the conflicts between those who believed the war was immoral and others who believed that it was a soldier's obligation to fight for his country. In this instance, Sassoon and Rivers believed each other's position, as well as their own. Rivers believed that a soldier had a duty to fight.

Although Rivers was able to coax Sassoon back to the war—in Palestine and finally back to the Western Front—Sassoon's long convalescence, first in Scotland and then in England, allowed him to pursue his poetry and keep up with his literary contacts, which were a Who's Who of literary Britain at that time. Among those he befriended was Thomas Hardy, who was living at Max Gate when Sassoon came calling.

The irony was not lost on Sassoon that he had gone into battle on the Somme with several of Hardy's Wessex novels, including *Tess of the d'Urbervilles*. He writes in *Siegfried's Journey*: "It seemed almost incredible that—after carrying a couple of the Wessex novels about with me during the Somme battle—I might have arrived at Burford to spend an afternoon in the presence of the great man himself!" He had often heard of Hardy from his mother's brother, Hamo, a sculptor who in 1915 had done a bust of the poet. Egremont writes that even in the trenches Sassoon longed for the connection to the idyllic aspects of Hardy's writing:

> But, as often with Sassoon, anger and energy were joined by nostalgia, a yearning for country life that turned him towards one of his greatest idols: Thomas Hardy. "Books about England were all I wanted,' he wrote later of his time at Flixécourt.... He had *Tess of the D'Urbervilles* and thought of the Sussex landscape round Ringmer as the bombardment intensified.

When Sassoon finally met the great man, he commented: "He liked good talk, of course, but preferred people not to be vividly intellectual at the tea-table." He went on: "Anyhow, what I carried away from Max Gate, both then and thereafter, was an impressive awareness that Hardy—who was, as I remarked to myself, 'the nearest thing to Shakespeare I should ever go for a walk with'—had no vestige of vanity, and wore his illustrious laurels with no more concern about them than if they had been his hat."

FRIENDS OF A KIND

Heytesbury's Sassoon: *A country gentleman*

LEAVING MELLS, I took another road than the one I had come in on, hoping that I might bypass some of the big hills that led back to Frome. For a while I rolled along country lanes but finally I walked the bike up a steep incline leading into Frome. Then I followed a cycle route through Frome, avoiding some of the traffic, and outside the town picked up the national cycle Route 24, which would take me in a slightly roundabout way to Warminster and Heytesbury, where Sassoon lived after he got married in the 1930s. (His marriage is another oddity in the Sassoon story, as throughout the 1920s he was homosexual.)

The advantage of following a prescribed cycle path is that one doesn't have to stop at each crossroads and study the map. (GPS can be accurate, but it is not compatible with historical wanderings.) Besides, the maps in my bag were long on literary allusions but short on details about where to turn. For about an hour, I wandered along country lanes in Wiltshire until the path led me directly to Longleat House, a baronial mansion that looks like a Scottish castle nestled in a valley of the Highlands.

Surrounding the manor house are hundreds of acres resembling a manicured croquet lawn, and I felt as though I was biking into a vision of medieval England. Because I was running late for Heytesbury, I decided not to tarry on the lush grounds. I got the distinct impression that while Longleat was still a drawing room of Empire, it doubled as a restaurant, museum, amusement park, and zoo, as I could see a long line of slow-moving cars—many with children's faces glued to the windows—driving the contours of the gardens, as if on the lookout for safari animals.

If Longleat was stocked with lions or tigers, I never saw any. Instead I suffered on a long hillside that climbed out of the parkland on the southern side. It went on for more than a mile, and about halfway up I was again reduced to putting my feet on the ground. It didn't help that I was biking around England with a computer and several hardcover biographies.

When I got to the top I had a near endless glide down the other side into Warminster, which is the market town before Heytesbury. There I stopped to refill my water bottles and buy a sandwich lunch from a gas station (I refer to this diet as "eating on the half Shell"). I also got directions to Heytesbury, about four miles farther down a national road. Sometime after 2 p.m., after making a few wrong turns in the village, I pulled up to the house of which Sassoon wrote, just after he bought it in 1930, that he felt like he was "walking calmly into the first volume of a Trollope novel."

After Sassoon died in 1967, the manor house was sold off and later subdivided into an elegant gated community of condominiums and single-family houses. (The gate is only missing a portcullis.) In addition, what the British call a "dual-carriage way" was cut through the front section of the property, separating it from Heytesbury. I doubt Sassoon would recognize his old home, which Egremont describes this way:

> A large, barrack-like, grey-stone Georgian mansion, surrounded by fine trees, set back from the village of Heytesbury in the Wylye valley, it was a much more substantial property than Fitz House or Weirleigh [where he grew up], with 90 acres of parkland and 130 acres of woods. His decision to buy it was, perhaps, a reflection of his experience of country-house life at Wilsford where, despite Stephen's [Stephen Tennant, his gay lover] moods, Sassoon had found an English paradise; now he would show Tennant that he could make a paradise of his own, this time a genuinely eighteenth-century one, not an Arts and Crafts pastiche.

In many ways, with the move to Heytesbury, Sassoon—the fox-hunting man—was coming home to his idealized image of England, although the postwar years were every bit as tumultuous for Sassoon as they were for Lawrence.

FRIENDS OF A KIND

Sassoon and Lawrence: *Postwar friends*

SASSOON SPENT ARMISTICE Day, 1918, at a dinner in London with a soldier who had, according to Egremont, "spent the war supplying the liquor board." Sassoon writes despondently in *Siegfried's Journey*: "Our moral advantage over him made the situation awkward. It was, no doubt, wrong for me to exclaim that the War had been a loathsome tragedy and that all this flag-waving couldn't alter it; but he wasn't in a position to support the opposite view with fine phrases."

Leaving the army, Sassoon tried his hand as newspaper editor, worked on his poetry, made a speaking tour in the United States (he tended to mumble on stage), cultivated literary giants, and embarked on a series of homosexual love affairs, most of which ended painfully.

At his first meeting with T. E. Lawrence, which took place in London, Sassoon had no idea who he was, only that he was friendly with Eddie Marsh and had asked to meet the celebrated poet and war critic. Egremont writes:

> At the Savoy, with Eddie, he found the small, fair haired young-looking T. E. Lawrence and discussed Doughty and Henry James, Marsh overflowing with appropriate anecdotes. Sassoon at one moment exclaimed to the quiet Lawrence, 'What I can't understand is how you came to be a Colonel!' Lawrence, who had asked to meet the author of *Counter-Attack*, felt charmed by the question, but Sassoon was not yet mesmerized by one of the most compelling influences of his life. The next day he went again to the Ministry of Munitions to see Churchill, who was 'full of victory talk', sounding, Sassoon thought, like the leading article of a newspaper, opposed to the idealistic Woodrow Wilson and intending (his audience surmised) that a victorious Britain should increase its power, with Germany skinned alive.

In time Sassoon and Lawrence, so similar in many ways, would find enduring friendship, but it took a while, despite their shared affection for Thomas Hardy. In 1922, Sassoon bumped into Robert Graves and Lawrence near Piccadilly Circus, thought they were laughing at him, and stalked off in a huff.

Unlike many Lawrence biographers, Egremont takes it for granted that Lawrence was homosexual and that this orientation is something he shared with Sassoon, although the two were never lovers. Egremont writes about their friendship in this way:

> An ascetic, homosexual masochist, Lawrence put into his friendships a hypnotic, often wordless, sense of mystical understanding. Small, of immense vitality combined with an emotional and physical awkwardness that made him—like Thomas Hardy—hate to be touched, he seemed to reach beyond the material world. For Sassoon, who was often uncomfortable with reality, his aura was especially strong. Lawrence knew the lasting demons of battle.

Two things changed Sassoon's life in the late 1920s: he published *Memoirs of a Fox-Hunting Man*, which established his reputation as a leading World War I memoirist (capable of more than anti-war poems), and he fell in love with Stephen Tennant, a scion of immense wealth whose mother was married to the former foreign minister, Sir Edward Grey (whom Sassoon blamed for leading England into the world war). Sassoon also learned to drive a car (apparently he was prone to thinking they could leap fences) and with Tennant embarked on a series of long drives across England and the continent. In France he made several detours to his former front lines and stopped at Ypres (where the war memorial at the Menim Gate prompted him to recall "the unheroic Dead who fed the guns"). Sassoon and Tennant also make a long trip through Italy and Sicily, where in early 1930 Sassoon finished the manuscript of *Memoirs of an Infantry Officer* in a Syracuse hotel.

Tennant, who often dressed in what looked like women's clothes, was prone to hysteria and paranoia, and the combination of his illnesses and Sassoon's insecurities drove them apart. On the rebound, Siegfried married Hester Gatty, an equally vulnerable woman but one with a fortune. The

FRIENDS OF A KIND

marriage resulted in a son, George, but little happiness; each had their own room at Heytesbury until Hester moved to the Scottish island of Mull. What could be expected in such a union if, on their honeymoon, Hester and Siegfried went to the same places and stayed in the same hotels that, three years before, Tennant and Sassoon had visited in Sicily?

Sassoon was at Heytesbury when Lawrence was killed on his motorcycle. Some years before, when motoring with Tennant, Sassoon had come across him on a visit to Thomas Hardy. Egremont writes: "They called at Max Gate, to find T. E. Lawrence there on his motorbicycle, over from Bovington Camp. Later they went to Lawrence's cottage, meeting his friend Russell—whom Sassoon assumed was 'T. E.'s sexual partner'— then through the Wylye valley, to Abbotsbury and H. M. Tomlinson, who had rented The Old Coastguard Station; this pastoral England seemed a world away from modernism."

On hearing the news about Lawrence, Sassoon immediately drove down to Moreton, where he joined the small circle, including Winston Churchill and E. M. Forster, at the burial. Later he wrote a poem about his departed friend that reads:

> *I'd heard fool-heroes brag of where they'd been,*
> *With stories of the glories that they'd seen.*
> *But you, good simple soldier, seasoned well*
> *In woods and posts and crater-lines of hell…*

They were words that could easily have been said about Sassoon.

SIEGFRIED SASSOON

Warminster: *Trainspotting memoirs*

NOTHING IN HEYTESBURY, at least that I could find, connects the village to Siegfried Sassoon, even though his poetry and memoirs have helped define the way that millions imagine World War I in the trenches. Today the war seems a pointless slaughter; then, at least as Sassoon expressed them from the frontlines, such sentiments were a revelation.

Heading to the train station in Warminster, I could have ridden back along the busy national highway, but the traffic was daunting. Instead, I folded up the Brompton and carried it onto a local bus, which dropped me near the railway station. There I learned that it would be impossible, later that night, for me to board the overnight train from Plymouth to London. The problem was that company policy did not allow anyone to make a reservation less than twenty-four hours before departure. As it was now too late to reserve a berth, I decided to head to Bristol, a city I had never seen.

The Bristol train was running late, and when it showed up, it was packed with Friday afternoon travelers. I found a seat where I could also stow the bicycle, but it was facing in the wrong direction, something I find disconcerting on a train. I had thought I might read some excepts from Sassoon on my Kindle or look out the window at the West Country; instead I sat motionless in my seat, unable to move or even to retrieve a book from my bags. New English trains look modern on the outside; inside, they feel like steerage on the *Titanic*.

What I wanted to see in Bristol was the university, but what I didn't know, until it was too late, is that it sits at the top of a hill of San Francisco proportions and the route I had chosen to get there meant more pushing of the bike up a steep incline. I did finally arrive, breathlessly, at the top and toured the colleges before coasting down the hill to the station.

Only when I was back in Switzerland did I spend more time with Sassoon's many memoirs, rereading *Memoirs of a Fox-Hunting Man*, which has a haunting ending. By this point Sherston has left the leafy glades of his childhood and is serving in the war in France. Sassoon biographer Max Egremont writes of the last line: "On the last page Sherston, hearing a bird sing beyond a destroyed wood in the trenches, stands 'deprived of everything he valued.'" Actually the ending is more subtle and lyrical. It reads:

> And here I was, with my knobkerrie in my hand, staring across at the enemy I'd never seen. Somewhere out of sight beyond the splintered tree-tops of Hidden Wood a bird had begun to sing. Without knowing why, I remembered that it was Easter Sunday. Standing in that dismal ditch, I could find no consolation in the thought that Christ was risen. I sploshed back to the dug-out to call the others up for "stand-to."

I read this passage as the opening of the next volume, *Memoirs of an Infantry Officer*, which covers the war years in detail.

Describing the horrors of war and the trenches, Sassoon's poetry is immediate, as much of it was written, literally, on the front lines, which explains the agony in so many verses, as, for example, when he writes in "They":

> *'We're none of us the same!' the boys reply.*
> *'For George lost both his legs; and Bill's stone blind;*
> *'Poor Jim's shot through the lungs and like to die;*
> *'And Bert's gone syphilitic: you'll not find*
> *'A chap who's served that hasn't found some change.*
> *'And the Bishop said: 'The ways of God are strange!'*

By contrast, the *Memoirs of an Infantry Officer*, written more than ten years after the war, although clearly based on his diaries, are distanced from the carnage, which Sassoon uses to ironic ends, writing in a language that, while not comic, at least conveys the humour that comes naturally to many soldiers serving on the front lines.

Here is a sampler of Sassoon's prose from the second volume of the memoir:

—On training: "I was like a boy going to early school, except that no bell was ringing, and instead of Thucydides or Virgil, I was carrying a gun."

—On patrolling in no-man's-land: "It was rather like going out to weed a neglected garden after being warned that there might be a tiger among the gooseberry bushes."

—On fighting: "My courage was of the cock-fighting kind. Cock-fighting is illegal in England, but in July, 1916 the man who could boast that he'd killed a German in the Battle of the Somme would have been patted on the back by a bishop in a hospital ward."

—On battle: "I didn't want to die—not before I'd finished reading *The Return of the Native* anyhow."

—On glory: "I wanted the War to be an impressive experience—terrible, but not horrible enough to interfere with my heroic emotions."

—On commanding officers: "I began to realize that in a Commanding Officer, amiability is not enough."

—On the ranks: "…modern warfare offered a niche for everyone, and many of them looked better qualified for a card-table than a military campaign."

—On anger: "I felt more annoyed with Battalion Headquarters than with the enemy."

—On religion: "The consolations of the Church of England weren't much in demand at the Advance Dressing Station."

—On God and country: "In war-time the word patriotism means suppression of truth."

—On reporters: "But somehow the newspaper men always kept the horrifying realities of the War out of their articles, for it was unpatriotic to be bitter, and the dead were assumed to be gloriously happy."

—On fate: "But I am no believer in wild denunciations of the War; I am merely describing my own experience in it; and in 1917 I was only beginning to learn that life, for the majority of the population, is an unlovely struggle against unfair odds, culminating in a cheap funeral."

Many biographers have criticized Sassoon for writing about his war in fictionalized memoirs, so that he can clean up the awkward bits.

For example, Egremont writes: "In the process, he created, in parallel with an autobiography, a utopia purged of his own awkward boyhood, his homosexuality, his Jewishness, his wish to be a writer, Theresa's [his mother] mental fragility and the socially demeaning, hideous Weirleigh [the house where he grew up]. Sassoon seals up this beautiful world, as he seals up parts of his true self." But I judge the *Memoirs* by a different standard, as for almost four years in World War II, my father was a company commander in a front-line Marine Corps battalion, and his stories about Pacific island combat sounded much the same as Sassoon's. Of leaving the Battle of Arras, Sassoon writes hauntingly:

> Their jargoning voices mingled with the rumble
> and throb of the train as it journeyed—so safely and
> sedately—through the environing gloom. The Front
> Line was safely behind us; but it could lay its hand on
> our hearts, though its bludgeoning reality diminished
> with every mile. It was as if we were pursued by
> the Arras Battle which had now become a huge
> and horrible idea. We might be boastful or sagely
> reconstructive about our experience, in accordance with
> our different characters. But our minds were still out
> of breath and our inmost thoughts in disorderly retreat
> from bellowing darkness and men dying out in shell-
> holes under the desolation of returning daylight. We
> were the survivors; few among us would ever tell the
> truth to our friends and relations in England. We were
> carrying something in our heads which belonged to us
> alone, and to those we had left behind us in the battle.

In a similar vein, although it was about another war in another part of the world, what my father wrote about his last days in the battle of Guadalcanal echoes Sassoon's style, which tells me that *Memoirs of an Infantry Officer* describes many wars. My father wrote in 1983:

> But we, too, were weakening. The adrenaline
> distilled by courage was running low. Our patrols
> slackened; we dreaded more than ever the agony of

evacuating the dead and wounded on stretchers through the jungle. Since August our battalion had been on the front line for more than four months—one of the longest stretches without relief in any modern war—and the strain was showing. All we could anticipate were fresh orders to rejoin the troops attacking westward and one more struggle up the long, bare ridges that rose from the jungle floor. In the midst of this weary resignation we received the electrifying word that we were leaving the island. It was a reprieve that seemed to come not only from division HQ but from heaven.

I am sure Sassoon would have recognized the emotions here.

Robert von Ranke Graves served in the Great War as subaltern in the Royal Welch Fusiliers, a regiment in the trenches in France. He fought in the slaughter that was the Battle of Loos—a British attack uphill into German guns. Before the 1916 battle of the Somme, Graves met another young regimental officer, Siegfried Sassoon, with whom he shared his passion for poetry and prose. Graves was badly wounded on the Somme, but he recovered, and in 1917, he appealed to the military tribunal hearing Sassoon's case that his friend be spared the death penalty. After the war, while a student at Oxford, he met T. E. Lawrence, and while there wrote one of the first books about his legend in the desert called *Lawrence and the Arabs*. Graves's memoir, *Good-bye to All That*, was published in 1929.

Section III

ROBERT GRAVES: HELLO TO ALL THAT

With Siegfried Sassoon

THE SOLDIER MOST associated with Siegfried Sassoon is his fellow poet and officer from the Royal Welch Fusiliers, Robert Graves, who published *Good-Bye to All That* about the time that Sassoon brought out *Memoirs of an Infantry Officer*. The two men met in April 1915, at Festubert on the front lines in France. Sassoon wrote in his diary: "Walked into Bethune for tea with Robert Graves, a young poet in Third Battalion and very much disliked." He might have stopped there trying to cultivate Graves, except the two became lifelong friends and sometimes rivals. Most of the time they got along fine, and after the war they exchanged long letters and visits. At other times they sniped at each other.

Sassoon felt that Graves had copied his narrative structure in *Good-Bye to All That*, although it came out before *Memoirs*. Egremont writes of Sassoon's reaction: "The book seemed egotistical, inaccurate, condescending, journalistic and falsely tough, the swaggering narrator different from the prim, shaky wartime Graves. *Good-Bye to All That* revelled in unpleasantness, as in the descriptions of soldiers' lechery and the resurrection of Owen's reputed cowardice." So angry was Sassoon—later he mellowed—that he and a friend spent an entire night going through the Graves memoirs, pointing out factual errors and other faults on 250 of the 448 pages in the book. Graves later returned the favor, panning some of Sassoon's writing, although that didn't stop him from borrowing money from the wealthier Siegfried.[2]

In looking at the two memoirs, it is hard to tell which of the writers most influenced the other. Graves has many sentiments and observations that Sassoon would later echo, although it is certainly possible that Sassoon had shown *Memoirs* to his friend as a work in progress. Each would have been valuable to the other in checking facts or the progress of some battle. Graves writes, in a very Sassoon manner: "In March I rejoined the First Battalion on the Somme. It was primrose season." He also writes: "Patriotism, in the trenches, was too remote a sentiment, and at once rejected as fit only for civilians, or prisoners."

I first read the Graves memoir as a freshman in college, when taking Professor Mark Neuman's seminar on European history. Unfortunately, that course (or maybe that professor?) was over my head, as he expected a room full of college freshmen to have read—even before the first class—all 1,072 pages of the small type in R. R. Palmer's *A History of Europe in the Modern World*. Taking the facts of European history "as read," the seminar would then spend each week on "original" texts, including Francis Bacon's *The New Organon* (which interested me not at all as a freshman) and the Graves memoir (which I liked but found "very English").

Only when I was in my forties did I go back to Graves and admire both the style of the writing ("The necessary supply of heroes must be maintained at all costs...") and the politics ("The troops with the worst reputation for acts of violence against prisoners were the Canadians (and later the Australians).... At all events, most overseas men, and some British troops, made atrocities against prisoners a boast, not a confession"). He is especially clear in stating that the Allies held no moral advantage over the Germans. He writes:

> We no longer believed the highly-colored accounts of
> German atrocities in Belgium; knowing the Belgian

---

2 Apparently another source of tension between the two men was Graves' published description in *Good-Bye to All That* of his visit in 1916 to Weirleigh, the house where Sassoon grew up in the Weald of Kent. It was just after Sassoon's younger brother Hamo had been killed in Gallipoli, and during the stay Graves heard what he described as "sudden rapping noises" and a "diabolic yell and a succession of laughing, sobbing shrieks that sent me flying to the door." The source of the racket turned out to be Sassoon's mother trying to raise the spirit of her dead son on the other side "by various spiritualistic means." Graves wrote: "In the morning, I told my friend, 'I'm leaving this place. It's worse than France.'" When the account came out in 1929, Sassoon resented Graves writing about his family's grief in this way, and it added to the list of grievances that both men nurtured against each other, despite being lifelong friends.

now at firsthand. By atrocities we meant, specifically, rape, mutilation, and torture—not summary shooting of suspected spies, harborers of spies, *franc-tireurs*, or disobedient local officials. If the atrocity-list had to include the accident-on-purpose bombing or machine-gunning of civilians from the air, the Allies were committing as many atrocities as the Germans.

He makes it clear that on both sides professional soldiers, even those who had been drafted or volunteered, were carrying out unpleasant orders. He writes: "The battalion cared as little about the successes or reverses of our Allies as about the origins of the war. A professional soldier's duty was simply to fight whomever the King ordered him to fight."

Because Sassoon's memoirs are fictionalized, he writes about Robert Graves through the character of David Cromlech, while Graves mentions Sassoon by name directly, and not always in the most flattering light. He notes that, after the death of a fellow officer, Sassoon tried to take revenge on the Germans. Although he was the battalion transport officer, he led patrols into no-man's-land, where he could toss grenades into German trenches. Perhaps the biggest disagreement between the men was over the role that Graves played when Sassoon issued his anti-war statement in 1917, with the assistance of Bertrand Russell. Graves wrote: "I found myself most bitter against the pacifists who had encouraged him to make this gesture. I felt that, not being soldiers, they could not understand what it cost Siegfried emotionally."

Graves was present when Sassoon was summoned before a medical board, which was convened to conclude that he had written his anti-war protest because of "nerves" or "shell shock," not because he was treasonous. Graves himself gave evidence to the panel and tried to assure Sassoon that in no way would he be court-martialed. (Graves was over his pay grade in making such a claim.)

Later the two men fell out (for a while) when Graves hinted in letters to Sassoon that his fellow Welch Fusiliers officers were skeptical that Siegfried was actually suffering from war shock and needed to spend time in an asylum. Sassoon resented that Graves had not joined him in denouncing the war more forcibly, which explains why Siegfried scoffed at this passage in *Good-Bye to All That*, when Graves writes: "Siegfried vehemently asserted that the [peace] terms should have been accepted;

FRIENDS OF A KIND

I agreed. We no longer saw the war as one between trade-rivals: its continuance seemed merely a sacrifice of the idealistic younger generation to the stupidity and self-protective alarm of the elder." Sassoon may have felt that Graves had left him hanging on the wire in no-man's-land, but throughout all of their disagreements they remained friends.

Graves at Charterhouse

AS I WAS planning my first trip, I intended to weave in a stop for Robert Graves. I knew that he had grown up in Wimbledon, where there was a plaque on the family's house, and that he had spent his summers in North Wales, near Harlech and its Arthurian castle. But none of those stops worked with my planning, and in the end it came on another trip that I spent a day out of London visiting his boarding school, Charterhouse. In the meantime, I also had a chance to reread *Good-Bye to All That* and volume one of a biography entitled *Robert Graves: The Assault Heroic 1895-1926* by Richard Perceval Graves, one of Robert's nephews.

The train station for Charterhouse is Godalming, and I had no trouble getting there. Richard Perceval Graves, who also went to Charterhouse, describes the trip in his biography:

> His train journey took him through the rolling hills of Surrey to the pleasant little country town of Godalming. Trunks were sent on 'in advance'; and from Godalming station most boys walked with their hand-luggage out of town and up the long winding road which climbs westward above the River Wey to the Charterhouse heights.

I struck out in finding a taxi at the station and ended up walking those same two kilometers, up a hill to the campus on the heights. I figured that Graves' portrait would be hanging in the school library but assumed that a private school didn't want strangers wandering around the campus. I presented myself to the admissions office, explained the nature of my research, and asked if I could perhaps meet one of the librarians on the staff. Just walking to the administrative offices, I got a sense of how imposing Charterhouse is and wasn't completely surprised that Graves wrote of his first days there: "From the moment I arrived at the school I suffered an oppression of spirit that I hesitate now to recall in its full intensity."

Unfortunately, on the day I was visiting, the Charterhouse archivist,

Mrs. Catherine Smith, was not available to see me, although she subsequently wrote me a long letter, explaining how I could access some of the prose and poetry that Graves wrote while he was a student. ("You will find articles and poems written by Robert Graves in both the School's magazines and I have attached a list of poems/letters that appear in *The Carthusian* and a list that includes the *Greyfriar* and a few other items that have not been digitized.") I was disappointed not to see his portrait hanging in a library or commons room, but her letter and my walk around the campus were the ideal way to get me started on the life of Robert Graves.

Graves was fourteen when he matriculated at Charterhouse. Ironically, as he would write a number of books and poems set in the classical world (*I, Claudius* was the most successful), his weakest subject on arrival was Greek. His family, by no means poor, lacked some of the inherited wealth of other students, and Graves' prickly personality combined with this disadvantage made it hard for him to integrate fully with his classmates. (Being good at boxing helped, however.) He was lucky to find among the masters George Mallory, who would achieve lasting and justifiable fame as a mountaineer. He may or may not have been the first person to reach the summit of Mount Everest (he died trying, so we shall never know conclusively if he made it).[3]

Mallory introduced Graves to climbing and to "the existence of modern authors I had never heard of people like Shaw, Samuel Butler, Rupert Brooke, Well, Flecker, or Masefield, and I was greatly interested in them." In 1919 Graves wrote about Mallory:

> But George, disliked and ragged though he may be,
> has always been the champion of everything noble and
> downtrodden and enemy of everything that is base and
> uplifted, and has been the only friend to a succession
> of Carthusian Ugly Ducklings who but for him would
> have gone under altogether.

Graves' descriptions of Mallory's brilliance as a climber make it clear that he certainly had the skills to get to the top of Everest. Graves writes:

---

[3] Mallory died on Everest in 1924 but only in 1999 was his body found on the mountain—but not his Kodak camera. So the debate continues whether he made it to the top.

No one knows whether he and Irvine actually made the last five hundred yards of the ascent, or whether they turned back, or what happened; but another who has climbed with George is convinced that he got to the summit and rejoiced in his accustomed way without leaving himself sufficient reserve of strength for the descent.

It was also at Charterhouse that Graves met the ubiquitous Eddie Marsh, Winston Churchill's private secretary and the patron of so many poets and writers. Richard Perceval Graves writes:

> ...Robert could still escape to the protective atmosphere of Mallory's rooms; and it was here that one date in late October or early November he was called in after lunch to have coffee with Edward Marsh, a distinguished civil servant who was also a poet and a patron of the arts. Marsh had already published the first volume of *Georgian Poetry* which contained works by many of the 'new' poets; Robert was introduced to him as 'a senior boy of literary promise', and when Marsh left the school he carried away for further study some of Robert's contributions to *The Carthusian*.

Perhaps more than formal schooling, what directed Graves toward prose and poetry were his summers in Wales, which suited his independent nature. He was away from his domineering father, in the company of his artistic mother, and he was free to read and write as he pleased. His nephew Richard writes: "It was here, on the hills behind Harlech, that Robert 'found a personal harmony independent of history or geography." Harlech is less than ten miles from Termadog, the village in Wales where T. E. Lawrence was born, and the proximity of their villages made me want to know more about their relationship, which I knew from the nephew's biography began postwar when both men were in Oxford.

FRIENDS OF A KIND

Graves, Lawrence, and Rory Stewart

WHILE WORKING ON this book, I had an email from my friend Edward Mortimer telling me that Magdalen College in Oxford was hosting an exhibition of T. E. Lawrence memorabilia. Would I like to come over and see it?

I jumped at the chance to come to Oxford, not only to see Edward, whom I had known for more than forty years, but because the invitation came with the offer to spend the night at All Souls College, where Lawrence wrote much of *Seven Pillars of Wisdom*. If I arrived on a certain evening, Edward said, we could attend a speech by Rory Stewart, then a member of Parliament who had written several bestselling books about his own travels around the Middle East—sometimes on foot. At the time, as Stewart was moving up in the ranks of the Conservative Party, he was thought to be this generation's T. E. Lawrence, someone who knew the Middle East from his own travels and war experience in Iraq.

I flew from Geneva to London Gatwick and then caught a bus directly to Oxford. I checked into my lodgings in time to meet Edward at the college for afternoon tea (laid out in the library after about 4 p.m.), and then we walked next door to Magdalen College to look through the Lawrence exhibit. The artifacts were arranged on the second floor of one of the college libraries, and the theme was "Lawrence of Oxford," which was appropriate as Thomas Edward (T. E.) had grown up not far from the High Street on Polestead Road, read history at Jesus College, Oxford, and, after the war, came back to Oxford as a fellow at All Souls, where he rewrote much of *Seven Pillars* (after the first draft disappeared in the Reading railway station).

On display at Magdalen were sketches, manuscripts, maps, and letters from Lawrence's war years in the Middle East. I found of particular interest a map, hand drawn by Lawrence during the Arab Revolt, that showed one of the routes he took alongside the desert rails of the Hejaz Railway on the way to attack Aqaba. According to the caption: "The map shows El Houl, a barren plain near the Hejaz railway about which Lawrence wrote: 'We, ourselves, felt tiny in it, and our urgent progress across its immensity was a stillness or immobility of futile effort.'" That said, Lawrence and his Arab allies did manage to seize Aqaba from its Turkish garrison.

Browsing through the excellent collection, I came across a 1927 first edition of Robert Graves' *Lawrence and the Arabs*, a book that had eluded me throughout my research. I knew that Graves had known Lawrence, but I didn't recall the precise details about either their Oxford friendship or the biography that Graves later wrote about him. During the war Graves' half-brother had served with Lawrence in Cairo, and liked him. After the war, when Graves went up to read classics at St. John's College, Oxford, he and his father met Lawrence in the lounge at All Souls. At this time Lawrence was not yet "of Arabia" and was known only in limited circles, but during 1919-1920 (after Lawrence was in Versailles with various Arab delegations to the peace conference) the two men drew close. Richard Perceval Graves writes:

> Robert…explained…he now spent 'most of my time at Oxford with Col. Lawrence the man who smashed the Turks in Arabia & Palestine: he is at All Souls & a great man on poetry, pictures, music & everything else in the world.' At their first meeting the previous November Robert had 'felt a sudden extraordinary sympathy' with Lawrence; and this feeling persisted, although was later told that everyone was fascinated by Lawrence, and therefore 'tried to dismiss [it]…as extravagant'. The truth is that Lawrence had a great gift for reflecting back to people the best of which they were capable; and he sustained Robert's sense of his worth both as a poet and as a human being at a time when he was increasingly full of self-doubt.

Next to the copy of Graves' biography of Lawrence was an annotation that explained their relationship in more detail. It read:

> Lawrence served in the Arab Bureau with Philip Graves, half-brother to poet and novelist Robert Graves. Lawrence and Philip Graves were early recruits to Cairo and were tasked with updating the Handbook of the Turkish Army. Robert Graves came up to Oxford in 1919 and found friendship with Lawrence, who was a new resident at All Souls, attempting to write up *Seven Pillars*. Following the success of the 1926 publication

of *Seven Pillars*, Lawrence was asked by Jonathan Cape to write an autobiography. Instead, Lawrence insisted that the publisher contract an impoverished Graves to pen a biography. *Lawrence and the Arabs* was immediately successful and helped Graves establish his name as an author and poet. The book, however, is full of inaccuracies which led Lawrence to comment later: "Do not take Graves' book as very true!... It would be hard in writing of a little-known but reputed figure not to dramatise one's subject a bit."

In due course, according to Perceval Graves, Robert would complete the circle and introduce Lawrence to "Hardy, Blunden, and Sassoon" (although Sassoon by then had met Lawrence through Edward Marsh). Perceval Graves adds:

> Between lectures Graves often visited All Souls where Lawrence, who never drank himself, 'used always to send his scout for a silver goblet of audit ale for me...'

Another panel in the exhibition showed a map of the Middle East as imagined by the 1916 Sykes-Picot Agreement that divided Lawrence's Pan-Arabic vision into colonial spheres of influence and mandates. The map shows France coming away with much of what is now Turkey, Lebanon, and Syria while Britain retained control of Iraq and the mandate over Palestine. The agreement was kept secret until it leaked to the press in 1917. The panel describing the map read:

> The Sykes-Picot map of 1916, though never implemented, has long endured as an imagery, variously interpreted as a symbol of imperial duplicity, the cause of a century of instability and authoritarian repression, and most recently a target for violent destruction by the apocalyptic Islamic State group.

When the war between Greece and Turkey—won by the Turks—overturned the 1919 Treaty of Sèvres (as close as Sykes-Picot came to implementation), the French concession was whittled in half while Britain realized that it could not rule Mesopotamia (Iraq) with a handful of military police. Even if Sykes-Picot was stillborn, it still imposed colonial boundaries over various tribal and religious divisions across the Middle East, the consequences of which we are still paying for today.

In his 2016 biography of his uncle Sir Mark Sykes, *The Man Who Created the Middle East*, Christopher Simon Sykes writes: "As one contemporary observed, 'Iraq was created by Churchill, who had the mad idea of joining two widely separated oil wells, Kirkuk and Mosul, by uniting three widely separated peoples, the Kurds, Sunnis and the Shiites.'" He ends the book with a quote from Field Marshall Wavell, who said of Versailles: "After the war to end war, they seem to have been pretty successful in Paris at making a Peace to end Peace."

In *Lawrence and the Arabs*, Graves describes some of Lawrence's coming estrangement from his government and politics. He writes: "In England, at his first coming, he had refused to accept his British decorations. He explained personally to King George that the part he had played in the Arab Revolt was dishonourable to himself and to his country and government. He had, by order, fed the Arabs with false hopes and would be obliged if he might be quietly relieved of the obligation to accept honors for succeeding in his fraud."

At Oxford, Graves and Lawrence talked about chucking it all and heading to Nepal to recover from their war weariness, but the trip never happened. Perceval Graves writes: "If Lawrence went, so would Graves. But Lawrence had declined. The strain of the war, and of the peace negotiations which followed, had finally caught up with him; the substantial successes which he had recently achieved for the Arabs had come too late, and he was on the verge of a severe mental breakdown." He decided to hide anonymous in the ranks of the air force, under an assumed name.

The Lawrence of the display cabinets was pretty much the Lawrence of our imagination. He's behind the lines in Arabia—drawing maps, blowing up trains, suggesting an alternative to conventional warfare involving tanks and marching brigades. In Rory Stewart's lecture that followed our walk around the Magdalen Old Library, Lawrence was a man of many more contradictions. He's a boy prince dreaming heroically of leading a benighted people—the Arabs—out of their desert squalor. He's a graduate archaeologist doing the bidding of his majesty's secret services in Aqaba and along the Hejaz railway. He's a middle-class Oxford schoolboy who at Versailles has a new vision for British colonial policies in the Near East. As Stewart said, he's an "armed prophet…a don going to war…someone who wants to be a hero, someone who wants to be a saint." In Stewart's take on the great man, Lawrence is Peter Pan with some machine guns and plastic explosives who, when he discovers the grown-up world of betrayal and corruption, prefers to retreat into the shadows of his bedroom wall, perhaps with a Scotsman "birching" him.

Unfortunately, Stewart's talk about Lawrence was truncated that evening, as earlier in the day he had heard from the prime minister, Theresa May, that he was to join the British cabinet with responsibility for overseas development. That bulletin was the buzzing news in the lecture hall before Stewart arrived, as it forecast his jump into power and the possibility that, if he could display the requisite political skills in cabinet, Stewart might well be positioning himself someday to become prime minster. I think the audience was settling into the Magdalen lecture hall with the expectation of a long evening of psychoanalysis about whether Lawrence knew he was being played by the colonial office or whether he enjoyed his violation at the hands of that Turkish commander in Dera'a. Instead what it got was one glass of wine in a plastic glass, some cryptic remarks (although well spoken) about Lawrence as a "truth teller," and then the backside of yet another Whitehall mandarin rushing from a hall to impress upon the audience his indispensability to the future of the kingdom.

Section IV

ACROSS THE LAWRENCE DESERT IN SAUDI ARABIA

The Legend Grows in Aqaba

I CAME AWAY from the Lawrence of Oxford exhibition with two convictions: I saw no political future for Rory Stewart, who, despite speaking eloquently about T. E. Lawrence, had come and gone from a crowd of admirers without pausing to shake any hands (or very few); and, secondly, that I needed to do more reading and travels relating to Lawrence's time in Arabia. In the cabinets of the Magdalen library I had spotted several books that interested me besides Robert Graves' *Lawrence and the Arabs*. Another was Michael Korda's *Hero: The Life and Legend of Lawrence of Arabia*.

As well, as I spent time studying various maps on display of the Hejaz Railway, I wondered if I could ever follow its tracks into Saudi Arabia and its terminus in the holy city of Medina. Together with my son Charles on our travels around Syria, I had seen its railway station in Damascus and its nearby museum, and in the 1980s I had seen the outside of its station in Amman. But after those stations the track bed went cold, and all I knew from maps was that the line crossed into the Saudi desert between Maan in Jordan and Tabuk in Saudi Arabia, across which Lawrence had led his band of Arab irregulars on their ride to attack Aqaba. Leaving Oxford, I wondered what might remain of Lawrence's railway footprints in the wilds of the Saudi deserts.

The problem I had following the tracks of the Hejaz Railway was that for both American and Swiss citizens it has been almost impossible to get a tourist visit for Saudi Arabia. I had tried a few years before, when flying to Kenya on Saudia Airlines. The airline allowed for a stopover in Jeddah, and I liked the idea of even spending twenty-four or forty-eight hours in the Red Sea city, but when I asked the airline and at the Saudi consulate if I would have any luck securing a transit visa, I was told the process would be endless, and that in the end I would be turned down. (At the time I thought how little the American alliance with the Saudi kingdom bought in return, at least for travelers curious to spend a few days along the Red Sea.) In the end, I had no choice when transiting through Jeddah but to remain cooped up in the airport, where I found the best place to sleep was in a transit lounge mosque.

I thought little more about Saudi Arabia or the Hejaz Railway until my eye fell upon a newspaper article indicating that the new governing regime in Saudi Arabia (including those who had authorized the killing of dissident journalist Jamal Khashoggi in the Istanbul consulate) were rethinking their approach to tourism beyond that of the hajj to Mecca and Medina, which accounts for billions in revenue for the desert kingdom. According to the article, in three or six months' time it might even be possible to apply for a Saudi visa online and receive instant accreditation. I had my doubts about such informality, but e-visas are the rage in Southeast Asia, and maybe the Saudis would see the advantages of encouraging Western tourists to cross its previously closed borders.

It took me a while to follow up with my application, but in winter 2023 I had a go at the Saudi "visa on arrival" program. I typed in my passport dates and numbers, uploaded a photograph, made a payment with a credit card, and expected to wait two weeks or even a month before hearing anything back. In the end, I took the view that I had not paid a lot for what I viewed as a Saudi lottery ticket. At least it had brightened my expectations on a dark January day. What I didn't expect was hearing back the next day that my e-visa had been approved, and that it was good for a year, in travel periods of ninety days. Immediately, I began daydreaming about a flight to Dammam and a train to Riyadh, or perhaps a bus to Al-Jouf, in the northwestern desert, and then an overnight train to the capital. I even wondered whether I could travel with my folding bicycle, and use it to get around Saudi cities. But little in the way of international flights, buses, or trains seemed to go anywhere near the line of the Hejaz Railway.

In all it took about a week of brainstorming (brooding might be another word for my one-man deliberations), but I came up with the idea of a direct flight from Italy to Aqaba, not far from which there is a land crossing into Saudi Arabia. From there—although the details were missing—I could go to Tabuk (a Hejaz Railway city) and follow the line south to Medina, one of the holy cities (the other being Mecca, which is off-limits to non-believers). In Medina (assuming it would have me), I could catch a new Chinese-built high-speed train to Jeddah, where, if my luck held, I could spend a few days beside the Red Sea and catch a one-way cruise ship for $211 that would take me to Yanbu, another port on the Red Sea, and up the Gulf of Suez to Ain Sokhna, one of the ports for Cairo. What I loved about my plan was that all stops along my convoluted route were places that Lawrence writes about in *Seven Pillars of Wisdom*, especially Aqaba and Jeddah, and if all worked as I hoped, I could read the Graves and Korda biographies and refresh my memories about the Lawrence legend.

From Italy it was a four-hour flight to Aqaba, the Jordanian port city that shares the same coastline as Eilat, the Israeli beach resort. En route I was happy to begin Graves' biography. My edition, published by Jonathan Cape in 1927, was elegant and cloth-bound, and when turning its brittle pages it was easy for me to imagine Graves and Lawrence getting to know each other in postwar Oxford, when Lawrence was a fellow at All Souls and Graves was an undergraduate at Jesus College, from which Lawrence had graduated in 1910. In the Michael Korda biography of Lawrence, there are several allusions to Graves "needing money" during his days in Oxford (*Good-Bye to All That* was not published until 1929), and that one reason Lawrence agreed to collaborate with the biography was so that his new friend could earn some income. Lawrence would also have wanted Graves to correct some of the errors made in Lowell Thomas' more sensational account, *With Lawrence in Arabia*, which could well have had the title *A Few Days with Lawrence in Aqaba*.

Not long before my plane to Aqaba landed, we crossed into Israeli airspace, and all passengers were required to remain seated with their seat belts buckled (a footnote on Israeli politics five miles below us). On our final approach we left the bleak, dry, mountainous landscape of the Sinai Peninsula and flew directly south over the town of Aqaba, which is divided between a working port and a beach resort.

Graves' biography devotes considerable attention to Lawrence's 1917 military campaign to take the city from the Turks. At the time he was a junior liaison staff officer to Prince Feisal's band of Arab fighters, and not under any orders to seize the strategic port. But he conceived of the attack from the "land side," as his Arab detachment was moving north from around Yenbo to cut the Hejaz Railway at various points (it supplied the Turkish garrison in Medina). Of that expedition, Graves writes: "One can well imagine Lawrence's loneliness on this ride. He was no longer merely a British officer; his enthusiasm for the Revolt on its own account had cut him off from that. Nor was he a genuine Arab, as his tribelessness reminded him only too strongly. He hovered somewhere midway between the one thing and the other…" Of Aqaba, Graves states:

> The importance of Akaba was great. It was a constant threat to the British Army which had now reached the Gaza-Beersheba line and therefore left it behind the right flank: a small Turkish force from Akaba could do great damage and might even strike at Suez. But Lawrence saw that the Arabs needed Akaba as much and more than the British. If they took it, they could link up with the British Army at Beersheba, and show by their presence that they were a real national army, one to be reckoned with.

Just to get his forces in position to attack Aqaba, Lawrence had to lead them on a long, roundabout ride through the desert, and slip past Turkish sentries in the mountains outside Aqaba, so that the attack would come as a surprise. In the film *Lawrence of Arabia*, Lawrence leads the attacking Arabs on camels in a cavalry charge out of the hills and down into the town, where the Turkish forces were encamped (their guns pointing toward the sea, from which they expected an attack to come). In the movie, it is a charge of Light Brigade proportions, with the Turks wiped out to a man, although in reality the Turkish garrison surrendered rather than fight. Here's how Graves describes the endgame:

> They were, it was said, only three hundred men and had little food (the Arabs were in the same fix), but were prepared to resist strongly. This was found to be true. The Arabs sent a summons to surrender by white flag and by prisoners, but the Turks shot at both; at last a little Turkish conscript said that he could arrange it. He

came back an hour later with a message that the Turks would surrender in two days if help did not come from Maan. This was folly; the tribesmen could not be held back much longer and it might mean the massacre of every Turk and loss to the Arabs too. So the conscript was given a sovereign and Lawrence and one or two more walked down close to the trenches with him again, sending him in to fetch an officer to parley with them. After some hesitation one came, and, when Lawrence explained that the Arab forces were growing and tempers were short, agreed to surrender next morning. The next morning fighting broke out again, hundreds of hill-men having come in that night knowing nothing of the arrangement; but Nasir stopped it and the surrender went off quietly after all. There were now no more Turks left between them and the sea. They raced on to Akaba in a driving sandstorm and splashed into the sea on July the sixth, exactly two months after setting out from Wejh.

Lawrence was among those who ended the campaign with a swim.

Leaving my flight, I wondered if getting a visa "on arrival" in Jordan would be a problem, but when my turn came at the booth, the border guard simply opened my passport and stamped it. (I learned later that Aqaba is visa-free, while a visa is required if you land in the capital, Amman.) I shared a taxi into town with some other arriving passengers, but at my hotel I spent a half-hour alone in the lobby, trying to find someone to check me in. Finally a sleepy clerk arrived. He had no advance word of my Booking.com reservation but showed me a few rooms. I took the one with a balcony and a distant view of the sea, and went in search of dinner, which was easy, as Aqaba has enough tourists to keep restaurants in business off-season.

By contrast, after Lawrence took Aqaba, he needed to get word to the British high command in Cairo, and the only way to do so, he concluded, was to ride and walk across the Sinai desert to the Suez Canal, which the British then held. Graves describes the epic ride:

Lawrence decided in the end to keep at a walk; if they could hold out, they would reach Suez in fifty hours. But in such cases the test of endurance is harder for the man than for the camel, and Lawrence was near the end of his strength, having ridden an average of fifty miles a day for the last month, with very little food. To make halts for cooking unnecessary they carried lumps of boiled camel and cooked dates in a rag behind their saddles....

At last in the middle of the afternoon of the third day they arrived at the Suez Canal. They had ridden for forty-nine hours without sleep and with only four short halts and had come a hundred and sixty-eight miles. When it is remembered that they were tired men before they started, and that the camels were exhausted too, this must rank as a good ride, though Lawrence surpassed it himself later....

At Suez, where he arrived verminous and filthy, with his clothes sticking to his saddle-sores, he went to an hotel and had six iced drinks, a good dinner, a hot bath, and a comfortable bed. He appreciated this dull hotel-comfort after having in the last four desperate weeks, though not yet recovered from a severe illness, ridden fourteen hundred miles on camel-back through hostile country. They were weeks of little sleep, poor food, frequent fighting and never-ceasing anxiety at the hottest time of the year in one of the hottest countries of the world. Later he found that he weighed only seven stone, nine stone being his normal weight.

In the movie, Lawrence is shown in full Arab dress pushing his way into the officers' club in Cairo to announce that he had "taken" Aqaba, while in reality he had landed back in British hands in the port city of Suez.

ACROSS THE DESERT

A Theoretical Route into Saudi Arabia

I DEVOTED SOME of my first evening in Aqaba (things were open late) to exploring with local travel companies how I might cross into Saudi Arabia and get to the Saudi city of Tabuk. I knew that in a car it would take about three hours to drive there, but in between was the border, and in my mind was the lingering question as to whether a Saudi e-visa would be accepted at such a remote border crossing (in some countries e-visas are only for arrivals at the main airport). At various kiosks and travel stalls in Aqaba, I heard the same thing: that at a roundabout near the old Turkish fortress (which Lawrence had claimed for Britain and the Arabs) there were minivans that, once they filled up, would head to the Saudi border and Tabuk. The cost of each crossing was about $260, divided by the number of passengers along for the ride.

The next morning after finding breakfast (no easy chore in my ghostly hotel), I set out for the fortress and roundabout, where I found a fleet of new Chevy Suburban SUVs lined up in a small lot waiting for customers. On each front door was an embossed green emblem indicating that the car made the correspondence between Aqaba and Tabuk, and clearly in style. Since I wasn't leaving until the next day, my driver negotiations were at the theoretical stage, but even from those I could tell that it wasn't going to be easy to find fellow travelers to cross the divide into Saudi Arabia.

Clearly, there wasn't much back-and-forth between Aqaba and Tabuk, nor, in a larger sense, between Jordan and Saudi Arabia. Lawrence knew that better than most. He spent a large part of his campaigns in the desert arbitrating feuds among various tribes, and no dispute was more pronounced than that between King Hussein (whose heirs would sit on the throne of Jordan) and ibn Saud, who took possession of Nejd (central Arabia) and who wrested control of the Hejaz (and its holy cities of Mecca and Medina) from Hussein. In all Lawrence biographies, Arab feuding is on every page. Here's what Graves writes about Syria:

> The six principal cities, Jerusalem, Beyrout, Damascus, Homs, Hama and Aleppo, were also each of them entirely different in character. The only possible bond

between most of these pieces of the Syrian mosaic was the common language, Arabic, and though at this time there was much talk of Arab freedom, it was impossible to think of Syria as a national unity. Freedom to the Syrians meant local home-rule for each little community in its valley or city, but a freedom impossible in modern civilization where roads, railways, taxes, armies, a postal system, supplies have all to be maintained by a central government. And whatever central government might be imposed on Syria, even though Arabic was the official language, would be a foreign government; for there was no such thing as a true or typical Syrian. How to spread the Revolt up to Damascus over this chequerboard of communities, each divided against its neighbour naturally by geography and history, and artificially by Turkish intrigue, was a most baffling problem: which, however, Lawrence set himself to solve.

Perhaps because he was an admired foreigner who was brave, resourceful, and passed out a lot of gold, Lawrence became a rallying personality in the Arab revolt—in the Hejaz and up the railway line to Damascus. In his presence, many tribal leaders overlooked their differences and decided to fight the Turks and campaign for independence under British (and Lawrence's) leadership, although London (under the secret terms of the 1916 Sykes-Picot Agreement) had other ideas about how to divide up the Middle East that it didn't always share with its junior officers in the field. When Lawrence left Arabia in 1918 at the war's end, the fighting and feuding resumed, not just between the many Arab tribes, but also among the rival colonial powers (Britain and France) in the region. And all of these discordant interests, in turn, collided with the Jews who, under the 1917 Balfour Declaration, were beginning to arrive in Palestine.

ACROSS THE DESERT

The Wadi Rum Stage Set

THE CAR AT the roundabout that I did engage was a local taxi, the driver of which, Ahmed, accepted $50 to take me to Wadi Rumm, a desert preserve an hour from Aqaba where Lawrence often was encamped during the war and where much of *Lawrence of Arabia* was filmed.

The road from Aqaba to Rumm climbs through a tortuous valley, through which Lawrence and his attacking Arabs would have navigated in 1917. At the head of the defile there were several military checkpoints, all of which made me glad I was in a taxi, not a rental car. Before entering the nature preserve, I bought a ticket from the visitor center, and then the driver dropped me at one of many tent camps around Wadi Rumm, where another driver with a jeep pickup truck was waiting to tour me around the cinematic rolling valleys.

Lawrence and his Arab forces often used Rumm as a base of operations from which to attack the Hejaz Railway and, on the way into the valley, we drove alongside some remaining stretches of track and stopped at a small stone station (now a museum), where rolling stock from the railway was parked. I got the impression that the line near Rumm is used occasionally for freight and tourist trains.

There's a passage in the Graves biography that describes Lawrence's camp at Rumm:

> They rode for hours the next day through the valley of Rumm, a broad tamarisk-grown avenue two miles wide between colossal red sandstone cliffs. The caravan felt awed and kept quite silent. Towards sunset there was a break in the cliffs to the right, leading to the water. They turned in here and found themselves in a vast oval amphitheatre floored with damp sand and dark shrubs. The entrance was only three hundred yards wide, which made the place more impressive still. At the foot of the enclosing precipices were enormous fallen blocks of sandstone, bigger than houses, and along a ledge at one side grew trees. A little path zigzagged up to the ledge and there, three hundred feet above the level of the plain, jetted the water-springs. They watered their

camels here and cooked rice to add to the bully beef which the sergeants had brought, with biscuits, as their ration.

As much as I respect Robert Graves, this description does not do justice to the vast and imposing landscape around Rumm, which is a mixture of lunar remoteness, vast tracks of sand, and rose-red rock formations that give the impression of the American Southwest and the Mojave Desert. More than a dozen movies, besides *Lawrence of Arabia*, have been filmed here, and my driver listed the movies he had worked in, including many in the *Star Wars* series. For the Bedouin around Rumm, filmmaking is a windfall, as the likes of Stephen Spielberg spend millions converting the Jordanian desert into a distant galaxy. On one rock formation there was a carved portrait of Lawrence; otherwise, the revolt in the desert has moved on to Hollywood.

Many visitors to Rumm sleep in one of the tent villages that dot the edges of the wadi. Some have luxury accommodations and hot showers; others are more primitive. After my jeep tour and some pictures of the Hejaz line, Ahmed and I headed back to Aqaba, where he said he could arrange my passage the next day across the border into Saudi Arabia. Ahmed told me that his brother was licensed to drive one of those hulking white Chevy Suburban SUVs, and that he would be happy to drive me to Tabuk. I said that would be fine, provided other passengers were found to defray some of the cost. Already I sensed I was being fitted in the garments of a mark, but I agreed to meet Ahmed and his brother the following morning at 8:30 a.m. at the fortress roundabout.

That afternoon in Aqaba I went to the town beach and swam in the headwaters of the Red Sea, here called the Gulf of Aqaba. In many Lawrence biographies there are references to sharks prevalent in these waters, so I chose a stretch of beach where others were swimming farther offshore. Another option at the beach was to rent a glass-bottom boat to see some of the nearby reefs. I was tempted to join one of the excursions, but grew weary of the hawkers following me up and down the beach, and decided I would rather read Graves under a straw umbrella and drink mango juice bought from a vendor.

ACROSS THE DESERT

A Frozen Desert Border

THE NEXT MORNING, exactly at 8:30 a.m., I found Ahmed at the roundabout, with his brother in the driver's seat of one of the gleaming Saudi cars. They were ready for me to fork over $260 immediately and to head to the border and Tabuk. Ahmed kept saying that if I dallied, I could be delayed at the border for several hours as it was a Sunday and people would be returning to work. Foolishly or not, I said I would only go when at least one other passenger turned up to share the cost. What followed was a standoff of wills that I knew I would lose, especially as the minutes passed and no one showed up looking for an international joyride.

In the end I caved. I agreed to pay $100 up front and another $100 when I was delivered to my Tabuk hotel three hours down the road and across the desert. Everyone in the negotiation circle—by now we were about five haggling under a shady tree—agreed to these terms. I paid the front money and was placed in the back seat of a Chevy that immediately set off for the border.

Where I live in western Switzerland, local border crossings into France are invisible affairs with empty huts and a gate that is closed in the evening, but the Jordanian-Saudi border had Cold War dimensions. Razor wire and concrete barriers lined the road for several kilometers even before we reached Jordanian immigration, and in the no-man's-land between the two countries there were sandbags and more obstacles that slowed the Chevy to a crawl.

Although there were only a few cars and trucks at the border post when we pulled up, it still took close to an hour for us to navigate all the procedures. At least my e-visa posed no problems. I was sent to one hut for photographs and fingerprinting (all ten fingers pressed hard onto an electronic reader), and at another checkpoint my backpack was scanned and searched. Finally, the driver and I were ushered into a small waiting room—like that at a car wash—while the Chevy was attached to a conveyor belt and towed through an x-ray machine. I have no idea if they were searching for guns or drugs, or both, but I wasn't temped to ask. Instead I spent my time watching vans and other cars dragged through the enormous scanner. Then we got back in the x-rayed car and presented our approved paperwork to not one last checkpoint but two, after which I was officially in Saudi Arabia.

I was glad that I was a passenger in a gleaming official car and had not tried to run the border in a gypsy cab. Now I looked forward to a three-hour drive across the desert to Tabuk. I celebrated the crossing with sips from my tea caddy and a few biscuits from the breakfast buffet, but no sooner had I settled back into my limo than it came to a halt in the parking lot of a frontier gas station, where with no explanation I sat for thirty minutes. I figured the driver was having his breakfast, or the cigarette and coffee breaks that punctuate driving in the Middle East, but then Ahmed's brother opened my back door and said I would be continuing my journey in another car—this one a broken-down sedan like some of my rental cars in Jordan from the 1980s.

The bait-and-switch of the white limo struck me as unfair, but at least the deal was that I would only pay the remaining $100 when I got to my hotel in Tabuk. Ahmed's brother whined a little about $200 being the fare, but since I was far from Tabuk, I refused to pay more, and there was more staring. In the end the driver of the old sedan agreed to the transfer fee, and off we went to Tabuk, with my backpack in the trunk and my briefcase at my side.

The three-hour ride to Tabuk was uneventful. The driver and I chatted some, but mostly I looked out the window at the desert, studied my maps, and read Robert Graves, although reading in cars is not a skill that I have mastered. The desert through which we drove was more rocky lava than a sandy expanse, and here and there we drove through towns and villages, all of which were the concrete equivalent of Bedouin tent camps. I caught no glimpses of the Hejaz Railway, which had run farther inland (from Maan to Tabuk), but the ride enabled me to better understand Lawrence's strategies during this stage of the war, which were to disrupt the railway with bombs and raids just enough to preoccupy the Turkish high command with keeping the line open. Lawrence didn't want to cut the rail line entirely and force the surrender of the Turkish garrison in Medina, as then the British and Arabs would have needed to feed a large number of Turkish prisoners and civilians.

Without the preoccupation of keeping the trains running to Medina, the Turks would have been free to re-take Aqaba or suppress the Arab revolt. Lawrence's mission was to distract as large a number of Turkish soldiers as he could while the main British Army, under General Edmund Allenby, advanced on the line from Gaza and Beersheba toward Jerusalem. In that campaign, Lawrence's forces were an annoyance to the Turks, and they anchored Allenby's right flank.

ACROSS THE DESERT

The Hejaz City of Tabuk

I DON'T WANT to make Tabuk sound like Mardi Gras in New Orleans, but I did enjoy being there. My Tabuk Ramada hotel was in the city center, although still on a six-lane boulevard that ruled out walking anywhere, and I could take all my meals in the dining room with a group of cheerful construction workers, doing their part for the Saudi building boom.

My first and only taxi ride proved frustrating—the driver was at a loss to find what I was looking for, the Hejaz Railway Museum—but when I discovered that Uber is alive and well in Tabuk, I took it everywhere. On a Sunday afternoon (a workday in Saudi), I was free to wander around the small historic quarter, find the Mosque of the Prophet (Muhammed stopped in Tabuk and drank from a spring), and tour the old Turkish fortress, which doubles as a city museum.

It was in the fortress museum that I came upon this quote from Arabist H. St. John Philby, who was not only a Lawrence contemporary and the British liaison officer to ibn Saud (the first Saudi king) but the father of Kim Philby, who from the 1930s to the 1950s betrayed Great Britain to the Soviets and eventually defected to Moscow. Father Philby wrote:

> It is assured that the land of Tabuk, since times of old, an excellent center on the road travelled by merchants on their way to the Mediterranean Basin...it is also the road travelled by pilgrims to the Holy cities....
> And the state of Tabuk shows progression in all fields, for the number of the Tabuk metropolitan inhabitants according to 1951 censes has reached 2,000 people, half of which are merchants and Government employees.

Now the city's population is close to seven hundred thousand.

Only the next morning did I get inside the Hejaz Railway Museum. It was closed on Sunday but would open on Monday at 8:00, giving me time to visit the station museum and still catch my bus to Medina at 10:00.

I cannot say that my Tabuk Ramada breakfast was inspiring, but it filled me up, and Uber delivered me promptly at 8 a.m. to the museum, where an indolent security guard pointed me toward a wall of storyboards and several restored freight cars and engines. One of the billboards read:

> On Sept. 1, 1906, a ceremony was held at Tabuk on the occasion of the arrival of the railway line. It was attended by an official delegation from Damascus, tribal shaykhs, nobles and merchants. After performing the morning prayer in the Mosque of the Prophet in Tabuk, all those in attendance proceeded to the tent set up for the inauguration ceremony. A number of speeches were delivered and animals were sacrificed, after which the special representative of Sultan Abdul Hamid read the telegram sent by the sultan on this occasion.

As it turned out, the Hejaz Railway opened just as the sun was setting on the Ottoman Empire. Less than two years later, the so-called Young Turks had overthrown the sultan, and only for about ten years would the Hejaz Railway connect Damascus to the holy cities. In theory, the line operated to carry faithful hajj Muslims on their way to Medina and Mecca, but that was a convenient cover story for something more geopolitical, which would reinforce Ottoman rule in the strategically important Hejaz along the Red Sea.

Although the rail line did follow the pilgrim's way from Palestine to Medina, it angered the Bedouin tribes along the route, as it cut into their profits earned (or stolen) along the holy trail. For Lawrence the Hejaz Railway and its ribbon of narrow-gauge track across the desert was low-hanging fruit in the great game between Britain and the Arabs, on one side, and Turkey and Germany on the other. As another poster in the museum reads:

> The Hijaz Railway did not survive for long; it was soon affected by the outbreak of the First World War (1914-1918). The revolt led by the Sharif with British support during the war brought in its wake the destruction of parts of the line between Amman and al-Madinah al-Munawwarah. Most of the bridges, equipment, and stations were ruined in actions in which the British colonel, T. E. Lawrence, played a major role.

ACROSS THE DESERT

As Graves makes clear in his biography, Lawrence saw the attacks on the line as steppingstones to bring his Arab constituents closer to Damascus, where he hoped they could declare their independence not just from the Ottomans but also from the colonial presence of Britain and France (who, to Lawrence's shame, were his overlords).

FRIENDS OF A KIND

The Closely-Watched Bus to Medina

MY BUS TO Medina—a nine-hour ride across the desert—departed on time. I had gone to the bus station the day before during my Uber-ing and knew it was little more than a parking lot with an adjoining waiting room in which touts hawked various services. At 9:45 a.m. I took a seat near a window in the back of the bus. The bus was about half full, and the passengers seemed to be a mixture of guest workers and pilgrims, although I was the only Western traveler. The landscape through which we passed was unending desert, although there was the occasional village and town off the four-lane highway.

About an hour outside Tabuk, a police car with flashing lights pulled over the bus. From my seat I could see the driver in conversation with the policeman, who never left his car or turned off his flashing lights. The driver had with him various documents, and after a while he returned to the bus and said he needed the passports of two passengers, one of whom was me. I gave him my passport and a printed copy of my e-visa (how could it hurt?), and watched from my seat window while the driver handed over my documents and while the cop verified them in whatever system he had in his car. At no point did anyone say anything to me, and after a while the policeman returned my passport to the driver, who gave it back to me, and we were on our way. I spent the rest of the bus ride wondering whether I was on a list that the driver or policeman was carrying. All during the long day on the road, I saw other police checkpoints with other buses and cars waylaid on the way to Medina, but we were never stopped again.

To get me across nine hours on "a dark desert highway" (I know its sounds like "Hotel California"), I had saved Michael Korda's *Hero: The Life and Legend of Lawrence of Arabia*, a full-length biography that was published in 2010. During my initial research on Lawrence, I had grown weary over the number of Lawrence biographies on the market, and I had thought I could make do without Korda's, although it turned out I was wrong, as his portrait of Lawrence is well written, if not definitive. Best of all, Korda directly answers many lingering questions about Lawrence: Was he homosexual? (More asexual and repressed.) Was he a British spy? (No, but happy to cooperate with his majesty's government.) Was he aware of Sykes-Picot as early as 1916? (Yes, but was in denial and hoped it would lapse.) What fueled his feelings of shame and guilt that he tried to expiate with caning? (Betrayal of the Arab cause.)

Korda has spent most of his life (he's now ninety) as a senior editor in New York book publishing, and I wondered how he acquired his fascination with Lawrence. Only toward the end of the book did I find the answer, which is that his uncle, celebrated filmmaker Alexander Korda, had bought an option in the late 1920s to turn *Revolt in the Desert* into a Hollywood film. (This was after Lowell Thomas had taken his own film footage and book on the road in London and New York, inventing the legend of "Lawrence of Arabia.") Alexander Korda and Lawrence met often to discuss the feasibility of the film, and in his gentle, diplomatic way Lawrence talked Korda out of the venture, to the point that Korda would later quip that he was "the nicest man I ever failed to do business with." No doubt the Korda family's affection for Lawrence passed down from uncle to nephew, to the point that when it came time for Michael to do military service in England, he enlisted in the RAF and drove around the UK on a powerful motorcycle. Only later did he become Lawrence's biographer.

In weighing Lawrence's life and legend, Michael Korda inevitably comes out on the side of his goodness; hence the title *Hero* and the firmness with which Korda dismisses some of the more outlandish allegations against his subject. To be clear, he exhaustively sorts through mountains of evidence before he states that Lawrence was probably asexual or that his work for the British government in the Middle East did not count as spying. Nor does he believe that Lawrence fabricated aspects of his military career or inflated accounts in his books, and he dismisses the charge that I had read elsewhere that as the war went on Lawrence developed something of a bloodlust and was happy at the prospect of massacring Turks. He believes his motorcycle death on the road was an accident, not an assassination, and he takes at face value Lawrence's description of what happened in Dera'a.

Nor does Korda think Lawrence was a poseur or a publicity hound going around London and Paris in Arab dress. He acknowledges that Lawrence suffered emotional distress upon the discovery of his own illegitimacy and that, come the end of war and the revolt, he became an unwitting instrument of the British government's claim to Middle Eastern lands and its appropriation of the political control that Lawrence had promised to the Arabs. Toward the end of the book, Korda describes him in these words:

> He was a hero, a scholar, a diplomat, a brilliant writer,

endowed with enormous courage and capable of reckless self-sacrifice, and behind the facade that Lowell Thomas and the newspapers built up around him, also the kindest, gentlest, and most loyal of friends, and that rare Englishman with no class prejudices of any kind, as at ease in a barracks as he was in Buckingham Palace, in the desert, or at Versailles.... He was partly instrumental in the creation of not one but *three* Middle Eastern kingdoms. Only one of these, Jordan, survives today in its original form; but much of the map of the Middle East was drawn by Lawrence, quite literally, as we have seen; and if he could not give the Arabs what they most wanted—a "greater Syria"—he at any rate helped to give them the states that now exist there, and, for better or worse, the dream of a larger, united Arab nation, which for a brief time led to the union of Egypt and Syria as the United Arab Republic, and which is still the motivating force behind much of the unrest and violence of Arab nationalism.

Above all, Korda admires Lawrence's intellectual brilliance (his guerrilla campaigns had aspects of art forms) and his modesty.

I am sure one of the reasons I so warmed to Korda's biography is that I was reading it in the Hejaz (now Saudi Arabia), where Lawrence first came in contact with King Hussein and his sons, and I could appreciate the bravery that it took to cross vast stretches of the desert on a camel with little food or water. All I had to do was to ride on a bus for nine hours and then—without GPS working on my phone—figure out how to find the hotel that I had reserved (clearly my roaming coverage had not made the hajj).

Eventually, after connecting to hotel Wi-Fi near the Medina bus terminal, I was able to summon an Uber, and it took me to my hotel, where I had to wait almost an hour at the front desk while three clerks checked in dozens of pilgrims ahead of me. But it was a warm evening and everyone was in a festive mood (Medina is something of a theme park), so I didn't mind watching the clerks assign rooms to three busloads of pilgrims, all of whom were eager to drop their bags and head to Mosque of the Prophet. (Nonbelievers in Medina, unlike Mecca, can enter the city, but they cannot visit the prophet's tomb.)

ACROSS THE DESERT

A High-Speed Haj

MUCH OF WHAT I did in Medina, I confess, was read my books, as I find mosques pleasant places to read and reflect, although in this case I was reading Korda, not the Koran. In the company of so many Arabs from so many differing cultures (dozens of languages are spoken in Medina), the passages of Korda that most caught my attention were those that describe Lawrence's endless patience and diplomatic skills in reconciling the differing goals of numerous Arab tribes and uniting them (however briefly) to fight alongside the British in liberating Arabia from the Turks. Korda writes:

> The Bedouin had no sense of time; they did not accept orders; they would break off fighting to loot, then ride home with what they had stolen; they thought nothing of stripping and killing enemy wounded; they wasted ammunition by firing *feux de joie* into the air to announce their comings and goings; when there was food they gorged on it, instead of thinking ahead; when there was water, they drank until their bellies were swollen, instead of rationing it out sensibly; they stole shamelessly, from friend and foe alike; their tribal quarrels and blood feuds made it difficult to rely on them when they were formed up in large numbers; by British standards they were cruel to animals; and they were distrustful of Europeans and Christians, even as allies. In order to lead them, Lawrence had to learn to accept their ways, to share their ribald and teasing sense of humor and their extravagant emotions and love of tall tales, to embrace the extreme hardships of their life, and to understand that because they were intense individualists any attempt to give a direct order to them would be treated as an insult.

Korda adds: "Nobody understood this better than Lawrence himself, who wrote: 'A man who gives himself to the possession of aliens leads a Yahoo life.... He is not one of them.... In my case my effort for these years to live in the dress of Arabs, and to imitate their mental foundation, quitted me of my English self, and let me look at the West and its conventions with new eyes, and destroyed it all for me. At the same time I could not sincerely take on the Arab skin: it was an affectation only.'"

I only spent one night in Medina, but I was happy to be there on a warm evening and a sunny morning, during which I walked everywhere and caught several buses. I went to the terminus of the Hejaz Railway, an elegant stone building that is now part of a museum complex complete with sidings, a few old rail cars, track, and, inside, a history museum about Medina. According to photographs on display, when the railway was finished in 1908, pilgrims could walk from the terminal to the Mosque of the Prophet in about twenty-five minutes. In those days Medina was more of a dusty town than what it is today—a city clustered with five-star hotels and festival lights around the central mosque. The contractor that renovated the Mosque of the Prophet in the 1970s and '80s was none other than the father of Osama bin Laden, Mohammed bin Awad bin Laden, who was a construction mogul.

The other engineering marvel in Medina is the new station for the Chinese-built high-speed rail line that connects Medina with Mecca in about two and a half hours. My train to Jeddah left around 2:30 p.m., and I got to the Medina station early enough to buy lunch in a restaurant, but despite the station's modern glittering architecture—closer to Vegas than the Hejaz Railway—I could not find any food before boarding my train. The others in the departure lounge looked more like business people than pilgrims, and I noticed that most got off in Jeddah rather than ride another half hour to Mecca, although in theory the Saudis commissioned the Chinese to build the new line with the hajj in mind.

After my all-day bus ride from Tabuk to Medina, I was happy for the high-speed service, which seemed to float over the desert. The only stop was at King Abdullah Economic City (KAEC), which is supposed to be an urban enterprise zone with a population of 1.4 million that will cost some $60 billion to construct, although from what I could tell from my train window, KAEC is a remote station in search of a population.

ACROSS THE DESERT

Seaside Jeddah on the Red Sea

UBER TOOK ME to my Jeddah hotel, which I had booked for its proximity to the Corniche, a residential suburb that has a walking path along the Red Sea. I thought I might even be able to walk from my hotel to a beach, but the desk clerk explained that dangerous currents kept most visitors out of the Red Sea in that area. Instead I did what everyone else does in that neighborhood, which is to walk by the water and enjoy picnics in the seaside parks.

When Lawrence first came to Jeddah in 1916, as part of a mission to explore an alliance with Arab tribes against the Turks, the city was little more than a small port miles down the coast. For me to get to Lawrence's Jeddah, I had to ride in an Uber for more than twenty minutes, depending on the rush-hour traffic. In that sense, Jeddah differs little from American cities in Southern California: it's an agglomeration of interstates, traffic jams, and air-conditioned malls.

Here's how Korda describes Lawrence's first glimpse of the port:

> Lawrence may have been the only person in Cairo who would have thought of a journey to Jidda as a lark. A stifling, dusty rail journey from Cairo to Suez was followed by a sea journey of almost 650 miles on board a slow steamer taken over by the Royal Navy, the heat made bearable only by the breeze of the ship's movement. "But when at last we anchored in the outer harbor," Lawrence wrote of his first sight of Jidda, of the white town hung between the blazing sky and its reflection in the mirage that swept and rolled over the wide lagoon, then the heat of Arabia came out like a drawn sword and smote us speechless."

In my Uber, I was dropped near Al-Balad, a neighborhood of traditional Arabic houses now undergoing a multimillion-dollar renovation, thanks to the Saudi government. When it's done, the historic quarter will have gift shops, restaurants, cafés, and hotels in historic buildings of stone and elaborate wooden shutters. Otherwise, about all there is to do in Jeddah is wander around the malls.

It was my good fortune to establish myself in an elegant outdoor café with plush seating, where I read Korda and fell into conversation with a local businessman and politician, who that afternoon drove me around the historic quarter in a golf cart so that I could see the house where Lawrence stayed in 1916. In turn, I showed them maps of Lawrence's desert campaigns and the line of the Hejaz Railway.

Korda writes at length about Lawrence's hope that he could get his irregular Arab forces into Damascus (the other end of the rail line) before the British Army got there, as a way to forestall the Sykes-Picot Agreement from devouring any Arab claims for independence. He writes:

> Lawrence's guilt at encouraging the Arabs to fight even though he knew they were not going to get what they wanted (and what they thought they had been promised) would become increasingly severe as the war went on and as his place in the Arab Revolt increased in importance. It was the reason why he would refuse to accept any of the honors and decorations he was awarded; it was at the root of his self-disgust and shame; it would eventually make him follow a strategy of his own, urging Feisal and the Arabs on in an effort to reach Damascus before the British or the French entered the city, and declare an independent Arab nation whose existence could not be denied at the peace conference—a grand, sublime gesture would, he hoped, render the Sykes-Picot agreement null and void in the eyes of the world.

In the end Lawrence's men did get there slightly ahead of an Australian division under the ultimate command of General Allenby, but it did nothing to prevent either Britain or France from staking their claims to the Middle East.

ACROSS THE DESERT

A Lawrence Cruise to Yenbo

IN PLANNING MY travels in Saudi Arabia, I held out hope that to go from Jeddah to Cairo, my next stop, I might hitch a ride on a northbound cruise ship plying the waters of the Red Sea. I had seen one such passage advertised on a discount cruise website that was offering three nights at sea (admittedly in a windowless cabin) for $211.

In theory, the ship was to take me from Jeddah to Ain Sokhna in Egypt, and it included a stop in Yanbu, another coastal port that Lawrence had gone to in his campaigns that is otherwise difficult for land travelers to visit. I signed up and paid for my discount Red Sea cruise, but spent the next month wondering if I had been scammed, as I never received anything that looked like a boarding pass or even a confirmation. Finally, from my hotel room in Tabuk I called a help number on the website, read in my credit card and passport numbers, and found, to my relief, that I was free to board the ship in Jeddah anytime between 1 and 2 p.m. on the day of our sailing. I might not be much of a cruise ship enthusiast (they strike me as floating Atlantic City hotels), but I asked myself how bad it could be to spend several days on the Red Sea in February, and to call in at Lawrence's Yanbu, which otherwise I would never see.

Even for $211, my cruise ship had every amenity: floor shows, restaurants, shops, swimming pools, aerobics classes, and jacuzzis. Feeding was nonstop, as were the memos that were slid under my door during the day and night, alerting me to lifeboat drills, coastal explorations, movie times, dancing classes, and disembarkation procedures. On arrival in Egypt, I had planned to hail a taxi by the docks and go up to Suez, where I figured I could watch ships transit the canal for a while and catch Lawrence's train to Cairo. But officialdom on the cruise ship nixed that drive-by-day notion, and instead put me on an official bus to the Cairo airport (not that I wanted to go to the airport).

Mostly what I did on board the MSC *Splendida* was search around the many decks for a book-reading nook that had sunshine but was sheltered from the stiff winds and still afforded me a view of the Red Sea. Aligning all those stars wasn't as easy as it should have been, but the ship was enormous and even on the third day I was discovering new decks and lounges where I could hide with my books. The only thing I dreaded was dinner, as I was assigned to a table with only one other passenger, an

American woman named Pam, who talked nonstop during each meal, which may explain why occasionally cruise ship passengers leap off their balconies.

The port call in Yanbu was scheduled so that many passengers could board buses and ride several hours inland to Medina. As I was spared that pilgrimage, all I did was disembark with the first wave (still a convoluted process involving passports and several scanners) and walk to the old town opposite the docks. There I took up a reading post in a local café that had sofas under broad awnings, which allowed me quiet time in the shade while I figured out how to find the Lawrence museum.

While I was fussing with Google Maps, a group of Arab men joined my shady corner, and after a while we fell into conversation. It turned out one of the men was retired from the local police force, and he was taking his nephew and another friend out for coffee. In joining me—besides running a stakeout of an obvious foreigner—what he wanted was a firsthand account of the cruise ship's amenities, so I entertained them with stories about twenty-four-hour buffets and piano bars that (in Saudi waters) only served lemonade and water. (I felt like I was debriefing Kojak.)

Before leaving, my police friends told me where to find the Lawrence house, although when I showed up on its doorstep—a construction site—I learned that the "museum" is only a dream at this point. There's another house museum close by that is featured in various Lawrence articles on the internet ("Visit the Magical House of Lawrence of Arabia in Yanbu"), but the kindly director there said that the claim was a hoax, although she allowed for the possibility that Lawrence might well have visited this particular traditional house on occasion.

I cannot say I minded the deception, as I had Michael Korda's account of Lawrence's visit in Yanbu (then spelled Yenbo), in which he writes: "Here Lawrence spent four days in the 'picturesque, rambling house' of Sheikh Abd el Kader el Abdo, Feisal's 'agent' here—at this point Yenbo was by no means safe, since the local sharif and emir was known to be pro-Turk. While waiting for the Royal Navy to appear, Lawrence wrote down everything he had seen [on his visit to the interior of the Hejaz and his meeting with King Hussein's son, Feisal]." It was easy for me to imagine why Lawrence had liked the small port of Yanbu—fresh breezes and turquoise waters on the edge of the steaming desert—and how it allowed him time to think and reflect on a strategy that might drive the Ottoman Empire out of the Hejaz.

ACROSS THE DESERT

Without having to linger over glass cabinets of Lawrence memorabilia, I decided to engage a local taxi driver to drive me to a nearby beach so that I could swim in the Red Sea. There are few good places for swimming near the port, so he drove about twenty-five minutes north of Yanbu to a public beach near some low-rise apartment buildings. I changed in what felt like a Turkish prison but the swim was magical. The Red Sea is salty, buoyant, and refreshing. I could easily imagine why, on taking Aqaba, Lawrence rode his camel from the desert fighting directly into the water.

The 1921 Cairo Conference Imagines Lines in the Sand

TO REACH AIN SOKHNA from Yanbu required thirty hours of sailing. Only near Sharm el-Sheikh did the *Splendida* approach the shore. The sun was warm, but the breeze kept the temperature cool in the shade, and I spent the day shifting my deck chair around to stay in a temperate zone. I had always imagined the Red Sea as a languid body of warm water, but on this particular day it was dotted with whitecaps and swells.

Without having to detour to the town of Suez, at the southern entrance to the canal, I thought I might use my free afternoon in Cairo to make sense of the 1921 Conference that Winston Churchill convened, together with Lawrence and Gertrude Bell among others, to sort out the borders of the new Middle East, at least those pertaining to the British Empire. Cairo is also where Churchill and his cohorts came up with the money-saving idea of maintaining rule in Iraq with the Royal Air Force bombing any insurgencies that might spring up—as opposed to keeping boots on the ground. (The idea worked no better than did American drones eighty years later.)

To track down the locations of the 1921 Cairo Conference, I hired a bicycle and a guide and gave him the coordinates of various waypoints, such as Shepherd's and the Semiramis Hotel, where the meetings often took place. I thought that on an expertly guided bicycle I might avoid Cairo-by-taxi, not one of life's more enlightening experiences, but instead all I got was a comedy of errors. The first two bikes I was offered were broken, and the third, on which I rode, had a defective saddle that felt like an electric chair. The guide decided to ignore my suggestions for a Cairo Conference ride and only took me to places that interested him, which always involved Cairo streets with deadly traffic. To imagine the conference I had to make do with accounts in my books, including this one in Korda's biography:

> Churchill not only was impressed by the young colonel, but would go on to become Lawrence's lifelong supporter. Perhaps nobody would describe better the effect Lawrence had on his contemporaries than

Churchill at the forthcoming peace conference: "He wore his Arab robes, and the full magnificence of his countenance revealed itself. The gravity of his demeanor; the precision of his opinions; the range and quality of his conversations; all seemed enhanced to a remarkable degree by the splendid Arab head-dress and garb. From amid the flowing draperies his noble features, his perfectly chiseled lips and flashing eyes loaded with fire and comprehension shone forth. He looked like what he was, one of Nature's greatest princes."

In both of their accounts of Lawrence, Graves and Korda make the point that the Cairo Conference resolved some of Lawrence's painful sense of betrayal for promising the Arabs independence and then delivering them up to the fate of Sykes-Picot and other colonial masters. Graves, in particular, emphasizes this point, quoting at length from a letter Lawrence sent to him about how the Cairo Conference assuaged some of his war guilt:

> 'I want you to make it quite clear in your book, if you use all this letter, how from 1916 onwards and especially in Paris I worked against the idea of an Arab Confederation being formed politically before it had become a reality commercially, economically and geographically by the slow pressure of many generations; how I worked to give the Arabs a chance to set up their provincial governments whether in Syria or in Irak; and how in my opinion Winston Churchill's settlement has honourably fulfilled our war-obligations and my hopes.'

Lawrence added: "I take most of the credit of Mr. Churchill's pacification of the Middle East upon myself. I had the knowledge and the plan. He had the imagination and courage to adopt it." When he quotes the same passage, Korda concludes: "This was, as it happened, a bold but accurate claim: Lawrence had a central role in shaping the borders of the modern Middle East and in placing Hashemite monarchs on the hitherto nonexistent thrones of Iraq and Jordan." As Lawrence elsewhere wrote to Graves:

My object with the Arabs was always to make them stand on their own feet. The period of leading things could now come to an end. That's why I was at last able to abandon politics and enlist. My job was done, as I wrote to Winston Churchill at the time, when leaving an employer who had been for me so considerate as sometimes to seem more like a senior partner than a master. The work I did constructively for him in 1921 and 1922 seems to me, in retrospect, the best I ever did. It somewhat redresses, to my mind, the immoral and unwarrantable risks I took with others' lives and happiness in 1917-1918.

'Of course Irak was the main point, since there could not be more than one centre of Arab national feeling; or rather need not be: and it was fit that it should be in the British and not in the French area. But during those years we also decided to stop the subsidies to the Arabian chiefs and put a ring-wall around Arabia, a country which must be reserved as an area of Arabic individualism. So long as our fleet keeps its coasts, Arabia should be at leisure to fight out its own complex and fatal destiny.

'Incidentally, of course, we sealed the doom of King Hussein. I offered him a treaty in the summer of 1921 which would have saved him the Hejaz had he renounced his pretensions to hegemony over all other Arabic areas: but he clung to his self-assumed title of "King of the Arabic Countries." So Ibn Saud of Nejd outed him and rules in Hejaz. Ibn Saud is not a system but a despot, ruling by virtue of a dogma. Therefore I approve of him, as I would approve of anything in Arabia which was individualistic, unorganized, unsystematic.

After my bike ride, I walked through Coptic Cairo and took a taxi to the Citadel and the Egyptian Military Museum, so that I could inspect some cabinets about the 1956 Suez Crisis and see if there might be some material about Lawrence and the Hejaz Railway (there was, but only in passing). Because it was a Sunday, many families were out strolling, although downtown Cairo is a traffic pinball machine. I did walk to the riverside location of the first Semiramis Hotel, which has been reincarnated as an Intercontinental that looks more like a corporate filing cabinet than a "grand dame" of a hotel. It was the closest association I could find in Cairo for Lawrence, Churchill, and their conference. In fact, when I later looked up where the Cairo scenes of the film *Lawrence of Arabia* were shot, I discovered that those locations were in Seville, Spain.

The movie ends with the Arabs in Damascus waving tribal banners in a makeshift parliament, foreshadowing the dysfunction that would dominate inter-Arab politics for the next hundred years, and with Lawrence motoring away from the war, worn out from the fighting. In World War I, the shelf life of junior field officers was generally about six weeks, but Lawrence managed to stay close to the front lines for almost two years. When he enlisted in the RAF under an assumed name and took a physical, the doctors had some doubts about his denial of prior military service (in keeping with his alias) when they inspected the many wounds (more than a dozen) he had endured in the campaigns.

The movie makes no mention of Lawrence's postwar literary associations, but they were extensive, as through Marsh he met Sassoon and then Graves, Buchan, Hardy, the Shaws, and Conrad, among many others. Korda writes:

> If Lawrence could inspire Churchill—a hardened politician; a former soldier himself who had ridden with the Twenty-First Lancers in the last major cavalry charge of the British Army at the Battle of Omdurman in 1893, Mauser automatic pistol in hand; and the grandson of a duke—to gush like a smitten schoolgirl, it is hardly surprising that lesser men were bowled over even before Lawrence's legend took hold. Apart from Churchill, Lawrence made an instant and lifelong friend of Edward ("Eddie") Marsh, Churchill's devoted and brilliant private secretary. Through Marsh, Lawrence met many of the literary figures who became his friends over the years, including Siegfried Sassoon. For somebody who already had the reputation of being reclusive, Lawrence had a genius for friendship—he was

a master of what would now be called networking, and an indefatigable correspondent.

Elsewhere Korda writes: "The notion of Lawrence as a lonely man is belied by his letters—he wrote to Edward Marsh, to Lord Trenchard, to Sir Edward Elgar, to C. Day Lewis, to Siegfried Sassoon, to John Buchan, to Lionel Curtis, and to Robert Graves. He met and liked Noel Coward (after being taken to a rehearsal of *Private Lives*), and sent Coward the manuscript of *The Mint* to read, a gesture of great intimacy and trust."

It interested me to read in Korda and Graves more about Lawrence's "self-identification" (as we would now say) with Ireland, although he would never visit the country where his father had lived in "a lordly fashion." In the 1920s, experimenting as he was with identity (no doubt Conrad would have approved), Lawrence spoke of himself as being Irish, which brought him some public rebuke, although not from Graves, who wrote (as is quoted in Korda) that his friend embraced "the rhetoric of freedom, the rhetoric of chastity, the rhetoric of honour, the power to excite sudden deep affections, loyalty to the long-buried past, high aims qualified by too mocking a sense of humour, serenity clouded by petulance, and broken by occasional black despairs, playboy charm and theatricality, imagination that overruns itself and tires, extreme generosity, serpent cunning, lion courage, diabolical intuition, and the curse of self-doubt which becomes enmity to self and sometimes renouncement of all that is most loved and esteemed." One of the postwar job offers that came Lawrence's way, which he declined, was to work for—as Korda writes—"the newborn Irish Free State, where his experience with guerrilla warfare, demolitions, and armored cars would no doubt have come in handy."

According to Korda, in the postwar period Lawrence also flirted with the idea of writing a biography of Sir Roger Casement, a figure every bit as daring as Erskine Childers. Korda writes:

> From time to time he was tempted by further literary projects, among them a life of Sir Roger Casement, the Anglo-Irish British consular official who had been among the first to expose and document the atrocities that were committed in King Leopold of Belgium's Congo Free State—the background and subject of Joseph Conrad's *Heart of Darkness*—where it was

routine to chop off the right hand of any native who was slow to collect or carry ivory and rubber.

In the end Lawrence's last book would be a prose translation of Homer's *Odyssey*, which came out in 1935, the year that Lawrence died. I might have thought that Lawrence would have been more drawn to re-translating the *Iliad*, a story of war, much closer to his own experiences in Asia Minor and *Seven Pillars of Wisdom* than the *Odyssey*, that of postwar wanderings, a search for family and tranquility. But Lawrence went with the latter, as he says in his foreword: "The shattered *Iliad* yet makes a masterpiece; while the *Odyssey* by its ease and interest remains the oldest book worth reading for its story and the first novel of Europe." When Lawrence was working on his translation, in the mid-1920s, he was closer to Odysseus—lost in the Royal Air Force as if at sea, searching for an imagined home—than he was to Achilles or Ajax, at war with the Trojans. No wonder Lawrence so warmed to the author who could write near the end of the *Odyssey*:

> *Now that royal Odysseus has taken his revenge,*
> *let both sides seal their pacts that he shall reign for*
> *life, and let us purge their memories of the bloody*
> *slaughter of their brothers and sons.*

In the battle for hearts and minds of the Great War, no one wrote more words in anger than **John Buchan,** also known as Lord Tweedsmuir. In what was then real time, he published a contemporaneous history of the fighting that ran to more than a million words and 24 volumes. At the same time, he worked in various war ministries and, if that wasn't enough, kept up with his own novels, including two bestsellers, *The Thirty-Nine Steps* and *Greenmantle*, which can be read as serious fiction and as war propaganda. One of Buchan's many gifts as a writer is that he could work anywhere—on commuter trains, at his breakfast table, at night in his club, etc. He was also gifted in that his books rarely needed major revisions; often they were print-ready after only one draft. For age reasons at the beginning of the war (he was close to 40), he could not serve as a front-line officer in the British Army, but he made up for it by traveling incessantly to many fronts as a war minister and correspondent, often putting himself in harm's way. He lost many friends in the war, although no one more dear to him than Raymond Asquith. They had met at Oxford, coming there from opposite ends of Britain's class structure, but bonding over a shared love for literature, language, and long walks.

Section V

THE JOHN BUCHAN WAY

Oxford: Unraveling Lord Tweedsmuir

ASIDE FROM LAWRENCE, the Oxford figure who most interested me, and for several reasons, was the writer John Buchan, who lived for much of his adult life in the nearby village of Elsfield. I had read and admired a number of his books. Furthermore, he was a close friend to T. E. Lawrence and took inspiration, as a writer, from Erskine Childers. *Greenmantle*, Buchan's thriller in the Richard Hannay series about what would now be called Islamic nationalism, can be read as a synthesis of the lives of Lawrence and Childers, although it came out in 1916, before Buchan knew Lawrence well. (Both had gone to Oxford.) In fact, much of the legend that grew up around Lawrence can be attributed to Buchan, who as a military intelligence officer and propagandist in World War I was always looking for feel-good stories about the fighting. He commissioned journalist Lowell Thomas to write about the war in the desert. From that assignment came the book *With Lawrence in Arabia*, and the "of Arabia" legend. (And in the late 1920s, Buchan recommended Robert Graves for a lectureship in Cairo.) Finally, I was interested in Buchan's friendship with Raymond Asquith, the son of the prime minister, Herbert Asquith, killed in the fighting on the Somme. Buchan writes movingly about Asquith in his memoirs, *Pilgrim's Way*, a book that I acquired in high school after I read somewhere that it was a favorite of President John F. Kennedy.

Buchan was born in 1875 and was almost forty years old when World War I began, which kept him out of combat, although he did enlist in the army, where he served in staff positions. During the war years Buchan produced numerous books, both fiction and nonfiction, and his contemporaneous narrative *History of the War*, which came out in twenty-four volumes, was largely published before the fighting was over, helping to shape public perception. But until Edward Mortimer and I were poring over the glass cabinets of Magdalen College's T. E. Lawrence exhibition, I had no way into Buchan's Oxford world. It was then that Edward mentioned that he was close to David Buchan, one of John's grandsons, who lived some of the year in Elsfield at the Buchan house. Edward said he would try to arrange a visit for me the next time I came to Oxford.

In the meantime I had to content myself with reading the works and interviewing one of Buchan's biographers, Andrew Lownie, whose day job was as a literary agent in London. In the 1990s, Lownie had noticed that no one had published a Buchan biography since the 1960s, and in 1995 he brought out *John Buchan: The Presbyterian Cavalier*, an allusion to a life that included both intense action and reflection. Not only did Buchan write more than one hundred books, but he also served as a colonial officer in South Africa, in military intelligence in World War I, in Parliament (representing the liberal wing of the Conservative Party), and, at the end of his career, as the Governor General in Canada, which is where he died in 1940. One of Lownie's conclusions about John Buchan is that few figures in modern British history, save perhaps Winston Churchill, were so successful in combining a career in politics with writing. (Buchan wrote: "Even a perverse career or action seemed to me better than a tippling of ale in the shade, for that way lay the cockney suburbanism which was my secret terror.")

Buchan grew up in Fife, north of Edinburgh, the son of a Scottish minister, and at seventeen was accepted at Glasgow University, where he read the classics, published books, and won a scholarship to Oxford. That leap across the class system changed his life, in that, as Lownie says in his biography, Buchan met the sort of people who would later come to populate his novels—government officials, spies, artists, writers, and businessmen. Among his friends at Oxford were Raymond Asquith and Aubrey Herbert, a larger-than-life figure—he was twice offered the throne of Albania—as a traveler, diplomat, and spy. He appears in some of Buchan's novels as Sandy Arbuthnot, who also has aspects of T. E. Lawrence. According to Lownie, Buchan was among the last persons to have seen Lawrence before he died.

Out of Oxford, Buchan went to South Africa, then in the throes of the

Boer War, and served as the private secretary of the high commissioner for South Africa, governor of Cape Colony, Alfred Milner. Many of his later novels would feature southern Africa, where, among others, he met Cecil Rhodes just before the founding colonist died. Buchan wrote: "He gave me various pieces of advice. One was to beware of the vain man. 'You can make your book with roguery,' he said, 'but vanity is incalculable—it will always let you down.'" Actually Buchan's dream was to combine the writing life with politics. To be "just a writer," he thought, might be a bad business. In his memoir *Pilgrim's Way*, he writes: "Then I thought of being a man of letters, with a home among the hills, but I remembered Sir Walter's saying that literature was a good staff but a bad crutch, and anyhow I did not fancy the business. It should be my hobby, not my profession."

For his profession Buchan tried his hand at the law, having passed the bar. But it held little appeal. He writes: "I sat in my semi-underground chambers in Middle Temple Lane, feeling as if I were in Plato's Cave, conversant not with mankind but with their shadows." What did appeal to him was elective office, and he first stood as a Unionist candidate in 1911, although something tells me the awkward campaign scene in *The Thirty-Nine Steps* was lifted directly from that first election. (In the film Richard Hannay says: "Ladies and gentlemen, I apologize for my hesitation in rising just now, but to tell you the simple truth, I'd entirely failed, while listening to the chairman's flattering description of the next speaker, to realize he was talking about me.")

Later Buchan would be elected to Parliament from Scotland. He wrote of his constituents: "I did not want to be just any kind of Member of Parliament; I wanted to represent my own folk of the Border. I have written of them in an earlier chapter that they had the qualities I most admired in human nature: realism coloured by poetry, a stalwart independence sweetened by courtesy, a shrewd kindly wisdom." Lownie, however, explains that Buchan only knew the area around the River Tweed from his school vacations and from staying at the homes there of relatives. In many ways that part of Scotland was an adoptive country.

The Great War hit Buchan hard, although he was spared having to fight in the trenches. Buchan did enlist in the armed forces during the war, but his talents marked him for Whitehall, and he served a number of ministers in intelligence and later for propaganda. It was also during the war years that he published several of his best-known books, including

The Thirty-Nine Steps ("Capital...had no conscience and no fatherland") and *Greenmantle* ("There is a dry wind blowing through the East, and the parched grasses wait the spark. And that wind is blowing towards the Indian border. Whence comes that wind, think you?")

In 1917 Buchan published *The Battle of the Somme*, an account of the "first and second phase." (In the third phase, the British called off the attacks, after having advanced less than ten miles at the cost of some 420,000 casualties.) Buchan was not a witness to the offensive on July 1, 1916, but described, nevertheless, the lines of battle with rose-colored glasses:

> At half past five the hill just west of Albert offered a singular view. It was almost in the centre of the section allowed to the Allied attack, and from it the eye could range on the left up and beyond the Ancre glen to the high ground around Beaumont Hamel and Serre; and in front to the great lift of tableland beyond which lay Bapaume; and to the right past the woods of Fricourt to the valley of the Somme.... For, on a twenty-five mile front, the Allied infantry had gone over the parapets.... But to one who visited the front before the attack the most vivid impression was that of quiet cheerfulness. These soldiers of Britain were like Cromwell's Ironsides, they "knew of what they fought for and loved what they knew."

During the war, Buchan was a one-man word factory of good news for the Allies. Not everyone thought he was acting for the public good, however. One who has taken exception to his efforts is historian and writer Adam Hochschild, who in his recent history *To End All Wars* has taken Buchan to task for the sin of commission (that of doing the government's bidding). Hochschild writes:

> A star of the literary war effort was the novelist John Buchan, who had gained a wide public following since his days in Milner's South African Kindergarten. For Thomas Nelson, an Edinburgh publisher, he put his agile pen to work writing a series of short books

that constituted an instant history of the war as it was unfolding. They downplayed British reverses, emphasized acts of heroism, evoked famous battlefield triumphs of times past, scoffed at pacifists, predicted early victory, and overestimated German losses.
The first installment of Nelson's History of the War appeared in February 1915; within four years, with some assistance, Buchan would produce 24 best-selling volumes totaling well over a million words—by far the most widely read books about the war written while it was in progress. Like the best propagandists, he was not just a manipulator but a believer, for his sunny personality allowed him to imagine the upside of absolutely anything. The inevitable British victory, he claimed, would produce a more democratic society, and so "this war may rank as one of the happiest events in our history."

Hochschild believes that Buchan should have known better than to spin the war as a noble quest, asking:

> Did Buchan believe all this? Surely not. He had close friends in infantry regiments who knew just how mindless the slaughter had been; indeed, the historian of propaganda Peter Buitenhuis speculates that it was "the strain of duplicity" in what he wrote about the Somme that soon afterward gave Buchan an ulcer attack that required surgery. But we will never know more, for any anguish Buchan felt on this score he kept entirely to himself; there is no sign of it in his published work, diary or letters.

But Buchan, like many of his friends in the lines, was a good soldier. He even had kind words to say about General Sir Douglas Haig, one of Alan Clark's "donkeys," noting: "His best epitaph is the sentence which Pope wrote about Harley: 'He was a steady man and a had a great firmness of soul.'"

FRIENDS OF A KIND

Buchan After the Great War

AFTER THE WAR, Buchan reflected on how few war veterans went into public service, writing: "No doubt a great number of able young men died, but of those who survived only a small proportion took to public life; the majority turned resolutely to private business and stayed there. They refused to bury themselves in what T. E. Lawrence used to describe as the 'shallow grave of public duty.'"

In 1927 Buchan was elected to Parliament, where he was exactly a contemporary of Winston Churchill. Although both men loved literature and politics, they were never close. Buchan, a more liberal Conservative than the war-mongering Churchill (in his view), actually thought Winston was—in Lownie's phrase—something of a "rogue."

In *Pilgrim's Way*, Buchan expresses his political philosophy in this way:

> When I examined my political faith I found that my strongest belief was in democracy according to my own definition. Democracy—the essential thing as distinguished from this or that democratic government—was primarily an attitude of mind, a spiritual testament, and not an economic structure or a political machine. The testament involved certain basic beliefs—that the personality was sacrosanct, which was the meaning of liberty; that policy should be settled by free discussion; that normally a minority should be ready to yield to a majority, which in turn should respect a minority's sacred things.

In 1935, he was appointed Governor General of Canada. Even while serving there, he continued to publish a number of books, including his memoirs. (His last book, *Sick Heart River*, is set in the Canadian wild and came out posthumously in 1941.) When I asked Lownie how a man with such important jobs could write more than a hundred books, he answered that he was ruthlessly efficient, scheduling his time so that he could write perfectly turned-out sentences and paragraphs at night or even on commuter trains into London. Apparently, he needed few drafts to complete a story, allowing him, some years, to come out with three books.

In 1939 Buchan was anti-war and leery of Churchill, but when the war came all three of his sons enlisted and, Lownie said, he thought both Britain and his family needed to be in the fight. Like Churchill, however, he would have been distraught to know that Britain would end the war with its empire close to liquidation (although he writes in *Greenmantle*: "That is England's way. She cares more for her Empire than for what may happen to her allies").

With Childers, Buchan helped to pioneer the political thriller. *Greenmantle*, the novel I know best, centers on the Germans sowing Arab nationalism in Ottoman Turkey, as a way to divide Britain from its Indian colony. He writes: "The ordinary man again will answer that Islam in Turkey is becoming a back number, and that Krupp guns are the new gods. Yet—I don't know. I do not quite believe in Islam becoming a back number.'" A citizen-spy, Hannay travels overland to the Middle East ("I saw what I took to be mosques and minarets, and they were about as impressive as factory chimneys") to determine the extent of German influence in Arab affairs ("I had heard of the East as a good place for people to disappear in; there were no inquisitive newspapers or incorruptible police"). He concludes: "There's a great stirring in Islam, something moving on the face of the waters." He continues:

> I've found out one thing, and that is, that the last dream Germany will part with is the control of the Near East. That is what your statesmen don't figure enough on. She'll give up Belgium and Alsace-Lorraine and Poland, but by God! she'll never give up the road to Mesopotamia till you have her by the throat and make her drop it.

I asked Andrew Lownie, who is also Scottish, what Buchan would have made of Britain's vote to leave the European Union and the possibility that Brexit could lead to another vote on Scottish independence. He said that Buchan, while a strong believer in Scottish nationalism, was also very much a Unionist and would want Scotland and England to remain together in the United Kingdom and also Europe. Buchan once said in Parliament: "I believe every Scotsman should be a Scottish nationalist. If it could be proved that a Scottish Parliament were desirable... Scotsmen should support it." But Lownie did not believe that he would now be a supporter of Scottish independence and said that on many issues, Buchan, a child of the British Empire, was conventional in his political opinions. He also said that Buchan was friendly with Franklin Roosevelt and an Atlanticist. That explains his pro-American sentiments in his memoirs, including this passage:

> The United States is the richest, and, both actually and potentially, the most powerful state on the globe. She has much, I believe, to give to the world; indeed, to her hands is chiefly entrusted the shaping of the future. If democracy in the broadest and truest sense is to survive, it will be mainly because of her guardianship. For, with all her imperfections, she has a clearer view than any other people of the democratic fundamentals.

Ironically, I was typing these words in the aftermath of the January 6 storming of the U.S. Capitol.

JOHN BUCHAN

Elsfield Manor, Oxford:
At home with the novelist

ONLY ON A subsequent visit to Oxford did I manage—thanks to my friend Edward—to get a look inside Elsfield Manor, where John Buchan lived with his family from 1919 until 1935 (when he was appointed Governor General of Canada). Buchan actually owned the sprawling home until 1940. Later on, the house was subdivided, and David Buchan, one of John's grandchildren, now lives in part of the manor, together with his wife Lisa and their children. The village is about four miles from the center of Oxford. When he bought the house, Buchan wrote: "The War left me an intense craving for a country life. It was partly that I wanted quiet after turmoil, the instinct that in the Middle Ages took men into monasteries. But it was also a new-found delight in the rhythm of nature, and in the small homely things after so many alien immensities."

At the house, David Buchan introduced me to his cousin Ursula Buchan, a well-known English journalist who was writing a biography of her grandfather, which was published in 2020 as: *Beyond the Thirty-Nine Steps: A Life of John Buchan*. David and Lisa walked me through their part of the house, pointing out the corners where Buchan had written or at least revised many of his books. We then had tea and talked in the kitchen, which David joked had been his grandfather's dressing room.

Ursula said she decided to write her grandfather's biography in part because she had never read all of his books: twenty-nine novels, four collections of poetry, forty-two works of nonfiction, and ten biographies. During some years in the 1920s, Buchan would publish two or three books a year, and when I asked Ursula (as I had Andrew Lownie) what accounted for her grandfather's ability to write so much and so clearly, despite having full-time work and a large family, she said that both his parents, plus the Scottish public schools in the late nineteenth century, gave him a grounding in the classics plus the works of such celebrated Scots as Robert Burns, Walter Scott, and Robert Louis Stevenson. Later I came across a passage that Buchan wrote, in which he stated: "The fatigue of the War, moral and mental, was passing, and my bodily ailments could be kept within bounds. The truth is that in my late forties I experienced a ridiculous resurgence of youth."

FRIENDS OF A KIND

Ursula said that the inspiration for many of his later characters, including Richard Hannay, came while Buchan was on service for Lord Milner in South Africa. For example, the life of William Edmund Ironside (a long-serving British officer in many battles from the Boer War to World War II) inspired many of the heroics later undertaken by Hannay in such books as the *Thirty-Nine Steps* and *Greenmantle*.

At the time of the Second Boer War, Buchan was working in London as a publisher. He wrote some articles about the crisis in South Africa, and they led to him being hired by Lord Milner, who ran the civil service in South Africa during the war (and many would say, a vast spy network). At one point in the war, Ironside disguised himself as an Afrikaans driver, and infiltrated German lines, the kind of caper that so appealed later, in fiction, to Richard Hannay.

In my conversation with Ursula, I recalled that in the *Thirty-Nine Steps* Richard Hannay (having escaped London) ends up in desolate country, probably in Scotland, seeking the kindness of strangers to avoid arrest by the police. She said that many John Buchan fans—I think I am one—routinely confuse or gently mix the book and the Hitchcock film. In the 1935 film *The 39 Steps*, Hannay finds himself footloose closer to Edinburgh and the Firth of Forth, while in the novel he takes a mail train toward Galloway and Solway Firth, an area that Buchan knew from his youth.

Buchan spent part of his childhood in the slums around Glasgow, where his father was a Presbyterian minister. While his parents came from distinguished Scottish families, Buchan inherited no money, and he ended up in Elsfield Manor purely because of his ability to write and sell books. Ursula said that he had sold his first novel even before he matriculated at Oxford.

I asked Ursula and David a lot of questions about Buchan's famous friendships, such as those with T. E. Lawrence and Winston Churchill. Ursula made the point that, politically, he was a centrist, and that when he first stood for Parliament, it wasn't clear whether he would run as a Liberal or a Conservative (then the Unionist Party). His support of women's rights and those of workers marked him as a Liberal, but in the end, his firm convictions against home rule for Ireland tilted him toward the Tories.

She confirmed what Lownie had said about his relationship with Churchill, saying that he was often infuriated with his friend, but added that Churchill was capable of having the same feelings about Buchan. About Lawrence's last days and Buchan, she was less clear, but did say that after the war it was Buchan's connections to Stanley Baldwin and his marshal of the Royal Air Force, Hugh Trenchard, that allowed Lawrence to enlist under the pseudonym J. H. Ross.

I asked Ursula about John Buchan's attachment to southern Scotland, an area often called the Borders, and she said that while, in adult life, he always lived in or near London, Buchan took a holiday every summer in Scotland. He loved to fish and hunt deer, or tramp on the moors, often in the company of his Oxford friends. Later he took his growing family to the village homes associated with both of his parents, and led them on hikes and adventures, many of which later found their way into his fiction. She mentioned *John McNab* as one of the stories that might have been inspired by his summer holidays. It's the story of three middle-aged London men who take to poaching, and then returning the stolen animals, as a way of bringing some excitement into lives punctuated with "ennui."

FRIENDS OF A KIND

Peebles, Scotland: *Tramping with Richard Hannay*

IT WAS ONLY after I went to the Buchan house in Elsfield that I made it to Peebles, in the Scottish Borders south of Edinburgh, not far from where Buchan's parents were born in Tweeddale.

For a long time I thought Buchan himself had lived for much of his life in Peebles, as that is the location of a John Buchan museum, and it also was where, in such books and films as *The Thirty-Nine Steps*, he invested much emotion in his stories. (He once said: "My chief passion was for the Border countryside, and my object in all my prentice writings was to reproduce its delicate charm.") But as Ursula had explained, Buchan's attachment to the area came from his childhood holidays with his parents and later in his life from his own trips there with his children, where he liked nothing more than to tramp around the hills. In his memoir *Pilgrim's Way*, Buchan describes his affection for the land:

> Those Border shepherds, the men of the long stride and the clear eye, were a great race—I have never known a greater. The narrower kinds of fanaticism, which have run riot elsewhere in Scotland, rarely affected the Borders. Their people were 'grave livers,' in Wordsworth's phrase, God-fearing, decent in all the relations of life, and supreme masters of their craft. They were a fighting stock because of their ancestry, and of a noble independence. As the source of the greatest ballads in any literature they had fire and imagination, and some aptitude for the graces of life. They lacked the dourness of the conventional Scot, having a quick eye for comedy, and, being in themselves wholly secure, they were aristocrats with the fine manners of an aristocracy. By them I was admitted into the secrets of a whole lost world of pastoral. I acquired a reverence and affection for the 'plain people,' who to Walter Scott and Abraham Lincoln were what mattered most in the world.

JOHN BUCHAN

To get to Peebles, my wife and I caught a local bus in Edinburgh that runs due south for about an hour. It left the Edinburgh bus depot at around 10:30 a.m. Before meeting up at the bus, I called on the owners of the house in Edinburgh in which Robert Louis Stevenson grew up and lived until the age of thirty. In a search of the internet for a Stevenson museum or society, I had come across the home, which at times doubles as a bed-and-breakfast. Stevenson fans can rent a room for the night, even though the house belongs to the family of John Macfie, a Scotsman with a lion's mane of facial hair that connects his bushy sideburns to his mustache. In one of the parlours on an upper floor, Mr. Macfie and I had a coffee and he talked about how "Louis" (the family name for Robert L. Stevenson) had grown up a sickly child, with his nose often in a book, and how telling ghost stories was an evening passion in the Stevenson household. He said that Louis' failure to join the family business—that of building coastal lighthouses around Scotland—had cast him as something of an outlier until his words, in such novels as *Kidnapped*, did more than the family lighthouses to illuminate the coastal highlands.

For much of the bus ride to Peebles, we rode through suburban Edinburgh, a long procession of shops and malls. Only as we approached Peebles (a small town on the River Tweed) did the landscape take on the barren, swept look of the Borders. Not knowing where exactly we would find the John Buchan Story Museum, we rode the bus to the last stop, where there was an eager crowd milling around to catch the returning bus into Edinburgh. It was someone in that (fairly loose) queue who pointed me in the direction of the museum, which occupies one floor of a house on High Street.

Inside, a Scotsman of few words was on duty. Without a lot of small talk, he collected the money for my admission ticket and pointed me in the direction of the exhibits, which tell the story of Buchan's life and his affection for the Borders. In one of the panels, Buchan recounts, in a letter to a friend, that it was a winter illness that got him started on the Richard Hannay series of "shockers;" that is, adventure stories revolving around a South African who is otherwise engaged in His Majesty's Secret Service. Buchan writes to his friend Tommy:

> You and I have long cherished an affection for that elementary type of tale which Americans call the 'dime novel' and which we know as the 'shocker'—the

romance where the incidents defy the probabilities, and march just inside the borders of the possible. During an illness last winter I exhausted my store of those aids to cheerfulness, and was driven to write one for myself. This little volume is the result, and I should like to put your name on it in memory of our long friendship, in the days when the wildest fictions are so much less probable than the facts.

Elsewhere Buchan has written: "I invented a young South African called Richard Hannay…and I amused myself with considering what he would do in various emergencies." In *The Thirty-Nine Steps*, Hannay is unjustly accused of murdering a man (in the film it's a woman). While fleeing the police, he succeeds in tracking down a spy ring that has it in mind to steal and send abroad British Air Ministry secrets. Unlike the sailors in Erskine Childers' darker adventure story about the German menace, Buchan's hero is an imperial inspiration, there to save king and country. But as someone who has read the novel, seen (several times) the Alfred Hitchcock movie, and even attended a musical of the story in London, I can say that Buchan's genius was to make Richard Hannay more Everyman than James Bond. Hannay manages to foil the plot with street smarts, good cheer, and the ability to trek a long way across the bleak Borders, as he shakes loose his many pursuers (which include more than a few police constables).

At the museum, I picked up a guide to The John Buchan Way, a walking path that tracks from Peebles to the town of Broughton, about fourteen miles west. Rather than walk in the direction of the setting sun, we decided, instead, to catch a local bus to Stobo—a way point on the walk—and find our way back on the trail. The women on duty in the tourist office said that we would have no trouble following the markers, which mostly turned out to be true, although at a few lonely intersections in the hills we spent considerable time trying to find our bearings.

The helpful bus driver dropped us at the kirk in Stobo, after which we climbed for several hours through the hills that roll above the valley of the Tweed. Never, however, were the hills as steep as many in the Alps, and for the most part the trail had the soft look of a green path cut by a lawn mower. Some of the fields had sheep and cows, and in one of the larger meadows near the crossroads labeled on the map as "The Glack," we found ourselves face-to-face with a herd of not-very-friendly black Angus cattle, including a massive bull. We tiptoed around the herd with the hope that neither of us would need to deploy matador skills or leap over a nearby stone wall. We resumed the walk, which reached its pinnacle at Cademuir Hill on a Roman road through the high ground of a forlorn but spectacular moor. The path across the highlands reminded me of this passage from Buchan's memoir:

> It was my custom in the long vacations to bury myself in the moorlands, taking up quarters in a shepherd's cottage….
>
> The chief episodes were the spring walking tours. Each year after much planning I would tramp with a friend or two on a circuit north of Tweed.… Those expeditions have given me memories of which time has not dimmed the rapture. There would be wild days among wet or snowy hills, or on moorland roads in the teeth of a hailstorm, and nights in inns before roaring fires, when, replete and content, we talked the rhetoric of youth.

Our walk ended with a long descent into Peebles, where the moors gave way to suburban trackhouses and paved roads, which led us to a café (for hot tea) on High Street and the bus back to Edinburgh. By late afternoon the summer day had turned into a premonition of fall, with a stiff breeze, low clouds, and passing squalls. It wasn't one of Buchan's hailstorms, but it was easy to imagine one. He writes: "I throve on a diet of oatmeal, mutton, and strong tea, and, with the habit to which I have already referred of linking philosophy to terrestrial objects, the works of Aristotle are ever bound up for me with the smell of peat reek and certain stretches of granite and heather."

Buchan and John F. Kennedy: *Kindred spirits*

My interest in John Buchan included a wish to learn more about Raymond Asquith, his friend who was killed in the Battle of the Somme and whose name is engraved in St. Andrews Church in Mells, where Siegfried Sassoon is buried. They had been close at Oxford, and Buchan writes about him at length in *Pilgrim's Way*: "No two friends were ever more unlike than he and I. He chaffed me unmercifully about my Calvinism, my love of rough moors in wild weather, my growing preference for what he called the Gothic over the Greek life, my crude passion for romance." Nevertheless, the two formed a bond that lasted until Asquith's death in 1916. They even married in the same year, and shared a bachelor party at the Hotel Savoy. Buchan was in awe of his friend's many accomplishments, writing:

> I have never met anyone so endowed with diverse talents. In sheer intellectual strength he may have his equals, and there were limits to his imaginative sympathies; but for manifold and multiform gifts I have not known his like.

Ursula Buchan had talked about how Buchan (not from a patrician family) was accepted into his Oxford set and said that Raymond Asquith was one of the college's stars. She repeated the story that when Raymond's father, Herbert Asquith, already a barrister and serving in Parliament, visited his son at Oxford, someone asked the older man if he was related to "our Mr. Asquith."

Clearly, based on his brilliance at Oxford and beyond, Raymond Asquith was marked as a future prime minister, and it was only a question of when, not if, he would stand for office. John Buchan writes that his profession, the law, bored him, and that no one could speak as effortlessly as Raymond. (Nor did it hurt that his father became the Liberal prime minister before the war. Buchan said of his friend: "His politics were hereditary, not, I think, the result of any personal enthusiasm.")

What seems to have set Asquith apart was his capacity for friendship. He wrote brilliant letters, and in conversation he was never shy when it came to *bons mots*. Buchan writes: "He loved the things of the mind—good books, good talk—for their own sake; he loved, above all, youth and the company of his friends." About the only thing that might have held him back from greatness was an absence of ruthless determination. "I have said," writes Buchan, "that he came up to Oxford with little ambition, and he went down with less."

At the outbreak of war in 1914, at age thirty-five, Asquith was commissioned as a second lieutenant in the Queen's Westminsters, and there found success as a junior officer. ("He was an excellent battalion officer, and so much in love with his new life that he sometimes spoke of going on with the army as his profession.") He died leading his men out of the village of Ginchy, which lies just beyond Mametz. The death of the prime minister's promising son, on the banks of the Somme, came to represent everything that the country lost in the war.

Among those haunted by Asquith's death was Lieutenant (junior grade) John F. Kennedy, who went to war in the Solomon Islands carrying with him a copy of Buchan's *Pilgrim's Way*. Since high school, I had known that Buchan's memoirs was among his favorite books, and as a child of the 1960s, who had seen Kennedy in person shortly before he was killed, I had tracked down a copy at a used bookstore in Sea Cliff, Long Island. I paid $2, although I didn't make it through the memoir until Easter 1994. But I had never known when and where Kennedy read the book until 2016, when I purchased Edward Renehan, Jr.'s *The Kennedys at War*, a well-written history of the family leading up to and throughout World War II. (It's best on Ambassador Joe's flirtations with Hitler and appeasement, and how JFK over time was able to distance himself from his father's pessimism about democracy's future.)

Renehan makes it clear that the young Jack Kennedy, at Harvard University while his father was ambassador to the Court of St. James (London), was very much at home among the English aristocracy and in its political world. Renehan also describes how JFK read Buchan's book on Tulagi, a small island opposite Guadalcanal, in spring 1943 when he was assigned to skipper *PT-109*. Renehan goes on at length about the meaning that Kennedy attached to Buchan's memoir and the fate of

Raymond Asquith.[4] He writes:

> He [JFK] was reading *Pilgrim's Way* that spring. Jack seemed mesmerized by, and talked incessantly to friends about, John Buchan's elegy for the fine crop of wellborn Brits—many of them friends not only of Buchan but also Billy Hartington's [his sister's boyfriend] father—who had found meaning (and, too often, death) on the battlefields of World War I. Personally, Jack perhaps related most to the tale of Raymond Asquith—son of the famed Liberal prime minister—who in 1915 grew bored with a safe job in intelligence, volunteered for the front, and there reveled in "the mingled bondage and freedom of active service." Asquith died in the Battle of the Somme, 1916. "For the chosen few, like Raymond," wrote Buchan, who had known Asquith at Oxford, "there is no disillusionment. They march on into life with a boyish grace, and their high noon keeps all the freshness of the morning." In his own copy of *Pilgrim's Way*, Jack—perhaps thinking of Mead and Howe [friends killed in the war]—circled a choice two lines of Buchan's tribute: "He loved his youth, and his youth has become eternal. Debonair and brilliant and brave, he is now part of that immortal England which knows not age or weariness or defeat."

At the time, although he was fighting the Japanese in Iron Bottom Sound, Kennedy himself was trying to reconcile the possibilities of a political life with an inclination to become a writer. Clearly Buchan's embrace of Parliament and his pen, and Asquith's valor on the front lines, resonated with him, then at war. Little did he know that Buchan's epitaph for his fallen friend, "One gift was withheld from him—length of years," would also one day speak for John Kennedy.

---

4 Another Kennedy biography, Nigel Hamilton's *JFK: Reckless Youth*, concludes that he had read *Pilgrim's Way* before embarking for the Solomon Islands and that he only sang its praises to the men in his circle, notably James Reed, who was the father of my friend and contemporary, Craig Reed.

FRIENDS OF A KIND

Like Thomas Hardy, **Joseph Conrad** (his full name was József Teodor Konrad Korzeniowski and he was older than many of those written about in this book) had an influence over this younger generation of writers and poets, notably T. E. Lawrence, who was drawn to some of the mystical elements of Conrad's novels. Both Lady Ottoline Morrell and her longtime lover, Bertrand Russell, visited Conrad at his country home in Bishopsbourne, just outside Canterbury. Although Polish by birth and a sailor by inclination and trade in his early life, Conrad was content to live in the countryside as an upper middle class Englishman. He wrote his novels in English, loving the flexibility that its words offered him, although he was more fluent in French.

Section VI

HEART OF JOSEPH CONRAD

Along the River Thames

FOR THE EARLY sections of this book, I made do with Bromptons from the rental scheme, retrieving bicycles from various lockers around Britain. But those Bromptons were limited to three gears, and none had rear luggage racks, which limited me to a front bag and whatever clothes were on my back. At some point, so to speak, I switched gears, and brought my own Brompton with me on these travels. It involved overland travel from Geneva to London, although occasionally I would take the folded bicycle on a flight. Usually, however, I would take the train to Paris, and then to get to London, depending on where I was headed, I would take Eurostar to St. Pancras or, if heading somewhere outside London, I might take one of the Channel ferries and land in Newhaven or Dover. In general, I preferred the ferries to the trains in the Channel Tunnel—who doesn't prefer the sounds and scents of the sea over a cramped seat?—but often it made for a long day, and not every Channel ferry accepts foot passengers.

After my Buchan travels in Scotland, I decided to bike around East London and out along the River Thames as it drifted toward the open sea—if only to see where Joseph Conrad filled into the literary puzzle that already had large pieces of T. E. Lawrence, Siegfried Sassoon, John Buchan, and Robert Graves. Often, in reading their biographies, if not their letters, poems, or novels, they would sing the praises of Conrad or make reference to visits with the great novelist who came to England by way of Poland and after a career at sea as a mariner. But I didn't know if or how he had influenced them until I pointed my bicycle toward the East End of London, and then toward Kent, where Conrad lived in the last years of his life. At the start all I knew for sure was that Conrad had greatly inspired the writing of Lawrence, and that was enough for me to head east along the Thames Estuary, a stretch of the river I most associate with Conrad's *Heart of Darkness*.

FRIENDS OF A KIND

It took me longer than it should have to warm up to Conrad's writing. In the tenth grade I was assigned to read *Heart of Darkness* and the *Secret Sharer*. I remember struggling with the sentence structure, much as I had with *Lord Jim* in the seventh grade. At times I felt I was reading something translated from Polish, or written with an open thesaurus.

In 1982, assigned to write an article on hurricanes for Pan American's in-flight magazine *Clipper*, I dug out my copy of *Typhoon*, hoping to find a good description of tropical storms. The book struck me as long on crashing waves but short on narrative development. I might never have gone further with Conrad except for two things: firstly I had a conversation with Columbia University scholar Edward Said, whom I had known since my days as a student there. I was editing an article that he had written for *Harper's Magazine*, and after we went over the galleys, he spoke at length and passionately about his love of Conrad and his understanding of the difficult questions of personal identity.

Said, a Palestinian who was born in Jerusalem (where he could no longer visit), had grown up in Cairo but attended boarding school in Massachusetts and college in Princeton, and now lived and worked in New York City. For Said, Conrad's personal diaspora was his own (Conrad wrote: "That mental feeling of being in two places at once affected me physically as if the mood of secrecy had penetrated my very soul").

My second breakthrough with Conrad happened when I bought several of his novels from Books-on-Tape. It had not occurred to me before that Conrad's language is so suited to being read aloud, but it makes perfect sense, as so many of his books, beginning with *Heart of Darkness*, are narrated at the fantail of a schooner, swinging at anchor in the gloaming. ("Marlow sat cross-legged right aft, leaning against the mizzen-mast. He had sunken cheeks, a yellow complexion, a straight back, an ascetic aspect, and, with his arms dropped, the palms of hands outwards, resembled an idol.")

As I worked my way through Conrad, I found it easiest to read particular novels in specific places. For example, I read *Nostromo*, about revolution, on a trip to Latin America ("The world rests upon the poor…") and *Under Western Eyes* in Geneva and Russia ("They turned to autocracy for the peace of their patriotic conscience as a weary unbeliever…"). But now standing on banks of the River Thames near Woolwich (one of my bike lanes ended on the riverbank), I reflected that I still did not know more than the bare outlines of Conrad's life. Like most, I knew he was

Polish, that he had gone to sea as a young man, and that later in life he lived in England and wrote his books in English, which was either his fifth or sixth language. But it was a revelation to me that he played an important role in the literature of World War I—if only from a distance, as he was born in 1857.

FRIENDS OF A KIND

Sailing Toward Poland

OVER THE YEARS I had collected several Conrad biographies, including the mammoth *Joseph Conrad: The Three Lives* by Frederick R. Karl. Occasionally I was tempted to dig into it, but I always found its 913 pages of dense type, and even denser prose, forbidding. Instead, on one of my trips I found a secondhand copy of Jeffrey Meyers' *Joseph Conrad: A Biography*. I knew there were better Conrad scholars in the market than Meyers, who is something of a professional biographer. But I had read and liked his biography of F. Scott Fitzgerald, and reasoned I was better off finishing a lesser biography than bogging down in a great one. At least I would come away with the outline of Conrad's life, which, when he went to sea, often traversed this stretch of the river. ("The estuary of the Thames is not beautiful; it has no noble features, no romantic grandeur of aspect, no smiling geniality; but it is wide open, spacious, inviting, hospitable at the first glance, with a strange air of mysteriousness.")

Conrad, a Pole, was born Józef Teodor Konrad Korzeniowski in 1857, but for most of his life Poland was a memory and an abstraction. Berdichev, where he was born, was famous for only one thing: in 1850, according to Meyers, the French writer "Honoré de Balzac had traveled through the countryside, 'sandy tracts studded with clumps of pines,' and had married Evelina Hanska in the Polish Roman Catholic church of Santa Barbara." Balzac brought Madame Hanksa back to Paris, where he died less than a year later. At the time Poland was under Russian rule. Meyers writes: "There were four possible attitudes toward Russian rule in Poland: loyalism, conciliation, resistance and emigration."

Conrad's father, Apollo, chose to emigrate, first to Warsaw, where he was arrested for organizing independence activities and sentenced to exile in Russia, a voyage as lonely as any in Conrad's novels. His father said: "We do not regard exile as a punishment but as a new way of serving our country. There can be no punishment for us, since we are innocent." Meyers writes: "Apollo's legacy to Conrad was a volatile temperament, an anguished patriotism, the bitterness of shattered hopes, the trauma of defeat and a deep rooted pessimism." Joseph's mother died when he was eight, and his father home-schooled him as they moved from place to place, usually in the bleak Russian winters. No wonder, later, did Conrad so delight in his home life outside London.

Apollo died, perhaps of a broken heart, when Conrad was eleven, and the boy moved in with an uncle, who despaired that the young Joseph showed so little aptitude at school or intellectually. He did like to read, was good with languages, and dreamed of the sea. His uncle decided that he was best suited for the life of a sailor, and to that end he sent Conrad, at age sixteen, to Marseilles, where it was hoped he could learn French and find work as a first mate. It also marked yet another exile in Conrad's already disrupted childhood. Meyers writes: "It is essential to emphasize and to remember the most crucial facts of Conrad's early life: the Russians had enslaved his country, forbidden his language, confiscated his inheritance, treated him as a convict, killed his parents and forced him into exile."

Philosopher Bertrand Russell (the lover of Lady Ottoline Morrell to whom we will come in this book) visited Conrad at the end of his life and wrote in his memoirs about the author:

> I travelled down to his house near Ashford in Kent in a state of somewhat anxious expectation. My first impression was one of surprise. He spoke English with a very strong foreign accent, and nothing in his demeanour in any way suggested the sea. He was an aristocratic Polish gentleman to his finger-tips. His feeling for the sea, and for England, was one of romantic love—love from a certain distance, sufficient to leave the romance untarnished. His love for the sea began at a very early age. When he told his parents that he wished for a career as a sailor, they urged him to go into the Austrian navy, but he wanted adventure and tropical seas and strange rivers surrounded by dark forests; and the Austrian navy offered him no scope for these desires.

Conrad was at sea for twenty years, sailing all over the world, although in his mind he was "always sailing toward Poland." He made eighteen long voyages, and countless shorter ones, in all the world's oceans. He took seriously his career as a seaman and passed his exams (in French and English) to serve as an officer. Later, when struggling as a writer and with a growing family, he dreamed of returning to his earlier career

FRIENDS OF A KIND

at sea. His temper and habits of independence marked him more as a freelance officer—he worked for many companies and served on many ships—and as he got older, a recurring theme in his letters was despair that more modern sailors were "little more than factory hands." They had not ascended the rigging during an ice storm to reef the main sail. Nor had they studied navigation or engineering with Conrad's diligence.

Perhaps with so much time on his hands (he wife once remarked that "his days ashore were intervals of utter loneliness"), Conrad became a reader and a writer. Meyers writes of an early shore leave in England:

> While waiting in Cornwall, Conrad took a brief leave and squandered all his money in London: "It took me a day to get there and pretty well another to come back—but three months' pay went all the same. I don't know what I did with it. I went to a music-hall, I believe, lunched, dined, and supped in a swell place in Regent Street, and was back to time, with nothing but a complete set of Byron's works and a new railway rug to show for three months' work."

I have no doubt that Conrad was good sailor. Nevertheless, Meyers writes that Conrad's nervous temperament was a liability in his chosen career: "…his extreme (almost shell shocked) nervousness, a lifelong characteristic, seemed a dangerous liability for a master who frequently had to deal with sudden emergencies." But the sea was a wonderful school for a writer. At sea about the same time was American writer Herman Melville, who wrote famously: "A whale ship was my Yale College and my Harvard."

Conrad's Yale and Harvard were the outposts of lonely Pacific islands, lee shores across Asian waters, and, perhaps most of all, the Congo River. Meyers writes: "He was strongly attracted to the theme of the degeneration of the white man in the tropics, and found it safer, for social and political reasons, to write about the Dutch rather than the English imperialists." He also draws parallels between a writer's solitary life and that of a seaman:

> The sea made Conrad "familiar with long silences," which, with the isolation, may have reminded him of the

long, depressing months with his moribund father. The loneliness of Conrad's childhood months was prolonged in his youth. As he realistically wrote in *Lord Jim*: "he had to bear the criticisms of men, the exactions of the sea, and the prosaic severity of the daily task that gives bread.... There is nothing more enticing, disenchanting, and enslaving than the life at sea."

I still have my high school copy of *Heart of Darkness*, and from the jejune marginalia I can see that mostly what I did while reading Conrad was look up words in the dictionary. Underlined with the ink of a Bic pen are such words as "diaphanous," "sedentary," "immutability," "ascetic," and "concertina." My only note appears on page 129, when in pencil I wrote: "Kurtz dies."

Among the passages I highlighted was one about the commercial exploitation of the jungle, which reads: "To tear treasure out of the bowels of the land was their desire, with no more moral purpose at the back of it than there is in burglars breaking into a safe." At the time, however, I am not sure how conversant I was with the ideas of colonialism or imperialism, and suspect that the disembodied heads staked along the riverbank made a bigger impression on my teenage sensibilities than did Conrad's alienation from the system he was serving.

Meyers writes at length about how the Congo changed Conrad. He quotes him as saying: "...before the Congo, 'I was a perfect animal.' Afterward, his new insights into the nature of evil turned his innate pessimism into a tragic vision: 'I see everything with such despondency—all in black.'" Meyers continues: "Only after he had reached the Congo and seen the brutal exploitation of the resources and the people did he realize it was 'the vilest scramble for loot that ever disfigured the history of human conscience and geographical exploration.'" Conrad reflected that Africa "has been 'opened up' (as if it were an oyster) and the Civilizers are now busy developing it with blood and slaying each other, and burning with hatred against me because I think their work is organized murder, far worse than anything the savages did before them." Meyers makes the point that: "*Heart of Darkness* is the first significant work in English literature to deny the idea of progress, which had been a dominant idea in European thought for the past four hundred years, and to question the very foundations of Western civilization."

FRIENDS OF A KIND

Canterbury Tales

MUCH OF CONRAD'S early works of fiction was a retelling of stories he had seen or heard at sea. He worked at his writing, much as he once had studied diligently for his master's exams. Of writing, he said, "You must squeeze out of yourself every sensation, every thought, every image—mercilessly, without reserve and without remorse…you must search the darkest corner of your heart, the most remote recesses of your brain." If there is a downside to Conrad's writing, it is that sometimes the densely packed images cascade down the page, making for a long afternoon of reading. Kipling said: "When I am reading him, I always have the impression that I am reading an excellent translation of a foreign author."

At the end of his life, Conrad—the successful author, and friend to the likes of Ivan Turgenev and Henry James—was perhaps more English than the English. He covered his small frame with dapper suits, wore a hat, and walked with a stick. He married a conventional English woman, Jesse George (Virginia Woolf called her a "lump of a wife"), and raised his sons in the Kent countryside to become English gentlemen, which proved harder than his own conversion.

I didn't ride all the way to Bishopsbourne, where Conrad lived, but took a train to nearby Canterbury, which charmed me for its French accents and, obviously, its cathedral ("Will no one rid me of this meddlesome priest?"). I ate lunch in a small bistro and walked around a Museum of Freemasonry. Bishopsbourne is a nearby suburb, where Conrad lived at the end of his life. In the center of the village there was a sign indicating that Conrad lived in the village, but no directions to the actual house, which is privately owned. Finally I asked directions from a pedestrian, and he pointed me toward the upscale house, known locally as Oswalds. A man was working in the yard, and he allowed me to take some pictures over the wall. I never got a clear view of the house through all the trees, but the village was sufficient to figure out that, at the end of his life, Conrad lived as an English squire.

Back in Canterbury, I headed to where Conrad is buried in the City Cemetery. I had printed out a photograph of his headstone, which seemed like a large slab of granite with an angular top, like the bow of a ship. The name engraved is Józef Teodor Konrad Korzeniowski. It was a January afternoon, and no one else was in the cemetery, and after about twenty minutes of searching in the cold I gave up to catch a train.

Back in London, to make up for my failure at the cemetery, I tracked down a copy of a short book, *Joseph Conrad: Interviews and Recollections*, which was edited by Martin Ray. The book is excerpts of primary source materials from people, such as his wife, who knew Conrad intimately or visited him at Bishopsbourne. One of the entries is from Lady Ottoline Morrell, who was among those who persuaded Sassoon to go public with his denunciations of the war. Of Conrad she writes:

> I visited him again once or twice, but as he was very patriotic I did not dare go during the war, as I felt sure he would disapprove of my views, but in 1923 while Philip [her husband] and I were staying with Bernard Holland not far from Conrad's new home in Kent we all went over to see him (he had not met Philip before). It was a perfectly happy day. We found him in a pleasant country house on the edge of a park, an old-fashioned house with large, low rooms, which he had furnished with great distinction and with something of the air, it seemed to me, of a Polish chateau. It was the sort of garden that you might find described, with its view over the rather monotonous landscape of the Park, in a Henry James novel, and Conrad with his polished air was, you might have supposed, very well set there. But the view was too narrow for his taste. He missed, as he said, one thing: 'It has no horizon.'

And then there is this passage taken from an interview with Jo Davidson, an American sculptor who came to England to make a bust of Conrad. It captures Conrad's writing method:

> The striking thing for me about Conrad was the way I found he approaches his work. He uses life as a point of departure. For instance, I was curious about how he got his characters for *The Secret Agent*. He told me that he used to go to restaurants in Greek Street or Dean Street or 'So' Square, where he watched the types—anarchists, agitators, charlatans, wretches of all sorts or

just arch-individuals of our genus fellow man. He didn't talk with them. He just sat looking, studying, reflecting on them.... If he saw a man with certain striking characteristics, with a certain sort of face, he didn't try to break into the man's life story. It wasn't necessary. He'd simply work it out to his own satisfaction that the man was a character and then he'd work out to his further satisfaction what sort of character did belong, ought to belong, with that sort of face....

In speech he is not fluent; he gestures continually and completes phrases with gestures. He speaks English in fact with a slight accent—not so well as he speaks French. When I asked him why he didn't write in French he said, "Oh, it's much more difficult. English is so plastic—you can do anything with it!"

Best of all, given my frustrations about missing his gravesite, I found in the book a description of Conrad's burial. The observer was R. B. Cunninghame Graham, who was head of the Scottish National Party. He was friends with Conrad for almost twenty years, sharing with him a loathing for colonialism. He remembered the burial in the City Cemetery:

> The voyage was over and the great spirit rested from its toil, safe in the English earth that he had dreamed of as a child in far Ukrainia. A gleam of sun lit up the red-brick houses of the town. It fell upon the tower of the cathedral, turning it into a great glowing beacon pointing to the sky. The trees moved gently in the breeze, and in the fields the ripening corn was undulating softly, just as the waves waft in on an atoll in the Pacific, with a light swishing sound. All was well chosen for his resting-place, and so we left him with his sails all duly furled, rope flemished down, and with the anchor holding truly in the kind Kentish earth, until the judgment day. The gulls will bring him tidings as they fly past above his grave, with their wild voices, if he should weary for the sea and the salt smell of it.

Conrad and Lawrence: *Confluent shipwrecks*

CONRAD WAS GENEROUS with his time for other writers, welcoming them for tea or writing long letters about their work. (Unlike Sassoon, he did not share his works in progress with anyone.) Myers writes: "Conrad had a genius for friendship, and his lonely occupation and intellectual isolation in the country made him especially sympathetic, responsive and hospitable."

Among those he met and influenced was T. E. Lawrence, who wrote in a letter to a London publisher about his idol:

> You know, publishing Conrad must be a rare pleasure. He's absolutely the most haunting thing in prose that ever was: I wish I knew how every paragraph he writes (do you notice how they are all paragraphs: he seldom writes a single sentence?) goes on sounding in waves, like the note of a tenor bell, after it stops. It's not built in the rhythm of ordinary prose, but on something existing only in his head, and as he can never say what it is he wants to say, all his things end in a kind of hunger, a suggestion of something he can't say or do or think. So his books always look bigger than they are. He's as much a giant of the subjective as Kipling is of the objective. Do they hate one another?

The friendship between Conrad and Lawrence, or, more importantly, Lawrence's admiration and fascination with Conrad, brings up one of the more fabulist conspiracy theories in literature, which is that Lawrence—in writing the Dera'a rape scene in *Seven Pillars*—made up the encounter and borrowed heavily from *Lord Jim* and other works by Conrad to explain the stigmata on his body and perhaps in his soul.

The indication that Lawrence struggled with the Dera'a material comes from biographer John Mack, who writes: "From 1919 to 1925, Lawrence wrote and rewrote the passage dealing with the episode in *Seven Pillars of Wisdom*—nine times he told Mrs. [George Bernard] Shaw." Lawrence said to her: "That is the 'bad' book, with the Deraa Chapter. Working on it always made me sick. The two impulses fight so upon it. Self-respect would close it: self-expression seeks to open it."

So ashamed was Lawrence about including the section in the book that it may explain his reluctance to publish the unabridged version of *Seven Pillars* in his lifetime. Mack writes that "the Dera'a episode also contributed to Lawrence's need for repeated acts of penance, which included severe whippings by a tough Scotsman named John Bruce."

If, indeed, Lawrence borrowed from *Lord Jim* to get over the hurdle of finishing the difficult chapter, he mined a story that was remote from the cruelties of a Turkish base in Syria. *Lord Jim* is the story of a seaman on a ship full of pilgrims. Believing that the ship is sinking, Jim and the rest of the crew abandon ship and the refugees to their fate. But the *Patna*, Jim's ship, does not go down, and Jim, who later faces a judicial trial (where the story is retold), has to live with the shame of desertion. Conrad writes: "When your ship fails you, your whole world seems to fail you; the world that made you, restrained you, has taken care of you. It is as if the souls of men floating on an abyss and in touch with immensity had been set free for any excess of heroism, absurdity, or abomination." The difference, however, between Lawrence in Dera'a and Jim aboard the *Patna* is that Lawrence did not betray his command in surrendering in Dera'a.

In the second half of the book, Jim confronts the question that torments Lawrence after Dera'a: "not how to get cured, but how to live." Jim believes, as does Lawrence, that his shame will color the rest of his life. Conrad writes: "Strange, this fatality would cast the complexion of a flight upon all his acts, of impulsive unreflecting desertion—of a jump into the unknown." This passage echoes the ending of *The Secret Sharer*, when the narrator's imagined, second self lowers himself into the water off the end of the boat:

> Walking to the taffrail, I was in time to make out, on the very edge of a darkness thrown by a towering black mass like the very gateway of Erebus—yes, I was in time to catch an evanescent glimpse of my white hat left behind to mark the spot where the secret sharer of my cabin and of my thoughts, as though he were my second self, had lowered himself into the water to take

his punishment: a free man, a proud swimmer striking out for a new destiny.

The only link I can imagine between Lawrence's account of Dera'a and various passages in Conrad is the possibility that Lawrence believed that Conrad was expressing the tortured duality that he felt about his sexuality. ("The Secret Sharer" begins: "But what I felt most was my being a stranger to the ship; and if all the truth must be told, I was somewhat of a stranger to myself.") Some recent critics have mined Conrad for homoerotic imagery, and some believe they may have found it in the description of Marlow taking Jim back to his hotel room. Conrad writes: "He followed me as manageable as a little child, with an obedient air, with no sort of manifestation, rather as though he had been waiting for me there to come along and carry him off."

Whatever happened between Marlow and Jim is far removed from the violence visited upon Lawrence in Dera'a. Here is the description of his violation, that which, presumably, he rewrote nine times:

> I remembered the corporal kicking with his nailed boot to get me up; and this was true, for next day my right side was dark and lacerated, and a damaged rib made each breath stab me sharply. I remembered smiling idly at him, for a delicious warmth, probably sexual, was swelling through me: and then that he flung up his arm and hacked with the full length of his whip into my groin. This doubled me half-over, screaming, or rather trying impotently to scream, only shuddering through my open mouth. One giggled with amusement. A voice cried 'Shame, you've killed him'. Another slash followed. A roaring, and my eyes went black: while within me the core of life seemed to heave slowly up through the rending nerves, expelled from its body by this last indescribable pang.

Lawrence only manages to survive his ordeal by separating his mind from his body, to view what was happening to him as if from a second self. But Lawrence might also have seen a parallel between his life and that of Jim's, who at the end finds himself as the protector of a native Malay tribe threatened by intruders. Jim gives his life for them. Certainly Lawrence would have related to that heroism.

What I do find overlaps in the works of Lawrence and Conrad are in Lawrence's descriptions in *Seven Pillars* of the desert, which echo Conrad's descriptions of the sea. If you substitute the word *sea* for *desert*, it could well be written by Conrad:

> To be of the desert was, as they knew, a doom to wage unending battle with an enemy who was not of the world, nor life, nor anything, but hope itself; and failure seemed God's freedom to mankind. We might only exercise this our freedom by not doing what it lay within our power to do, for then life would belong to us, and we should have mastered it by holding it cheap. Death would seem best of all our works, the last free loyalty within our grasp, our final leisure: and of these two poles, death and life, or, less finally, leisure and subsistence, we should shun subsistence (which was the stuff of life) in all save its faintest degree, and cling close to leisure.

FRIENDS OF A KIND

Although **Erskine Childers** was English, he died for the cause of Irish independence in 1922, when his erstwhile compatriots sentenced him to death for the illegal possession of a gun. Being found in possession of a handgun was hardly a capital crime, even in the tense atmosphere between England and Ireland in the struggle over Irish independence, but by that point the English aristocracy—which once made room for Childers in various government jobs in London—had had enough of the maverick supporter of Irish independence, and he was stood before a firing squad. In particular, what galled his old comrades—including Churchill and John Buchan, both of whom he knew well—was that during the Irish risings during World War I, Childers had run guns on his sailboat *Asgard* from the continent to Dublin. The literary irony of his gun running is that earlier in the 20th century, Childers wrote a prophetic novel, *The Riddle of the Sands,* that predicted an Anglo-German naval conflict over the North Sea and some of its coastal, Frisian islands. Initially, Churchill had dismissed this prophecy as the speculations of a novelist, but as it turned out, Childers was right about Germany, and right about Ireland, even though he had to pay for his clear judgment with his life.

Section VII

THE RIDDLES OF ERSKINE CHILDERS

Dublin

AFTER ONE OF my visits to London, I headed to Ireland, where Erskine Childers was executed in 1922, fighting for the cause of Irish independence even though he was English. In *The Damnable Question: One Hundred and Twenty Years of Anglo-Irish Conflict*, George Dangerfield summarizes his life well:

> But Childers combined a sternly logical mind with a vaulting imagination: his *The Riddle of the Sands* is one of the classical mystery stories of pre-War England, indeed of any England. Then again, he had spent many happy hours in his mother's Wicklow Hallow [in Ireland]. Around 1908 he began to conceive a sympathetic feeling for Home Rule and in 1911 wrote a most able book in its defense. On the whole, in the controversy over the Provisional Committee, he supported John Redmond. In World War I he fought loyally in the Royal Naval Reserve. Almost anything might have come out of all this: what did happen was that Childers boxed the political compass and, in 1922, a captain in the service of the Irish Republic, died with quiet composure before the rifles of a Free State firing squad. ("Come closer, boys," he said to his unnerved executioners. "It will make it easier for you.")

It was thought at the time that Winston Churchill, who knew Childers and had once admired his writing, could have stopped the execution, but did not.

FRIENDS OF A KIND

The "Irish question" (as it was called in British politics in the early twentieth century) touched the lives of many in this story. T. E. Lawrence's father was an Anglo-Irish aristocrat, a fact that his son struggled to understand. Irish politics mattered not only to the gun-running Childers, but also to John Buchan, such that he refused occasionally to side with the Liberal Party because of its support for Home Rule (Irish self-governance). Winston Churchill was another who could not see straight when looking at Ireland. He believed the future of the Empire hinged on Ireland's retention in the imperial galaxy. Finally, as I read about and traveled to the Somme battlefields of World War I in France, I discovered that much modern anger in Ireland can be traced to the events there in summer 1916. I thought that by traveling from Dublin and Belfast I might better understand not just the historical question that dogged so many in this story.

To go from London to Dublin, I decided to take the overnight train-ferry. I liked the idea of departing Euston Station (as opposed to, say, Gatwick or Luton airport) and arriving early the next morning in Dublin. I also thought that from the ferry deck at 5:30 a.m. I might see Howth, where Childers delivered the guns he was running in summer 1914 to Irish rebels.

What I did not count on in booking the ferry was that I would have to sit for several hours in a plastic chair in the middle of the night at the Holyhead terminal, waiting for the night boat to load all its trucks and cars. Up to that point, I had enjoyed the evening train ride through the English Midlands and Wales (near to where Lawrence was born and where Graves spent his summers), and I was looking forward to a berth on the ferry.

Only around 1:30 a.m. were the foot passengers given access to the boat, by which time it made no sense to hire a stateroom for three hours. Instead, I rushed around with some other passengers who were scouting places to sleep and picked a section of lounge flooring that was covered with thick carpet. Using my briefcase as my pillow, I stretched out against a warm wall and went to sleep immediately, waking in time to see Howth from the fantail.

Early the next morning, I had the top, open deck to myself, when I climbed some stairs and watched the sunrise against Howth's steep hillsides. Childers moored his yacht *Asgard*, which was loaded with German rifles, on the far side of the peninsula that stretches east from

Dublin Harbour. For his efforts, more symbolic than militarily strategic, Childers' yacht is now on display in the National Museum, and one of my plans for that day in Dublin was to visit the *Asgard* exhibition.

FRIENDS OF A KIND

England at Sea: *Childers issues a warning*

MY INTEREST IN Erskine Childers dated to summer 2000 when I spent part of a vacation reading *The Riddle of the Sands*. The novel recounts the cruise of an English sailboat—similar to *Asgard* but this one is called *Dulcibella*—to the Frisian Islands that form a necklace off the Dutch and German North Sea coasts. The waters around the islands are subject to fickle tides, and sailors lacking the right charts or navigational aids can find themselves aground on a sandy shelf, waiting for high tide. The tension in the novel comes from the discovery by the English yachtsmen that the German navy is using the mud-flats and hidden harbors among the Frisian Islands to assemble a strike force that could attack England with the surprise that struck Port Arthur or Pearl Harbor.

Until the novel was published in 1903, no one—not even the belligerent Winston Churchill—considered the possibility that Germany could represent a naval threat to the United Kingdom. The narrator of the story, a junior officer in the British foreign office, postulates what is then unthinkable when he says:

> 'Well, think of Germany as a new sea-power.... The next thing is, what is her coast-line? It's a very queer one, as you know, split clean in two by Denmark, most of it lying east of that and looking on the Baltic, which is practically an inland sea, with its entrance blocked by Danish islands. It was to evade that block that William built the ship canal from Kiel to the Elbe, but that could be easily smashed in war-time. Far the most important bit of coast-line is that which lies west of Denmark and looks onto the North Sea. It's there that Germany gets her head out into the open, so to speak. It's there that she fronts us and France, the two great sea-powers of Western Europe, and it's there that her greatest ports are and her richest commerce.

Eleven years later England would be at war with Germany, and the North

Sea would see the largest naval encounter in history, with the Battle of Jutland (1916).

In addition to projecting the Kaiser's Germany as a geopolitical threat to England, Childers also sought, with his novel, to change the direction of British naval policies. Like T. E. Lawrence in the 1920s, he wanted to bring a form of guerrilla warfare to the seas, utilizing smaller, faster torpedo boats—think of the PT boats in World War II—against the larger capital ships that cost a fortune to build and to protect. Childers sounds like Lawrence when he writes: "What you want is boats—mosquitoes with stings—swarms of them—patrol-boats, scout-boats, torpedo-boats; intelligent irregulars manned by local men, with a pretty free hand to play their own game. And what a splendid game to play!"

There were other parallels between the lives of Childers and Lawrence. Childers' biographer Leonard Piper writes in *Dangerous Waters: The Life and Death of Erskine Childers*: "It is interesting to compare Erskine with that other, even odder, romantic T. E. Lawrence. There are curious similarities between the two men: the same fondness for bleak, lonely, inhospitable places; the same asceticism; the same search for danger and love of speed. The same adoption of a nationalist cause that was not their own. And both men seem to have been haunted by an inner demon that denied them rest."

Childers and Lawrence: *The making of Irish rebels*

LIKE MANY OTHERS in this book, including Conrad and Sassoon, Childers grew up knowing early sorrow. His father died of consumption when he was six, and a year later his mother, Anna, contracted the same disease and left the family to live in a sanatorium for the next seven years. Never again would she see her children.

Piper writes: "Having no outlet for the depth of unhappiness that he felt, Erskine reacted the way children do in such circumstances—he turned in on himself." He was sent to school in Hertford and did well, showing an aptitude for languages (again, not unlike Lawrence) and literature. Piper explains: "By now Erskine's character was set. Much of it he had clearly inherited from his father, the good and the bad. His particular type of intelligence for instance: his easy acquisition of languages, his great attention to detail, and his amazing powers of concentration. Everyone who came to know him throughout his life was struck by the same thing, his ability to concentrate on what he was doing to such an extent that he became totally oblivious to everyone and everything around him."

For university he went up to Trinity College, Cambridge, where among the many friends he would make was Eddie Marsh, the future private secretary to Winston Churchill and the close friend in the war years to Siegfried Sassoon and later many others in this book. Through March, Childers would meet both Sassoon and Churchill.

From Cambridge, Childers scored well on the placement examination and took a job in the civil service, but mostly what he did during these years of government service was teach himself to sail long distances in the waters around Britain. Childers was a natural with a tiller in his hand. He spent weekends and holidays sailing, and one trip to the Frisian Islands with his brother Henry gave him the idea for a novel not just about small-boat handling—although there is much about that—but "the German threat and British ill-preparedness to deal with it." Sounding like an early Winston Churchill (they were contemporaries), Childers said: "We have no North Sea naval base, no North Sea fleet, and no North Sea policy."

As soon as the Boer War was declared, Childers rushed to enlist, not wanting to miss any of the action. It was the latest installment in the

Victorian wars (the Queen said: 'We are not interested in the possibilities of defeat...") and promised to be over once the Boers saw a British regiment march off the boats in Cape Town. Instead the war lasted three years, and while it ended with a nominal British victory, the costs, in terms of men lost and dawning disillusionment with the empire, were significant.

Childers was among those who came back from South Africa with a growing skepticism about the benevolence of imperial Britain. He had seen men in his unit killed, Boers rounded up in concentration camps, and generals ill-equipped to lead modern armies. ("I am getting used to the state of blank ignorance in which we live.") It also opened his eyes to Britain's class system. He wrote of his service in the lines that "more might be done in the army to lower the rigid caste-barrier which separates the ranks."

In the years after the Boer War, Childers returned to his parliamentary job, married Mary Alden Osgood (an American), and took some of his summer leave at the family property in Ireland (part of his family was Irish). Returning from Glendalough in 1907, he wrote to a friend: "I have come back finally and immutably a convert to Home Rule as is my cousin, though we both grew up steeped in the most irreconcilable sort of Unionism." Never again would his life be the same.

As with sailing, or anything else Childers set his determined mind to, Irish Home Rule became an obsession. Piper writes: "If ever a man was headstrong, that man was Erskine Childers. So far as we know, only once during their marriage did Molly seriously attempt to divert him from his chosen course; and on that occasion she failed completely."

Perhaps for that reason, she joined on the sailboat and in his growing radical politics. In 1912, the Liberal Party selected him to stand for Parliament, as he was pegged a war veteran, an accomplished and successful author, and someone who was pro-Navy. Instead he ran on the single platform of Irish Home Rule. Piper writes: "The result of this fundamental misunderstanding was to be a disappointment for everyone."

Childers spent the war years, 1914-1918, with a divided soul. On one hand he was a loyal British subject, eager to fight the war against the Germans (that, he alone, had predicted years before would be a threat). On the other, his obsession for Irish Home Rule colored his thinking. In July 1914, he and Mary sailed *Asgard* to the German coast to pick up the German rifles and then back to Howth, where it must have been clear to

Childers that, someday, they would be used against British soldiers.

In the war, as a first lieutenant in Winston Churchill's Admiralty, Childers found himself, ironically, having to deflect many of Churchill's harebrained schemes to raid the European coast, precisely the kind of warfare that he had suggested in *The Riddle of the Sands* would be the best way to fight the Germans. He proved invaluable in North Sea reconnaissance, especially along the German coast, and in 1915 he was transferred to Gallipoli, where Churchill had planned to rush the Straits and capture Constantinople.

In 1917, Childers was awarded the Distinguished Service Medal for his heroism as a spotter in planes scouting the Mediterranean. He had an excellent sense of navigation, which he brought to the air corps when transferred to the new service from the navy. And he was good at gathering intelligence. He remained in the thick of the action until the last days of the war, briefing a bomber group that was to attack Berlin on November 10, 1918.

When the war ended the next day, Childers could be proud of his rank (major), his decorations, and his valor in numerous theaters—any of which should have set him up for a postwar career at the highest levels of the British government. Instead, as his wife Mary feared, he longed for more adventures, and he fulfilled that hunger by aiding the fight for Irish independence. Piper writes:

> The Erskine Childers who soon committed himself once more to the cause of Ireland was a new Erskine, an Erskine who had lost the most attractive elements of his character. His sense of humour, his good nature, his courtesy, his sense of proportion, all were effectively gone or distorted beyond recovery. At the same time, those other elements of the Childers character, the tendency towards obsession, the intolerance of other people's point of view, the sheer pigheadedness that prevented him from changing a course once set, all were now dominant. Above all, he developed an addiction to danger that amounted almost to a death-wish. Together they led him inevitably to destruction.

Childers faced a problem in supporting Irish independence similar to the one that MI5 defector Kim Philby had with the Russians: few in Ireland could quite believe that a decorated English officer, with a distinguished record in the Boer War and World War I, was truly committed to an independent Ireland. (There were some who believed until the end that he was a British spy.) That, in turn, prompted Childers to take ever more extreme positions—putting him on the radar of English intelligence. He rejected the agreements of a 1921 conference that allowed Britain control of Ireland's ports for another five years in exchange for limited self-government. As George Dangerfield writes:

> Erskine Childers, as became a convert, was far more uncompromising. He condemned the cession of the ports—which the Dail Cabinet's 'Amendments' of 4 December had at least accepted for five years—as 'the most humiliating condition that can be inflicted on any nation claiming to be free.' The Treaty was basically vicious—'it places Ireland definitely and irrevocably under British authority and the British Crown.'

Nor did he stop there: He encouraged the Irish leadership into open armed conflict with the British government.

Shortly before he was executed, American journalist Elizabeth Lazenby, who was covering the Anglo-Irish conflict, saw Childers in person, and she was appalled at his appearance. She wrote:

> The photographs I have seen of Erskine Childers have little prepared me for the shock which runs over me as I turn towards him. Thin almost to emaciation, he looks ill, and unhappy to the point of death. I can only liken his face to a mask, to which the eyes alone give life. Restless they show him, and haunted, as if he is driven by an inner soul-consuming fire. However courteous, he is aloof, and seems hardly aware of what is taking place about him. One emotion only lightens the intensity of his eyes—his very real devotion to his wife.

The charges that led to his execution were exaggerated, to say the least. Although he was active in the civil war against Britain, what got him arrested (by the Irish Free State) was his possession of a small revolver that he said had been a gift from the revolutionary leader Michael Collins.

British and some Irish authorities were looking for any excuse to deal with Childers, and they seized upon the weapon possession to have him court-martialed, although at that time he was a civilian and should have been subject to civil courts. By then, neither the English nor the Irish Free State wanted him around. Hearing of his arrest, Churchill weighed in with a stinging memo, saying: "No man has done more harm or shown more genuine malice, or endeavored to bring a greater curse upon the common people of Ireland, than this strange being, actuated by a deadly and malignant hatred for the land of his birth." Piper concludes: "To the British he was a traitor; to the Irish a spy. A curious end for an honest man."

Between the Easter Rising in 1916 and Irish independence in 1922, Britain hoped that it could contain the separatists by the liberal use of prison and the firing squad. By no means was Childers the only rebel who was arrested or shot. Many of those who rose on the steps of the Dublin general post office in 1916 were immediately executed, which proved only a temporary setback to the movement. Dangerfield quotes one observer to the British government crackdown, similar to that which claimed the life of Childers. He writes:

> It is true…that the rebellion has miserably failed. But the military executions which have been its consequence have raised the victims to the status of martyrs…the sorrows of Ireland now fill the front page. Had the executions ceased in the first few days, the excitement would no doubt have died down.

Another epitaph was more direct. It was said: "Some tragic fatality seems to dog the footsteps of the Government in all their dealings with Ireland…." In the case of Sassoon, Eddie March had intervened with Churchill to save his friend; but in the case of Childers, his Cambridge classmate, there was nothing that could be done.

Like Erskine Childers, T. E. Lawrence was another Englishman conflicted about this Irish roots. It was when I was visiting the Lawrence cottage in Dorset and met his niece that I first heard about Lawrence's tortured connections to Ireland, which came through his father, Thomas Chapman, an Anglo-Irish baronet who had lands outside Dublin (before he ran off with his housekeeper, who became T. E. Lawrence's mother). It made me want to see the house in which Lawrence's father had lived.

In Dublin, as I was pondering the schedules of Irish Rail (the nearest stop to the house is Mullingar) and wondering how the roads would be on a bicycle, I learned through an email that a close friend from high school, Kevin Glynn (who lives in Los Angeles), was not just traveling in Europe, but that he had rented a car and was footloose in Ireland, where both his parents were born.

Would he be interested, I wrote back, to drive me on my appointed rounds to the Lawrence homestead? He agreed, and I put aside my train and bus schedules for a road map of Ireland. In his rental car, Kevin and I had no trouble finding Chapman's house, called South Hill. It was about an hour west of the Dublin Airport, where we met up. But instead of rolling up the pebble drive of an Anglo-Irish estate, we pulled into the parking lot of what is now St. Mary's Hospital.

The old mansion is still visible—I could recognize the original entrance—but the rest of the stone building is covered with industrial-strength stucco, and the paved parking places out front are delineated with white lines. If there is a plaque indicating that this was once the family home of Sir Thomas Chapman, the seventh and last baronet, I missed it. But the story of Lawrence's Irish connection is this:

Lawrence's father's full title was Sir Thomas Robert Tighe Chapman, 7th Baronet, and his pedigree came with enough (underpaid) tenants to work these (somewhat modest) baronial lands, in Delvin, County Westmeath, which is west of Dublin in rolling farmland. As Thomas Chapman, Lawrence's father had four daughters with his wife, Edith Hamilton, who by all accounts turned into a religious zealot and morose companion the longer they were together.

In the late 1870s, after their fourth daughter was born and Thomas was drinking heavily—to the nagging complaints of his wife, who was tired of such sinning—he had an affair with his children's governess, Sarah Lawrence, who became pregnant. Thomas packed Sarah off to rooms in Dublin, where she could have the baby and where he could visit her on the side. When the stern Edith got wind of the affair, Thomas refused to repent and ran off with Sarah, who in all was to bear him five sons.

Thomas Edward was born in Wales, not far from where my ferry had sailed from Holyhead.

By all accounts the family of Thomas and Sarah was a happy one, but, as Thomas had never divorced Edith, the so-called "Lawrences" were never married—a fact that their son picked up during his adolescence or while at Oxford (when he was living in his bungalow in the backyard). As much as Lawrence loved and admired his father, he was also ashamed of his family's illegitimacy. That might account for his search for atonement, his almost monkish devotion to self-inflicted pain and isolation.

Some Lawrence biographies—John E. Mack's *A Prince of Our Disorder: The Life of T. E. Lawrence* is one of them—highlight this aspect of his tortured psychology. Personally I find the point exaggerated, given Lawrence's otherwise sunny childhood, much of it spent hunting archaeological fragments around Oxford. Whatever the motivations of his asceticism that characterized parts of his life, his capacity for isolation, combined with intellectual curiosity, stood him in good stead when he walked across Syria to visit Crusader castles or when he rode his bicycle some two thousand kilometers around France. Without those qualities of determination, he might not have been able to withstand the rigors of the irregular war in the desert. And it should be noted that Lawrence had vast capacities for friendship at all levels of society. He earned the affections not just of mess mates and Bedouin villagers, but of Winston Churchill, Thomas Hardy, Siegfried Sassoon, Robert Graves, and Gertrude Bell, among many others.

That evening in Ireland, poking around the internet, I came across a mention of Lawrence and his Irish connections, in the *Irish Times*:

> Lawrence later became somewhat fascinated with Ireland. His surviving letters contain references expressing a desire to visit his father's homeland. In one letter Lawrence even remarked that he would like to buy a few acres in Westmeath. His letters are also full of references to the writings of Sean O'Casey, James Joyce and George Bernard Shaw. Indeed, he would later seek out Shaw and his wife, Charlotte, who would become close confidants. In 1925, Lawrence changed his name for the second time and was known thereafter as TE Shaw.

T. E. Lawrence never made it to Ireland, or seemingly came to terms with the shadows cast by his baronial or illegitimate past. And it may only be coincidence, but during the Troubles and after, the disenfranchised peoples of the Middle East, notably the Palestinians, were among the closest allies of Irish republicanism, a sentiment that Lawrence would have grasped immediately. As we drove west, Kevin mentioned once seeing the Hezbollah flag flying in Derry, and he reminded me of the IRA's connections, long ago, to Gaddafi's Libya.

When **Winston Churchill** was serving as an officer in the British Army, he often thought of himself as a foreign correspondent, and when he was assigned as a journalist to one of Britain's wars, he preferred to think of himself as a Sandhurst graduate and frontline officer. He endlessly juggled the two professions, except during World War I, when he divided his time between the war cabinet in London and then, after Gallipoli proved a failure, as a battalion officer in the Belgian sector of the trenches. Churchill's time on the front lines, however, allowed him to see the war from the sharp end, and that, in turn, established bonds between this senior British parliamentarian and many of the junior officers who figure in this book as writers and poets. When the serving officer Siegfried Sassoon denounced the war, Churchill had done his time on the front line, and could put himself in Sassoon's muddy shoes. Likewise, throughout the war Churchill sought the company of officers—Siegfried Sassoon and Raymond Asquith among them—who "spoke the language of the front lines." Churchill's own memoirs of the war may lack the stylistic flair of those of Sassoon, Graves, and Lawrence, but it speaks well that the future British minister—through the good offices of his personal secretary Sir Edward Marsh—gave himself freely to the company of so many war poets and writers, especially as many of them emerged from the trenches horrified by the experience Churchill arguably had a hand in creating.

Section VIII

WINSTON CHURCHILL IN THE TRENCHES

Plugstreet

AFTER DUBLIN, WHAT became clear in my mind is that this story needed to continue in France, along what remained of the Western Front of World War I. Many of the writers and poets that had come to interest me—notably Sassoon, Graves, Churchill, Asquith, and Wilfred Owen—had fought there, and those experiences had shaped their literature. For everyone in this book, World War I was pivotal in their lives.

The problem I had in getting there was that in between my visit to Dublin and my next trip to France, the Great Pandemic had closed down Europe, including the French-Swiss border, which is less than a mile from my house. In normal times, the French frontier is nothing more than a curiosity on the road, where there is a small (unmanned) guard post and a gate that closes at night. Now the same crossing was blocked with concrete barriers and strands of barbed wire, as though Vichy France was once again on the far side of the border. All I could do was daydream about traveling, although occasionally—during a lull in the virus—France would reopen and that would allow me (fully vaccinated) to board a French train in Saint-Julien-en-Genevois and carry on with my exploring. I often wasn't gone more than a week, and I tended to ignore crowds, which was easy as by this point I was going everywhere on the bike. I stayed at Airbnbs that had "self check-in," carried much of my own food, had picnic lunches on the road, and slowly covered the ground that the likes of Sassoon, Graves, and Owen had covered on foot.

I started my bike rides along the trenches at what the British and Commonwealth troops called "Plugstreet," aka the Belgian town of Ploegsteert, which lies near the French border in southern Belgium. Winston Churchill served his time in the trenches there, for about five months in 1916. I had wondered if his time at the front lines (and in political disgrace) was the reason that he found friendship with the likes of T. E. Lawrence and Siegfried Sassoon. It might also explain his anger at Erskine Childers and Irish republicanism, for what he believed was treason against the crown. At the very least, having Plugstreet as my starting point would allow me to focus my map and book reading on yet another corner of a foreign field that is "forever England." During the war years Ploegsteert Wood had trench lines with such names as Hyde Park Corner, Charing Cross, the Strand, Oxford Circus, Regent Street, Piccadilly Circus, and Hampshire Lane.

To reach Ploegsteert, I took a succession of trains from Saint-Julien-en-Genevois to Arras and then Lille before alighting (as the English like to say) in Armentières, a French town on the Belgian border. Unfortunately, as I was traveling in January, much of the train journey took place in fog and darkness. My train from Arras dropped me in the large modern station called Lille Europe, which was built to handle Eurostar traffic. From there, I rode my bike over to Lille Flanders, the older city station, where I warmed myself with coffee in a waiting room and caught a two-car local train heading in the direction of Calais but which dropped me in Armentières, forlorn in the misty rains.

Even though I was traveling with several Michelin and battlefield maps (the latter I had copied from books in my library), I got lost riding from the station to the canal that runs near the Belgian border. I had thought that I could follow, in a northerly direction, the arrow on the bicycle compass that I had bought, via eBay, in China. But I guess paying $1.95 wasn't sufficient to acquire a working compass, and that meant having to stop in the back streets of Armentières to check the more accurate compass on my iPhone. It got me across the canal and into the Belgian border town of Bizet (where the national boundary runs along a main street), and from there I errantly followed signs to Motor Car Corner Cemetery, thinking that it was in Ploegsteert. Instead, I discovered that it lies in a bleak Belgian hamlet near Comines-Warneton. Apparently Motor Car Corner had done brisk sniper business during the fighting, and many of those buried in the small British cemetery had been caught in the open, trying to move along the trench line between Armentières and Ypres.

On a road outside of Comines-Warneton, I flagged down a postman, and he straightened me out, in terms of finding Ploegsteert. He said, in heavily accented French, "Right...left...right," and indicated that I was about three miles from the war memorial near the Wood, once part of the British front lines. He added that there were small cemeteries scattered all over the area but that the main memorial was outside the town of Ploegsteert, on the road to Messines.

Modern Ploegsteert is a line of shops, houses, and businesses on either side of a main street, but in the misty rain I was not able to find the convent that Churchill made his headquarters. In his excellent book, *Churchill in the Trenches*, Peter Apps writes: "The battalion HQ—including Churchill—settled into some convent buildings in the center of the village. Several nuns were still in residence and were soon co-opted—"seduced," in Churchill's words—into providing cooked food for the occupants. The other companies, meanwhile, bedded down in outlying farms." I did find the famous plaque on the wall of the *mairie* (town hall) that shows an older Churchill—with a bowler, walking stick, and cigar, and dressed in a business suit—surveying the ruins of the town and trenches, as if about to give a campaign speech during a by-election.

For Churchill the road to Ploegsteert ran through the military disaster at Gallipoli and in the Dardanelles, where the British and French navies—and later an army of Allied ground troops—suffered horrific losses while trying to seize the Ottoman capital at Constantinople and knock the Turks out of World War I. For that operation—at least the naval portion—Churchill was the inspirational godfather. He conceived of a flying column of British and French ships forcing open the narrow straits of the Dardanelles, steaming into the Bosphorus Sea, and shelling the tottering Ottoman government into submission. It was a bold plan, intended to break the stalemate in the trenches on the Western Front, and, as First Lord of the Admiralty, Churchill was its spokesman in the war cabinet of Prime Minister Herbert Asquith. Not long after the war started in August 1914, the prime minister had said of his dashing, younger colleague: "I can't help but be fond of him," Asquith wrote in October 1914. "He is so resourceful and undismayed, two of the qualities I like best."

Gallipoli turned into the costliest battle of the war—in a war made up of disasters—and by November 13, 1915, as the Allies were withdrawing from the peninsula, Churchill had resigned from the cabinet in disgrace. Apps writes:

> Churchill always maintained he did nothing wrong, that the strategy was a reasonable risk undermined by colleagues who gave it inadequate resourcing. But he felt destroyed. "I am finished," he told his friends.

Not even his wife's pleading letter to the prime minister, whom she knew well, could save him. (She wrote: "Winston may in your eyes and those with whom he has to work have faults, but he has the supreme quality which I venture to say very few of your present or future Cabinet possess—the power, the imagination, the deadliness to fight Germany…") But by then her husband was equipping himself for the front lines, which meant getting tailored for several new uniforms and putting together a wine cellar that could make the Channel crossing.

Sir John French, the British commander on the continent, had thought of making Churchill a general and giving him command of a brigade (about four thousand men), but such were the concerns in the army about showing political favoritism that Churchill was taken on as a major and only given temporary command of a battalion (about eight hundred men) in the lines at Plugstreet. Initially Churchill was assigned to the Queen's Own Oxfordshire Hussars (literally a family regiment, made of footmen and others from around Blenheim, the Churchill family manor house) and then to the Grenadier Guards, in which his friend Raymond Asquith was serving. But Churchill only went into combat with the Royal Scots Fusiliers, who were fed into the line at Ploegsteert, which was then one of the quieter sectors of the front line. It was still a trench line facing the Germans, and Churchill's battalion was assigned a sector to defend, which meant enduring numerous shellings and patrols into no-man's-land. He never did "go over the top" in a frontal assault.

Although Churchill had graduated from the Royal Military Academy at Sandhurst, and had seen combat in Cuba, the Northwest Frontier Territory, South Africa, and at Omdurman in Sudan, most of the fighting he had endured occurred while he was covering colonial wars for a newspaper. Yes, he had his military commission, but he was not an active military officer when he went forward in the Boer War or at Omdurman. By the time he arrived at Ploegsteert with his men, he was a forty-year-old major who, for the last seventeen years, had served in Parliament and written a number of bestselling books about military adventures (including some of his own). He was now in the trenches not so much to bring the fight "to the Hun" but to rewrite the narrative arc of his political career so as to blot out the stain of Gallipoli. At Ploegsteert Churchill was in search of political redemption, and he thought the best way to find it was to patrol no-man's-land with satchel bombs, much the way Siegfried Sassoon had tried to assuage his own anger after his friend David Thomas was killed.[5]

Needless to say, Churchill was not a typical battalion commander of the Great War. Often, while he was serving in the trenches or at rest behind the front lines, he would entertain visiting cabinet officers, newspapermen, publishers, and parliamentarians who were out on fact-finding missions. At other times, Churchill would slip away from the action to return to London, where he remained a member of Parliament. During his time on his lines, Churchill kept up his vast correspondence with friends and colleagues. In one letter home to his wife, he asked her to send him a typewriter, so that his correspondence would be more presentable.

For all that Churchill had the look of a stuntman at the front—there to show British voters that even cabinet officers were taking their turn in the trenches—he turned out to be an excellent battalion commander and someone his men grew to admire and respect. To be sure, he got off to a rough start with the Royal Scots Fusiliers, when he told his 6th Battalion that he would "break" anyone who challenged him. And more than a few of his fellow officers must have wondered about a commanding officer who came to the lines with a portable bathtub and hampers from Fortnum & Mason. But Churchill was generous in sharing his perquisites with his men, and he visited all the men of the battalion three times daily, no matter how much artillery was in the air. According to Apps, his routine was this:

> Their initial spell in the front line had been only forty-eight hours. Thereafter, the Fusiliers would spend six days in and six out. It was a broadly typical pattern—the average British soldier would spend perhaps 100 days a year in the trenches, the rest in training or reserve. The reserve positions at "Plugstreet," however, were so close

---

5 On his way to the front lines Churchill was briefly attached to the headquarters of the 2nd Battalion Grenadier Guards so that he could "study the trenches." Near Laventie (I believe) he was in proximity to his friend Raymond Asquith, a line officer with the Guards, who wrote home to his wife on December 12, 1915: "Absolutely no news except that Winston rode over to see me. He is still with our 2nd Battn. and thoroughly enjoying himself and the war, very gloomy about Salonica, but at the same time very happy because he has always said that the troops we sent there ought to have gone to the Dardanelles instead."

to the front that they too would be under near perpetual shellfire.

Not only was Churchill personally brave in commanding his men and in sharing their discomforts, but he also, better than many front line officers, grew to understand the qualities of leadership that were needed in the British Army if it was to win the war. In particular, he believed that officers needed to show their men that the misery of the war would not get the best of them, and that they could carry on, despite the rats, high water, and dead bodies that filled the trenches and no-man's-land. Churchill liked to say to his subordinates: "Laugh a little, and teach your men to laugh—great good humour under fire. War is a game that is played with a smile. If you can't smile, grin. If you can't grin, stay out of the way till you can." In turn, the men came to respect Churchill as someone who could deal with artillery attacks or nighttime patrols. Apps quotes one officer on his commander in this way:

> One night, under a heavy barrage, Gibb recalled Churchill looking over the parapet and asking, "in a dreamy voice: 'Do you like War?' The only thing to do was to pretend not to hear him," wrote Gibb. "At that moment I profoundly hated War. But at that and every moment, I believe Winston Churchill revelled in it. There was no such thing as fear in him."

Even as a major commanding a battalion along one stretch of trench in Flanders, Churchill thought about the war as if he were the commander-in-chief. On nights when he was away from the line, he wrote letters to colleagues in London, suggesting strategies that might shorten the war or improve conditions for the army as a whole. In the cabinet and then on the front lines, he was a proponent of the weapon that turned into the tank—a truck on caterpillar tracks that could breach the opposing wire—and he thought that only conscription could bolster the depleted Regular Army.

From his foxholes or crumbling farm house headquarters, he was endlessly banging the drum for the better use of submarines, air power, and amphibious assaults behind German lines. He hated the stalemate war, and was forever suggesting ways to get around the wires in front of him, much as, in World War II, he set up second fronts in such places such as North Africa and Anzio. He even suggested another landing in Asia Minor, this time at Alexandretta (current day Iskenderum, in Turkey), but by that point no one was listening to him. (Although if you ask me, the idea had merit.)

As an ambitious politician, Churchill spent much of his time in Belgium plotting the best time to return to London and Parliament. He needed to serve long enough on the lines to look like any other officer doing his time at the front, but he did not want to be gone so long that he would be forgotten in Parliament or overlooked for an available job in the cabinet. He hoped that his earlier enthusiasm for Gallipoli had been superseded in the public's memory by more appreciative sentiments about his time in the trenches fighting "the Boche." He wondered if the issue of general conscription might put him in a more favorable London light. Apps writes: "As a frontline battalion commander, Churchill was all too aware that the volunteer army was exhausted. As a politician, he wondered whether the dispute might speed him back to power."

After several months on the line in Ploegsteert, he wrote to his wife Clementine to say that he thought it was the right time for him to come home. She discouraged him, saying he needed to stay longer or risk being seen as yet another an opportunist who was getting his "ticket punched" in the war zone and then heading back to London. Apps quotes her heartfelt letter:

> "Dear Winston I am so torn and lacerated over you," she wrote on April 6. "If I say 'stay where you are' a wicked bullet may find you where you might but for me escape." To be truly great, she told him, his actions must be understandable "by simple people".... I do long to see you terribly. Your last visit was no help to me personally. I must see you soon."

He was home for good in May 1916, and soon appointed as the minister in charge of munitions—a job well suited to his interest in technology that would shorten the fighting. It was after he came back from the trenches that he befriended Siegfried Sassoon, among others. One wonders if he would have been as lenient with Sassoon, after his public letter denouncing the war, if Churchill had not himself done duty on the front lines. Years later he wrote: "Before the war it had seemed incredible that such terrors and slaughters, even if they began, could last more than a few months. After the first two years it was difficult to believe that they would ever end."

WINSTON CHURCHILL

The 1914 Christmas Truce

TO FOLLOW IN Churchill's footsteps around Ploegsteert, my plan was to begin at the museum known as "The Plugstreet 14-18 Experience," a military museum in a modernistic pyramid structure. Since Motor Car Corner, I had been following signs for the exhibit, and there I thought that I could get directions to Churchill's trenches, which I knew were close to the town. But after locking my bike to a railing, I discovered that the 14-18 Experience was closed until the end of January. So too was the café across the street and another "for tourists" down the road. The only thing left for me to do was wander among the headstones in the nearby cemeteries and inspect the imposing war memorial that overlooks the entrance to Ploegsteert Wood. It was at one of these stops that I wrote down the following horrifying passage:

> Nearly 750,000 Commonwealth soldiers, sailors and airmen died on the West Front—200,000 in Belgium and over 500,000 in France. They are commemorated upon headstones marking graves in over 1,000 war cemeteries and 2,000 civil cemeteries, or one of the six memorials in Belgium and twenty in France which carry the names of more than 300,000 who have no known grave.

The inscription reminded me of a passage in Peter Apps' book about Churchill, in which he remarks on Churchill's fatalism, quoting a remark he made about a close call in the trenches: "You walk to the right or the left of a particular tree and it makes the difference whether you rise to command an Army Corps or are sent home crippled or paralysed for life."

With the museum closed and no coffee at hand to warm my cold fingers, I set off on the bike into the Wood, following a small sign indicating the route toward the "Christmas Truce"—that spontaneous truce in December 1914 during which Allied and German soldiers exchanged gifts, shared drinks, and played football. Before finding the truce lines, I rode past a number of cemeteries buried in the gloom of the forest. They had names such as Toronto Avenue Cemetery and Rifle House Cemetery, and most of the enclosed graveyards held only a handful of headstones, as if to mark the loss of a particular company or platoon. In the January cold and mist, the Wood itself had qualities of a miasma, as if I had ridden into a vortex of dead limbs and fallen leaves. In summer Ploegsteert Wood must be a pleasant place in which to walk a dog or go for a picnic, but in winter it's an underworld of decaying fortifications and bivouacs of the dead.

On the far side of the Wood I emerged from the forest and rode up an incline to the Christmas Truce memorial. In a small field next to the Prowse Point Military Cemetery, I came across a decorated Christmas tree set between two rows of trenches, complete with barbed wire and firing steps. I have to assume that the trenches are not original, but they show the proximity of the British and German positions (less than one hundred yards apart). There was a rack of soccer balls, left behind by visitors paying tribute to the spirit of the Christmas Truce. A plaque indicated that UFEA (the Union of European Football Associations) had recently honored the memory of the Christmas match in the lines, perhaps to make the point that football is synonymous with world peace (rather than bribes paid to World Cup selectors).

Only when I was home did I remember that my friend Dr. David Holmes had long ago given me Stanley Weintraub's *Silent Night: The Story of the World War I Christmas Truce*. I read through the book in several sittings. I was surprised to discover that Weintraub's version varied from the story told at the memorial. (He writes: "The Christmas Truce has lingered strikingly in memory even when its details have disappeared into myth.") I had assumed that only one truce took place at Christmas 1914 and that only one football match was played between the lines, but, according to Weintraub, there were numerous spontaneous truces all along the Western Front and at many locations the soldiers improvised a soccer ball and began playing matches that were, for the most part, "friendly."

In reality, the no-man's-land between the trenches was not an ideal setting for football. It was littered with shattered corpses, pools of water, and unexploded ordnance. As a result, the opposing armies, where they agreed upon a Christmas Truce, used the time to bury their dead and to exchange food and cigarettes. (Weintraub writes: "Up and down the line in Flanders, Christmas morning would be marked by religious observances marking birth and death.") A popular trade involved British tobacco for German beer. And there was the singing of Christmas carols and other popular songs. Football was a part of some truces, but it would be misleading to think of the pause in the fighting as the martial equivalent of a spontaneous Champions League. One soldier said the scene resembled: "...what on first sight looked like a crowd on a football field during the interval of a match."

Depending on the sector, the truce ended either after New Year's Day or whenever senior commanders got wind of the fraternization and ordered the shooting to resume. It says something about the distance of the British high command from the front lines that it took so long for them to realize that on Christmas Day the combatants were exchanging gifts and singing Christmas carols. (Weintraub writes of the Germans: "As on the British side, before any higher-ups 'could quite realize the situation and the necessary steps of discipline to insure a continuous state of war,' the war had taken a holiday.") Before parting, many on both sides had promised to look up new friends after the war. Addresses were exchanged. And both sides offered friendly, sometimes humorous advice on ways that the war could be fought going forward. One Bavarian, according to Weintraub, said to the British: "Oh, by the by, on Thursday"—New Year's Eve—"we are relieved by the Prussians. Give 'em hell; we hate them."

A great what-if of the war is whether the spontaneous Christmas truces could have been turned into a more durable peace. Of course it is wishful thinking to imagine a negotiated end to the fighting coming from the impulses of men in the lines. The war began because of treaty violations and hubris of European statesmen, not because the average Briton or German had any real reason to dislike each other. Once the fighting and dying began, the carnage became self-perpetuating. Within a few days of the Christmas lull, both sides believed that they had more to gain by giving war another chance. Weintraub writes: "The erosion of the 1914 truce as weather improved and unbloodied units moved into the line had closed off the last practical opening for negotiating an abbreviated war."

Messines: *Ireland on the Western Front*

FROM THE CHRISTMAS truce memorial I biked toward the main road and weighed whether or not to include Messines in my ride. I remembered the name of the town from my visit to Ypres and associated it with the explosion of several tunnel bombs under German lines that had, for a little while, created a gap along the Western Front (one that the Germans quickly filled). I hesitated because of the damp cold in the air and because the town appeared on my map to be at the top of a steep hill. But when I got out to the main road, I could see the Messines church tower on the hilltop, and concluded that the road was not as steep as indicated on my map. It was a long climb in a low gear on the bike, but in twenty minutes I had scaled the heights of Messines, something that took the Allies four years during the war.

Messines (Mesen in Flemish) is a somber town that runs along the crest of a ridge line. It was here that the German offensive stalled at the beginning of the war in August 1914. Instead of pushing toward the English Channel, the German columns turned south toward Paris. Had they captured Messines, the road would have been open for them to take Antwerp and other channel ports, which would have altered the course of the war (in their favor). During the stalemate of the trenches, the front lines ran through the once prosperous town, although Allied artillery had reduced the soaring Messines church to rubble that the Germans used for pillboxes and screens to hide their snipers. According to a brochure in the local museum, it was in the ruins of the Messines church that, early in the war, Private Adolf Hitler was treated for wounds. And it was under the ridge line that Allied sappers dug their tunnels in 1917 to set off one of the largest (non-nuclear) explosions in world history, which was timed to coordinate with the offensive to the north from Ypres toward to the village of Passchendaele (the Allies never got that far).

I did a loop about the town on my bike and spent time in the excellent local museum, and then rolled back down the hillside to what is called the Island of Ireland Peace Park. On my ride into Messines, I had seen the looming conical tower at the center of the memorial but had no idea what it marked until I pulled off the road and read a roadside tablet explaining the connection of the round tower to Irish nationalism and Irish suffering along the Western Front, notably in front of Messines.

From reading one of the many markers at the memorial, I learned that the Irish president, the queen of England, and the king of Belgium had dedicated the "peace park" on November 11, 1998, six months after England and Ireland concluded their Good Friday Agreement to end the Troubles in Belfast and Northern Ireland. The memorial (clearly paid for with EU funds) is an attempt to paper over the differences between Great Britain and Ireland by putting up a monument on a hillside in a remote corner of Belgium and acknowledging Ireland's suffering on behalf of the Allies in World War I. The three Irish divisions serving between Ypres and the Somme during the war lost 69,947 men, the reason that streets in Belfast subdivisions are named after battlefields in Belgium and northern France.

I hoped to climb the Irish tower and look out over the surrounding landscape, as if some artillery spotter, but I could find no stairs. The tower is built from the stone of an old barracks in Tipperary (yes, "it's a long way to go..."), and houses a list of all the Irish soldiers who died or were lost in the war. I wandered among the many headstones and markers that surround it, some with verses of Irish poetry and others that read like EU budget directives (erected to ensure peace in future generations, as per Article 4 of EU appropriation request number 1015...).

Needless to say, the poems, written by soldiers in the lines here, were more evocative of the war than were the explanations about the memorial's funding. I wrote down the verse of one poem by Tom Kettle, who served with the 9th Royal Dublin Fusiliers. It reads:

> *So here, while the mad guns*
> *curse overhead,*
> *and tired men sigh, with mud*
> *for couch and floor,*
> *know that we fools, now with*
> *the foolish dead,*
> *died not for Flag, nor King,*
> *nor Emperor,*
> *but for a dream born in a herdsman's shed,*
> *and for the sacred scripture of the poor.*

FRIENDS OF A KIND

I was at the peace park on a cold day in January. I am not surprised that I was the only visitor. But something tells me that neither Irish nationalists nor British royalists spend much time in Messines, reciting the peace pledge, which reads in part:

> As Protestants and Catholics, we apologise for the terrible deeds we have done to each other and ask forgiveness. From this sacred shrine of remembrance, where soldiers of all nationalities, creeds and political allegiances were united in death, we appeal to all people in Ireland to help build a peaceful and tolerant society. Let us remember the solidarity and trust that developed between Protestant and Catholic soldiers when they served together in these trenches.

These are noble words, to be sure, and few can argue with the sentiments, but around the tower I found something forced in the presentation, almost as if a project needed to be found for some appropriations that would be lost, if not spent on a war memorial in Flanders.

Section IX

GRAVES AND SASSOON GO TO WAR

Some Desperate Glory

HAD THERE BEEN a café or bistro serving homemade soup, I might have stayed in Messines for an early lunch. Instead I decided to bike back toward Armentières and continue from there my search for the villages near Aubers and Loos where Sassoon and Graves met and where they were posted during the early months of their wars. I rode with my head down and into the wind through Ploegsteert, Bizet, and Armentières, too often on national roads with dangerous roundabouts. When I arrived in Laventie, a nondescript small town with yet another oversized church, I hunted up and down the main street until I finally found a small restaurant that was open for lunch. Everything else in Laventie had the appearance of being closed for the winter.[6]

Lunch was pizza and a carafe of cold water, and my reading was a guidebook by Helen McPhail and Philip Guest entitled *Sassoon & Graves: On the Trail of the Poets of the Great War*. Years before I had bought the book at the Imperial War Museum in London, but this was my first chance to use it on location. Before leaving home, I had highlighted many of the villages in the area where either Graves or Sassoon had fought, and now, over lunch, I was putting together a bike route that would connect the dots of their lives along the Western Front. I am sure that the others in the restaurant thought that I was a daft Englishman—on a bike tour in midwinter, researching war poets—but they kindly indicated distances on my route when I asked, and the owner was pleased when I explained that I was, in fact, American, as though he could later expect other Americans under billowing ponchos to crowd into his restaurant during lunchtime squalls.

---

6 It was near here that Winston Churchill saw his friend Raymond Asquith in December 1915.

Even if the modern rendition of the town held little appeal, at least in the rain, I made a few stops along the main street of Laventie, notably in front of the bulked-up church, and then rode in the direction of Aubers Ridge and Neuve Chapelle, both of which were early British war disasters. Graves first encountered the trenches around Laventie, but it's impossible to locate the 1915 front lines, as no-man's-land between Laventie and Aubers is now cultivated farmland and clusters of suburban housing. Instead, I decided to head toward Aubers Ridge, as one of my books indicated that Adolf Hitler was on the lines there when the war exploded on this front in the spring of 1915. For much of the war Hitler was a runner or messenger for the Bavarian Reserve Infantry Regiment 16 (1st Company of the List Regiment). He first served near Ypres, but then his battalion (which was largely wiped out) was shifted south to Aubers, where on many days his regimental duties posted him several miles to the rear, although he would have endured artillery barrages and other horrors of battle.

Clearly Hitler was an odd soldier, although he did as he was ordered and won several decorations for valour. He was moody, aloof at times, prone to patriotic rants, and intolerant. He was one of the few in the ranks who disapproved of the Christmas Truce, saying: "Such a thing should not happen in wartime." To his fraternizing colleagues, he said, contemptuously, "Have you no German sense of honor?" (These sentiments came from someone born in Austria.) Weintraub writes of his service in the trenches: "He received no mail or parcels, never spoke of family or friends, neither smoked nor drank, and often brooded alone in his dugout." At some point, he adopted a stray dog (a Fox Terrier he named Foxy), who seems to have filled his requirements for affection. During his free time he would teach the dog tricks.

Toward the end of the war, gas temporarily blinded Lance Corporal Hitler, who needed several months in the hospital to recover. He came away from his wartime in (or near) the front lines embittered at civilians who had never served and angry at politicians (and Jews) whom he believed had "stabbed" infantrymen "in the back" for agreeing to the armistice. He thought the peace treaty of Versailles was a sellout, and for the rest of his tumultuous life he remained—to use the words of Paul Fussell—"a pissed-off infantryman" who felt alienated from all those who had not endured what he had at the front. That a corporal eventually rose to command the German Army infuriated many professional soldiers and career officers. But in his rise to power, Hitler spoke for many German servicemen whose time in the trenches was a descent into hell. In *All Quiet on the Western Front*, Eric Remarque writes: "It is very queer that the unhappiness of the world is so often brought on by small men."

In some of the books about the British campaigns in 1915, Aubers "ridge" is dismissed as nothing more than a gentle incline breaking the bleak farmland between Armentières and Givenchy. On my folding bike, however, I found the ridge to be slightly more pronounced, and it took me about five minutes or so to ride in low gears to the crest, where now the small town of Aubers spreads out on what was once the trench line.

Among the British battalions that were cut to ribbons attacking Aubers Ridge was Graves' Royal Welch, which tried to dislodge the Germans from the higher ground. Graves later remarked in his memoir that during World War I some twenty thousand men had passed through his battalion, which never had more than eight hundred men on the roster at any one time. My guidebook to the war locations of Graves and Sassoon has this description of the front lines between Laventie and Aubers Ridge, where I was riding:

> A long low hill-crest some 80 feet high, lying just under
> a mile in front of the British trenches, was Aubers
> Ridge, the objective of the disastrous attack by the
> British on 9 May 1915 in which the 2nd Welch had lost
> so heavily. The trenches were invariably waterlogged, as
> the original land drainage system, already inadequate,
> had been destroyed by shellfire.

Graves only joined that battalion in July 1915, so his baptism of fire would come in the trenches around Givenchy, Cambrin, and Vermelles, towns that later formed the extreme northern edge in the battle of Loos, which was fought in late September 1915 and in three days cost the British some sixty thousand casualties.

Lions Led by Donkeys

TO GUIDE ME from Aubers Ridge to Loos, I followed a map that appears in *Riding the Routes of the Great War*, a guidebook that I had purchased at the tourist office in Armentières. It charted a course on small backroads from Aubers to Festubert along what would have been the front lines in the battles of Aubers and Neuve Chapelle. I liked the idea of following contours of the fighting, but in short order—maybe because of the mist and rain—I was lost in the fog of war and drifting around such villages as Ligny-le-Petit and Lorgies. It was only when I got home and dusted off my copy of Alan Clark's *The Donkeys*, a history of incompetent British command in 1915, that I figured out where I had been and what I had seen.

I purchased *The Donkeys* when it was reissued in 1996, although the book was first published in 1961. I remembered seeing the book on my father's shelves when I was growing up, but in those days I had other interests than incompetent British generals in World War I. After I bought my copy, I read in the London newspapers that the author, Alan Clark (both a historian and a Conservative Member of Parliament), had been a sexual predator, an admirer of national socialism, and (as a government official) an enabler in the arms trade with Saddam Hussein—qualities that had not made it onto the book's back jacket. When I looked up an account of Clark's life, I came across these passages in *The Independent* newspaper, in response to a remark that the minister and diarist was "wonderful":

> Alan Clark was not wonderful. He was sleazy, vindictive, greedy, callous and cruel. He was also a thoroughgoing admirer of Adolf Hitler, although his sycophants persisted in thinking that his expressions of reverence for the Fuhrer were not meant seriously. They absolutely were....
>
> In 1981 his diary records: "I told Frank Johnson that I was a Nazi; I really believed it to be the ideal system, and that it was a disaster for the Anglo-Saxon races and for the world that it was extinguished."

GRAVES AND SASSOON

The Donkeys lay unread on my shelf for twenty years, but when I came back from Aubers Ridge, I discovered that the battles Clark discusses in his 1961 history took place in the same terrain that I had visited on my bike. So I decided to give the Hitler-loving sexual predator one more chance, at least to gather his views on trench warfare along the Western Front in 1915. After all, the quote at the beginning of the book reads:

> Prelude: On the Aisne
>
> Sir John French: "The British Army will give battle on the line of the Condé Canal."
> Sir Horace Smith-Dorrien: "Do you mean take the offensive, or stand on the defensive?"
> Sir John French: "Don't ask questions, do as you're told."

The title of the book is taken from an exchange between two German generals, who said that British soldiers in World War I fought "like lions" but were "led by donkeys."

On the subject of the British high command, I found myself in agreement with Clark, who states that the likes of Sir John French and Sir Douglas Haig were over their heads in leading the British Army to war in France. Between the Battle of Ypres through the offensive against Loos (all in 1915), British casualties exceeded several hundred thousand from sending the men "over the top." Not only did the top British generals make no gains against the entrenched Germans, but they wiped out the professional British Army and learned nothing about how to defeat an enemy dug into ridges such as those that stretch to the north from Aubers to Loos. Clark writes: "The losses of the one day's fighting that was the 'Battle' of Aubers Ridge were 458 officers and 11,161 men. It had been a disastrous fifteen hours of squandered heroism, unredeemed by the faintest glimmer of success."

At Neuve Chapelle, where I rode around a suburban subdivision (the trenches lines are long gone but small cemeteries indicate their presence), the British launched an assault against the Germans and made brief progress at several places in the line. As subsequent waves of attacking troops were held up by the congestion in the trenches, as the dead and wounded were brought to the rear, there was no chance to exploit any gaps in the German line. By the time the second wave came forward, the enemy were waiting with machine guns to rake the slowly advancing Allied forces (many were from India). Clark describes the carnage:

> When the time came for the second attack the stricken and disordered condition of the leading brigades made it impossible to achieve the same degree of co-ordination and numerical strength as had characterized the first. None the less a few officers managed to group together the remnants of various units and gallantly led these once more over the top when the bombardment stopped. All these individual groups, however, were cut down in No-Man's-Land within minutes of leaving their own trenches.

What's even harder to comprehend is that Sir John French and Sir Douglas Haig—the British commanders—learned nothing from their encounters with German trenches, wire, and machine guns. After Neuve-Chapelle, according to Clark, Haig said to a War Council meeting: "The machine-gun is a much over-rated weapon and two per battalion is more than sufficient." (After the war he would say: "I believe that the value of the horse and the opportunity for the horse in the future are likely to be as great as ever.... Aeroplanes and tanks...are only accessories to the man and the horse.") Nor did the high command have any ideas on the best way to get across the lines of German trenches and barbed wire, which in some cases around villages such as Ligny-le-Petit had a depth of more than five rows. Clarks describes the endless slaughter that was repeated on numerous battlefields, such as this assault at Neuve-Chapelle:

> They attacked in three successive waves, climbing out into a storm of point-blank fire, and some measure of their bravery may be taken from one sentence in the Official History: 'It was thought at first that the attack succeeded in reaching the German trenches as no one behind could see and not a man returned.' In fact every man, and there had been nearly a thousand, was killed.

All along the line from Armentières to Loos during 1915, the British generals thought that one more assault against the German trenches would lead to a breakthrough and end the war, as Allied forces would stream through the gaps and encircle the German armies. I am sure that the plans always worked out on paper or on the tables of sand at headquarters. But on the boggy slopes under Aubers Ridge or on the vast plain before Loos, the British were annihilated to the point that even the Germans were writing, among themselves, of their enemy's hopeless situation. One report reads: "The English troops, in spite of undeniable bravery and endurance on the part of the men, have proved so clumsy in action that they offer no prospect of accomplishing anything decisive against the German Army in the immediate future."

From Neuve-Chapelle, I rode into Festubert, where Graves and Sassoon first met. Sassoon wrote about their friendship:

> At his best I'd always found him an ideal companion, although his opinions were often disconcerting. But no one was worse than he was at hitting it off with the officers who distrusted cleverness and disliked unreserved utterances. In fact he was a positive expert at putting people's backs up unintentionally...

It's a more tactful account than what he first wrote in his diary about the encounter: "Walked into Bethune for tea with Robert Graves, a young poet in Third Battalion and very much disliked." Of their first meeting Graves wrote:

> A day or two after I arrived I went to visit 'C' Company mess, where I got a friendly welcome. I noticed *The Essays of Lionel Johnson* lying on the table. It was the first book I had seen in France (except my own Keats and Blake) that was neither a military textbook nor a rubbishy novel. I stole a look at the fly-leaf, and the name was Siegfried Sassoon. Then I looked around to see who could possibly be called Siegfried Sassoon and bring Lionel Johnson with him to the First Battalion. The answer being obvious, I got into conversation with him, and a few minutes later we set out for Béthune, being off duty until dusk, and talked about poetry.

FRIENDS OF A KIND

During the war, Festubert was reduced to rubble. Today it's just another suburban village in northern France, with faint echoes of the Great War. I did not find any plaques that read: "In Festubert, in April 1915, the writers Robert Graves and Siegfried Sassoon first met, beginning their lifelong, if often tempestuous, friendship. Both would write eloquently in their memoirs about the trench fighting that took place near here and in the surrounding villages." I detoured to ride past the Post Office Rifles Cemetery and took a picture of the church that was rebuilt after the war. Then I set my sights on the battlefield of Loos, which I wanted to see before more rain or darkness fell.

From Festubert, I passed from Givenchy-la-Bassée to Cuinchy, passing over the Canal d'Aire à la Bassée and near to a train station on the line from Bethune to Lens. In *Good-Bye to All That*, Graves writes about his many patrols into no-man's-land around the canal, including this horrifying passage about rats. He writes:

> Cuinchy bred rats. They came up from the canal, fed on the plentiful corpses, and multiplied exceedingly. While I stayed here with the Welch, a new officer joined the company.... When he turned in that night, he heard a scuffling, shone his torch on the bed, and found two rats on his blanket tussling for the possession of a severed hand.

Cuinchy today is a sprawling French town, no longer lethal French farmland. I thought for a moment of bailing on my bicycle tour in the January freezing rain and taking the train to Arras, where I had a room for the night. Instead I pointed my bicycle in the direction of Vermelles (where Graves once took communion, according to the guidebook) and Loos.

The only through road to Loos was D 943, what the French call a "route principale," with a stream of cars, trucks, and buses, all of which threw up rooster tails of rainwater. It had, in stretches, a bicycle path (okay, some painted symbols) on the shoulder of the road, although before riding up the long hill to Loos (the British had followed this direction in their attack) I stopped my bike and attached to the frame all sorts of blinking red lights. I must have looked like the Christmas Truce heading up a busy road. But the flashing lights got me in one piece to the Loos Memorial, on the crest of a hillside that looks down on Loos-en-Gohelle, which was at the center of the battle.

FRIENDS OF A KIND

The Black Hole of Loos

LOOS WAS YET another battle in which the British forces were shot in rows by the thousands as they marched, arm-in-arm, across barren farmland. In this case, as Loos is a center of French coal mining (Zola set his novel *Germinal* not far from here), the Germans could hide spotters and snipers on coal tipples, making the fire that much more deadly. As it was, the British only breached the German lines in one place. Loos was an illusion that turned into a nightmare, and it cost Britain and her allies some sixty thousand casualties in three days of fighting (most on the first day of carnage). Graves, on the far left flank, writes about the delusional orders that came down through the ranks from Sir John French to Graves' C Company:

> 'Tomorrow morning we go back to dump our blankets, packs, and greatcoats in Béthune. The next day, that's Saturday the 25th, we attack.'… I still have the map, and these are the orders as I copied them down:
>
> FIRST OBJECTIVE—*Les Briques Farm*—The big house plainly visible to our front, surrounded by trees. To get this it is necessary to cross three lines of enemy trenches. The first is three hundred yards distant, the second four hundred, and the third about six hundred. We then cross two railways. Behind the second railway line is a German trench called the Brick Trench. Then comes the Farm, a strong place with moat and cellars and a kitchen garden strongly staked and wired.
>
> SECOND OBJECTIVE—*The Town of Auchy*—This is also plainly visible from our trenches. It is four hundred yards beyond the Farm and defended by a first line of trench halfway across, and a second line immediately in front of the town. When we have occupied the first line our direction is half-right, with the left of the battalion directed on Tall Chimney.

THIRD OBJECTIVE—*Village of Haisnes*—
Conspicuous by high-spired church. Our eventual line
will be taken up on the railway behind this village,
where we will dig in and await reinforcements.

Most battalions got nowhere near their first objective, let alone the second or third, and the horror of Loos was compounded when the British generals decided to release poison gas during the attack. They didn't wait until the wind was blowing in the direction of the German trenches, and some of the chlorine gas floated back into the British positions or filled no-man's-land with its deadly vapours.

Many battalions were cut down in the vast open spaces between the well-fortified German trenches and the British lines down the hillsides. Clark writes:

> One of the German battalion commanders spoke later of the revolting and nauseating impression made on them all as they watched the slaughter; so much so that after the retreat had begun they ceased fire. Before them was the 'Leichenfeld [field of corpses] von Loos', and, as among them dozens of khaki-clad forms rose up once again and began to limp and crawl back to their own lines, 'no shot was fired at them from the German trenches for the rest of the day, so great was the feeling of compassion and mercy for the enemy after such a victory.' There had been twelve battalions making the attack, a strength of just under ten thousand, and in the three and a half hours of the actual battle their casualties were 385 officers and 7,861 men. The Germans suffered no casualties at all.

From the large cemetery of the Loos Memorial, I could see the village of Loos, numerous coal pits, and, in the distance, the skyline of Lens, a dreary provincial city. In less than an hour, I had ridden from pastoral France to an industrial wasteland, which the freezing rain did nothing to improve.

The British attack at Loos was meant to liberate the coal mines held by the Germans—they were needed for the war effort—and to relieve some of the pressure on French lines to the south. General Sir John French played the role of the loyal ally, but in so doing he destroyed his army and ended his career. He was relieved of his command after the massacre and replaced by Douglas Haig, every bit as much of a donkey as French—except Haig had the king's ear while French was dallying with other officers' wives.[7] Haig's contribution to military history would be the blunders of the Somme and Passchendaele, which were reruns of the disaster at Loos. In effect, both generals adopted the suicidal templates of Neuve-Chapelle and Aubers, as if those operations had been victories.

Trying to understand why the British government put up with such incompetence, Clark writes:

> For the generals were far away; they could make no trouble; and their prowess, as it seemed, reflected glory on the home Government. Thus a popular tradition of heroic infallibility had been established which was to mate disastrously with the amateurish good humour and ignorance of contemporary military theory that was reality. For the adulation that had been their lot from Press and public had deluded the commanders with notions of their own ability and made them at the same time secure against dismissal by the politicians.

But then Margaret Thatcher, when she was prime minister, appointed Clark to her government, which goes to show that old soldiers never die; they simply change offices.

---

[7] According to Sir John French's biographer, George H. Cassar, one of French's colleagues found him to be "unstable, petty, jealous, unreliable, and professionally incompetent."

THE WESTERN FRONT

Arras: *A forlorn plan of attack*

I SPENT TWO nights in Arras, which is about halfway between Lille and Paris. My Airbnb room was in an elegant townhouse near the station, so that it was easy to come and go on the local rail network, which fans across northern France. Even though the weather remained damp and cold, I loved the feeling around the old town, and I found a vegetarian café near the station, which served homemade pasta and reasonable wines.

Late one afternoon, I went on my bike in search of the Battle of Arras, where in spring 1917 Siegfried Sassoon was wounded by a German sniper as he was returning from a patrol in no-man's-land. It was after this that he returned to London and wrote his famous protest letter, which begins: "I am making this statement as an act of wilful defiance of military authority, because I believe the war is being deliberately prolonged by those who have the power to end it. I am a soldier, convinced that I am acting on behalf of soldiers. I believe that this war, upon which I entered as a war of defence and liberation, has now become a war of aggression and conquest."

Sassoon was only in the trenches at Arras for less than a week when he was wounded. According to the Graves-Sassoon guidebook, Sassoon was hit around the Héinel-Croiselles Road, which I figured out was southeast of Arras in the direction of Beaurains and Hénin-sur-Cojeul, two villages.

I left downtown Arras from the New Zealand Monument, which pays tribute to the "tunnelers" who dug shafts under the German lines and planted explosives to open gaps in the trenches. I had no choice but to ride along the route principale, D 5, which was lined with those tall poplar trees that were planted to shade the passage of Napoleon's marching armies in the summer sunshine.

I got to Héinel by turning left at the crossroads in Hénin-sur-Cojeul and riding under the lines of the TGV (Train à Grande Vitesse) and the French autoroute, both of which run parallel to the front lines of what was once the Western Front. In Héinel I found a marker pointing to no fewer than eight British cemeteries in the area, and I later I read that Commonwealth casualties in the Battle of Arras were about 150,000, yet another staggering figure for fighting that lasted about a month in spring 1917.

FRIENDS OF A KIND

When Sassoon was wounded, he was serving with the 2nd Battalion of the Royal Welch Regiment, and as he liked to do, he was freelancing with hand grenades in the gruesome no-man's-land between the opposing trenches. In this sector of the battle of Arras, the objectives were the so-called Hindenburg Line and the "Tunnel Trench," which backed up the German fortifications on a ridge line similar to that around Aubers.

My guidebook has a passage that describes Sassoon's way forward through the British trenches. It reads:

> With his usual impulsive independence Sassoon left his company and set off on his own, luckily finding a party of Royal Engineers who were able to give him directions. They were in the midst of the British and German dead, many from the fighting of April 9 and 10—as Sassoon recorded in his diary, 'the most ghastly sights…beyond description'. In later months, these sights would weed through directly and indirectly into a number of poems of bitter intensity.

At one point in the battle, Sassoon was ordered forward with about twenty-five men, to assist a detachment of the Scottish rifles that was low in ammunition and hard against the Hindenburg Line, the vestiges of which have been plowed under in the broad plain around the Héninel-Croisilles Road. According to the guidebook, what happened next is this:

> Whilst his men were consolidating he went exploring down a side trench—and peered over the trench parapet during a lull in the enemy machine-gun fire. It was a foolish move, for he was immediately seen by a sniper and hit in the shoulder by a rifle bullet. Faint with shock, he was quickly discovered by Sergeant Baldwin leaning against the trench wall and led back to the main trench.

In his *Memoirs of an Infantry Officer*, Sassoon has a long passage on his wounding, in which he writes:

> 'This [putting his head above the parapet] was a mistake which ought to have put an end to my terrestrial

> adventures, for no sooner had I popped my silly head out of the sap than I felt a stupendous blow in the back between my shoulders. My first notion was that a bomb had hit me from behind, but what had really happened was that I had been sniped from in front.

When he realized he was not dead from the bullet, he consoled himself, hoping that the wound would be his ticket out of the war. He writes:

> A German bullet had passed through me leaving a neat hole near my right shoulder-blade and this patriotic perforation had made a different man of me. I now looked at the War, which had been a monstrous tyrant, with liberated eyes. For the time being I had regained my right to call myself a private individual.

Sassoon was moved back, in successive steps, to various aid stations until he found himself in a hospital back in England. Along the way, he recorded: "I remember listening to an emotional padre who was painfully aware that he could do nothing except stand about and feel sympathetic. The consolations of the Church of England weren't much in demand at an Advance Dressing Station." The guidebook adds: "His participation in the Battle of Arras was even briefer, a mere five days, but his experiences during those days remained vivid in his mind for the rest of his life." The Sassoon poem most associated with the battle of Arras is entitled "The General," and it reads:

> *"Good-morning, good-morning!" the General said*
> *When we met him last week on our way to the line.*
> *Now the soldiers he smiled at are most of 'em dead,*
> *And we're cursing his staff for incompetent swine.*
> *"He's a cheery old card," grunted Harry to Jack*
> *As they slogged up to Arras with rifle and pack.*
>
> *But he did for them both by his plan of attack.*

After poking around the Héninel-Croisilles Road Cemetery, I should have turned my bicycle toward Arras and ridden home. Instead, I continued on toward Fontaine-les-Croisilles and Croisilles, neither of which Sassoon ever saw but which are mentioned in some of his dispatches. When it came time to ride back to Arras, I found that the winter sun was dropping below the clouds and the dark horizon and that I had little choice but to stick to main (very busy) roads.

Between Croisilles and Hénin-sur-Cojeul, I found myself sharing the narrow D5 with speeding cars and trucks. Once again, I loaded up my bike frame with flashing lights, and over my biking jacket I added a yellow vest (*gilet jaune* in French), with the hopes that I would be recognized as a cyclist and not run off the road as an anti-Macron protester.

At Hénin-sur-Cojeul I bailed from the D5 and on my map found an agricultural lane to Neuville-Vitasse and Tilloy-lès-Mofflaines. It started well, as a paved road through the fields, and to be in rural France, in the cold darkness under glistening stars, made me feel closer to the men who had camped so often in winter months in these very same fields. Then my lane turned into a cow track, and I was forced to walk my bicycle through the patches of mud, as if dragging artillery to the front.

Only after a heavy slog through the darkness did I come to a secondary road, which I followed into Arras, thinking of a poem, "Lights Out," by Edward Thomas, which reads in full:

> *I have come to the borders of sleep,*
> *The unfathomable deep*
> *Forest where all must lose*
> *Their way, however straight,*
> *Or winding, soon or late;*
> *They cannot choose.*
>
> *Many a road and track*
> *That, since the dawn's first crack,*
> *Up to the forest brink,*
> *Deceived the travellers,*
> *Suddenly now blurs,*
> *And in they sink.*
>
> *Here love ends,*
> *Despair, ambition ends;*

THE WESTERN FRONT

All pleasure and all trouble,
Although most sweet or bitter,
Here ends in sleep that is sweeter
Than tasks most noble.

There is not any book
Or face of dearest look
That I would not turn from now
To go into the unknown
I must enter, and leave, alone,
I know not how.

The tall forest towers;
Its cloudy foliage lowers
Ahead, shelf above shelf;
Its silence I hear and obey
That I may lose my way
And myself

Thomas, a friend of Robert Frost and other so-called Dymock poets, was killed on the first day of the Arras offensive, April 9, 1917. It has been said that Frost wrote his poem, "A Road Not Taken" ("Two roads diverged in a wood, and I—/I took the one less traveled by,/And that has made all the difference") to chide his friend for not enlisting at the outbreak of the war, although by the time that Thomas had been commissioned, at age thirty-nine, into the Royal Garrison Artillery, Frost was back on his farm in New Hampshire and getting ready to march to sounds of teaching English at Amherst College.

An entry of the Poetry Foundation records Thomas' death this way:

> Thomas turned down an offer to remain on the permanent staff as an instructor at Hare Hall camp and volunteered for a commission at the front. On Easter Monday, 1917, the first day of the Arras Offensive, he paused for a moment to fill his pipe. A shell passed so close to him that the blast of air stopped his heart; he died without a mark on his body. Or at least, this is what his widow was told at the time and was believed

to be true for many years. However, a letter from his commanding officer that was discovered years later [in the New York Public Library] revealed that Thomas was actually "shot clean through the chest."

As best as I could determine, Thomas was in the lines near Monchy-le-Preux, which is a village in the fields through which I was pushing my bike in the mud. He was buried in Argy Cemetery, which is across the D5, in the Arras suburbs.

THE WESTERN FRONT

Craiglockhart War Hospital:
The battle for Sassoon's soul

IT WAS AFTER his wounding in the Battle of Arras and the publication of his letter of protest that Sassoon was shipped off to Craiglockhart War Hospital, in the Edinburgh suburbs, where officers, in particular, were treated for shell shock so that they could return to the front lines. At Craiglockhart Sassoon came under the care of Dr. W. H. Rivers, and the relationship between the two men has been described in novels, plays, movies, poetry, and numerous memoirs. Sassoon was at Craiglockhart for three months, during which time he played golf with another patient, wrote poetry with Wilfred Owen (who would die in action near the Sambre-Oise Canal, east of Arras, in November 1918), and underwent treatment with Rivers, who turned into a mentor, friend, and father figure to the fragile Sassoon, although the doctor's somewhat confused goal was to cure his patients so that they could be fed back into the sausage machine.

Only after I had been to Arras did I make it to Craiglockhart, which is now part of Edinburgh Napier University. It was after school hours when I arrived and the doors were locked, but a student let me in a back door and pointed me in the direction of a small museum dedicated to the memory of the war poets. Included in the collection are many first editions of the war poets' books, as well as original letters and drafts of poems by the likes of Sassoon and Owen. On arrival Owen wrote to his mother: "A Taxi brought me up here about 2 1/2 miles from the Town. There is nothing very attractive about the place. It is a decayed hypo, far too full of officers, some of whom I know. I shall not see the M.O. [Medical Officer] till Tomorrow: I am going out now to take the lie of the land." In her novel *Regeneration*, which is set at Craiglockhart and describes the dynamic between Sassoon and Rivers, Pat Barker writes: "Nobody arriving at Craiglockhart for the first time could fail to be daunted by the sheer gloomy, cavernous bulk of the place. Sassoon lingered on the drive for a full minute after the taxi had driven away, then took a deep breath, squared his shoulders, and ran up the steps."

By the time I rolled up to Craiglockhart and came in through the back door, I had read numerous accounts of Sassoon's stay at the hospital, including two that he wrote himself (it appears in *Siegfried's Journey* and *Sherston's Progress*), as well as Robert Graves' long description in *Good-Bye to All That*, which recounts the battalion and British Army politics that landed Sassoon in the care of Dr. Rivers rather than before a firing squad (the normal proscription for anyone who denounced the war, senior command, and British government). Sassoon resented Graves' insinuation that he (Graves) had been responsible for securing Sassoon a place in the hospital by persuading the medical board that Sassoon was suffering from shell shock when he wrote his protest letter. Sassoon, himself, never believed that he had acted against the government except with a clear head and purpose: to end the killing in the war.

In his memoir Graves makes a link between Sassoon's wounding at Arras and his protest against the war:

> Heavy fighting in the Hindenburg Line broke out soon afterwards. Siegfried's platoon went to support the Cameronians, and when these were driven out of some trenches they had won, he regained the position with a bombing-party of six men. Though shot through the throat, he continued bombing until he collapsed. The Cameronians rallied and returned, and the brigadier sent Siegfried's name in for a Victoria Cross—a recommendation refused, however, on the ground that the operations had been unsuccessful; for the Cameronians were later driven out again by a bombing-party under some German Siegfried. Back in London now, and very ill, he wrote that often when he went for a walk he saw corpses lying about on the pavements. In April, Yates had sent him a note saying that four officers were killed and seven wounded in a show at Fontaine-les-Croiselles—a 'perfectly bloody battle.' But the battalion advanced nearly half a mile which, to Siegfried, seemed some consolation. Yet in the very next sentence he wrote how mad it made him to think of the countless good men being slaughtered that summer, and all for nothing. The bloody politicians and ditto generals with their cursed incompetent blundering and callous ideas would go on until they tired of it or had

got as much kudos as they wanted. He wished he could
do something in protest, but even if he were to shoot
the Premier or Sir Douglas Haig, they would only shut
him up in a mad-house like Richard Dadd of glorious
memory.

Other accounts of Sassoon's protest attribute much of his letter and general anti-war sentiments to Bertrand Russell, Lady Ottoline Morrell, and other London activists who, speculation goes, used the sensitive Sassoon (then recuperating from his shoulder wound) for their own, anti-war ends. But this passage, in Pat Barker's *Regeneration*, had Sassoon differing with Rivers on the source of his discontent:

> [Sassoon] 'I can guess what Graves said. What a
> fine upstanding man I was until I fell among pacifists.
> Isn't that right? Russell used me. Russell wrote the
> Declaration.'
> [Rivers] 'No, he didn't say that.'
> 'Good. Because it isn't true.'
> 'You don't think you were influenced by Russell?'
> 'No, not particularly. I think I was influenced by my
> own experience of the front. I am capable of making up
> my own mind.'

In her novel, Barker includes a long passage that consists of a report that Rivers wrote about his patient:

> When he became fit to return to duty, in July of
> this year, he felt he was unable to do so, and that it was
> his duty to make some kind of protest. He drew up a
> statement which he himself regarded as an act of wilful
> defiance of military authority (see *The Times*, July 31st,
> 1917). In consequence of this statement he was ordered
> to attend a Medical Board at Chester about July 16th,
> but failed to attend. It was arranged that a second
> Board should be held at Liverpool on July 20th, which
> he attended, and he was recommended for admission
> to Craiglockhart War Hospital for special treatment

for three months. The patient is a healthy looking man of good physique. There are no physical signs of any disorder of the Nervous System. He discusses his recent actions and their motives in a perfectly intelligent and rational way, and there is no evidence of any excitement or depression. He recognizes that his view of warfare is tinged by his feelings about the death of friends and of the men who were under his command in France. At the present time he lays special stress on the hopelessness of any decision in the War as it is now being conducted, but he left out any reference to this aspect of his opinions in the statement which he sent to his Commanding Officer and which was read in the House of Commons.

The inflection point in Sassoon's treatment was whether he would agree, on his own, to return to front-line duty, which was the goal that Rivers had set for his patient. It was a subject that they often discussed together, and after a while, without too much pressure from Rivers, Sassoon took the position that he would agree to a return to the trenches, but would refuse a home guard posting or garrison duty in Ireland. (He said to Rivers: "I refuse to garrison Ireland, which is entitled to self-determination under our peace terms.") Pat Barker in her novel captures the precarious world that Rivers inhabits with his patients. She writes: "Normally a cure implies that the patient will no longer engage in behaviour that is clearly self-destructive. But in present circumstances, recovery meant the resumption of activities that were not merely self-destructive but positively suicidal. But then in a war nobody is a free agent."

While coming around to his voluntary position on his own fitness to serve, Sassoon played a lot of golf (a Craiglockhart brochure reads: "It is much more beneficial for patients to play even once round the course daily—than to be perpetually immured in a picture house, or to parade Princes Street, for the gratification of their own vanity…"), and he befriended another patient at the hospital, Wilfred Owen, whose greatness as poet was then unknown.

Painfully shy, Owen asked Sassoon to inscribe one of his books, and then worked up the courage to invite Sassoon to contribute some poems to the hospital magazine, *The Hydra*. Barker imagines the scene in *Regeneration*:

> Sassoon reached the last book. Owen felt the meeting begin to slip away from him. Rather desperately, he said, 'I l-liked "The D-Death B-Bed" b-best.' And suddenly he relaxed. It didn't matter what this Sassoon thought about him, since the real Sassoon was in the poems. He quoted, from memory, "He's young; he hated War, how should he die/When cruel old campaigners win safe through?/But death replied: 'I choose him.' So he went." That's beautiful.'

Barker goes on to describe in their first meeting how Owen admits to writing his own poetry, which Sassoon later reads and admires. During their overlapping time at Craiglockhart, the two men work together on their poetry, with Sassoon making some suggestions on language to Owen. And it was Sassoon who introduced Owen to Robert Graves, who in his memoir writes about the Craiglockhart friendships:

> Siegfried and Rivers soon became close friends; Siegfried was interested in Rivers' diagnostic methods, and Rivers in Siegfried's poems. On my return from Edinburgh I felt much happier. Siegfried began to write the terrifying sequence of poems, some of them published in the Craiglockhart hospital magazine, *The Hydra*, which appeared next year as *Counter-Attack*. Another patient was Wilfred Owen of the Manchester Regiment. It preyed on his mind that he had been unjustly accused of cowardice by his commanding officer. Meeting Siegfried here set Owen, a quiet, round-faced little man, writing war-poems....

Sassoon was discharged from the hospital in October and cleared for front-line duty. Barker's *Regeneration* ends with Rivers writing up his last report on Sassoon: "His [Rivers] thoughts wandered as he wrote. He wasted no time wondering how he would feel if Siegfried were to be maimed or killed, because this was a possibility with any patient who returned to France. He'd faced that already, many times. If anything, he was amused by the irony of the situation, that he, who was in the business of changing people, should himself have been changed and by somebody who was clearly unaware of having done it."

The Man Who Shot Sassoon

INSTEAD OF RETURNING to France, Sassoon was posted in early 1918 to the Middle East and participated in General Allenby's liberation of Palestine, one reason he must have enjoyed getting to know T. E. Lawrence after the war. Only later in 1918 was he sent back to France, to Saint Floris, which is about twelve miles northwest of Festubert, where Sassoon's war had begun three years before. By that point, the German war machine was exhausted and shortly thereafter rolled back to the Belgian frontier. It was while serving in Saint Floris that Sassoon was wounded by one of his own men, who, while on sentry duty early one morning, shot at the officer as he was coming back through the mists from one of his raids in no-man's-land.

The sentry's bullet grazed Sassoon's head, but the wound was sufficiently serious for him to sit out the rest of the war. The shooting became the subject of a historical novel, John Hollands' *The Man Who Shot Siegfried Sassoon*. The book struck me as a memoir dressed up as fiction so that none of the Royal Welch veterans who Hollands interviewed could later sue him for damages or libel. ("My novel is based on actual events, augmented by my imagination.") I found a copy on Amazon, and read it with amazement.

The narrator of the novel is Hollands himself, and he pieces together the Sassoon shooting while visiting his wife's family in Wales, where many of the neighbors had served in the Great War with the Royal Welch Fusiliers. Included among them is a former private, known as Jones 617 (his full name was Rhys Jones), who was the one who shot Sassoon—deliberately, according to the novel. Jones 617 was the twin brother of Jones 618 (Davey Jones), who, like his brother, served with Sassoon in the Royal Welch on the Western Front

Hollands has this dialogue in his book:

> 'Jones [617] shot him but he didn't kill him. He only grazed Sassoon's skull, hardly even a wound. If he'd shot him straight between the eyes, as he intended, he wouldn't be like he is now.' [Jones was unable to speak.]
> 'You mean they would have strung him up.'
> 'No, no. It would have been hushed up. Strictly

speaking he was entitled to shoot him. The brass hats would have been glad to see the back of Sassoon at that stage. It would have been just another accident, a trigger-happy sentry shooting a man returning from no-man's-land.'

'How can you be so sure it was intentional?'

'Because I saw everything that led up to it. Sassoon was a popular officer with his men but Jones 617 had a special reason for hating him.'

According to Hollands, the special reason was this: Davey Jones 618 was a man of limited intellectual abilities (he might have been autistic), but he looked up to his commanding officer (Sassoon), as did most in the company. While Sassoon was away from the battalion after his wounding at Arras in 1917, Davey Jones found some of his commander's anti-war poems in a book and, wanting to remember them, copied them down in his own notebook, where another officer found them.

As a consequence, Jones 618 was court-martialed. During the trial he admitted to writing the poems himself. He was pronounced guilty and sentenced to death. After his brother was shot by a firing squad, Rhys Jones 617 vowed to revenge his brother's death. He got his chance when Sassoon came back to the regiment in Saint Floris toward the end of the war. The only reason that Sassoon wasn't shot "between the eyes" as he returned at dawn from his nighttime patrol in no-man's-land was that another soldier, "Khyber" Morgan, sensed what was happening and threw a Mills bomb in the direction of Rhys Jones. It exploded near the would-be assassin, who then, according to the novel, never said another word in his life. Hollands writes: "His failure to kill Sassoon had caused such deep-seated psychiatric damage that he was struck dumb. Not a single word passed his lips."

Jones 617 might well have become a lifetime patient at Craiglockhart, except that he was sent home to Wales, to be cared for locally. Ironically his anger matched Sassoon's own, as he expressed to Rivers in Barker's novel:

> A pause. Rivers waited. After a while Sassoon went on, almost reluctantly. 'A friend of mine had been killed. For a while I used to go out on patrol every night, looking

THE WESTERN FRONT

for Germans to kill. Or rather I told myself that's what I was doing. In the end I didn't know whether I was trying to kill them, or just giving them plenty of opportunities to kill me.

Belfast on the Somme

TO GET FROM Arras to the Somme battlefields, I caught an early morning local train heading to Albert and got off with my bicycle in Miraumont, a hamlet on the banks of the River Ancre. I had thought I might buy coffee in Miraumont before setting off toward the Ulster Monument, but little was stirring around the station when I checked my maps and settled on D151 in the direction of Grandcourt, yet another forgotten battlefield on the left flank of the 1916 Somme offensive.

During much of that fighting from July to November 1916, the British struggled to control the road down which I was biking, just as they struggled to cross the Ancre, a meandering stream in the nearby woods. As with so many "pushes" on the Somme, these failed to dislodge the entrenched Germans, who whenever they were forced to cede ground would counterattack in a nearby sector—to balance the score.

Had I been cycling in July, I am sure that I would have loved riding along a small, winding road near fields, a forest, and a stream. Instead I was pedaling through a cold winter fog, apprehensive any time headlights appeared in front of me. Occasionally, I passed signs for Beaumont-Hamel, remembering that in summer 2000 I had taken some members of my family, including my parents, to Beaumont-Hamel, where we walked among the preserved trenches of the Newfoundland Regiment, which was nearly wiped out in the folly of the attack on the first day, July 1, 1916.

In theory, the attacking Allied soldiers went forward after a week's worth of artillery barrages had cut holes in the German lines. Unfortunately, British artillery had not entirely dislodged the German barbed wire or the machine-gun crews. When the shelling stopped, the Germans emerged from their bomb shelters and gunned down the waves of approaching regiments, including that of Newfoundland (which only joined Canada after World War II).

At the crossroads in Hamel, I took pictures of the Ancre (which the Germans had tied into their defenses) and began biking up a long, steep hillside toward the Ulster Monument. Until that ascent, I had thought of the Somme battlefield as relatively flat, blocked only by trenches and wire. Instead, I discovered that the Germans had been masters of the terrain. They had dug their fortifications along hilltops and ridgelines, forcing the British and Allied troops, wherever they broke through the forward trenches, to fight their way up steep ravines and broad, exposed slopes, on which the Germans registered their big guns and canisters of shrapnel.

Without having to walk my bicycle (always an achievement on steep roads), I made it to the top of the hill and to the Ulster Monument, which looks like a truncated Irish castle and tower that somehow floated into northern France. (In fact, it's a replica of Helen's Tower, a nineteenth-century baronial pile in County Down, not far from Belfast.) On a sign by the road I was happy to read that the museum inside served coffee and tea, and I looked forward to warming myself. Only after locking up my bicycle and approaching the front door did I see a small, hand-printed notice that indicated the monument was closed until the end of January. All I could do was take pictures of the gloomy tower and move down the road toward the Thiepval Memorial and Museum.

The Thiepval Museum was also closed in January. I peered through the windows into the dark gift shop. Wanting to piece together what happened to the 36th (Ulster) Division, I waited for the rains to stop and rode in the direction of Schwaben Redoubt, which, along with the village of Grandcourt, was the objective of the 36th on D-Day, July 1, 1916. For a change in the history of the Somme battle, the Ulstermen met most of their objectives on that first day and stormed the redoubt, which was on the crest of a broad, open hillside beyond the present-day monument. Instead of marching with arms linked together into German machine guns (standard practice on D-Day along the Somme), the 36th attacked in small waves, going forward, from shell hole to shell hole close to the so-called creeping barrage. Not only did they make it up the long hillside, but they carried on to the redoubt and attacked it with small arms and bayonets. Had the British high command not been squired away in châteaux miles from the front lines, it might have exploited the success of the 36th and reinforced the breakthrough with more troops. Instead it called a halt to the forward progress of the 36th, as on either side of the Ulstermen (Newfies to the left, and British troops to the right), no progress had been made. As the 36th pulled back its lines, the Germans enfiladed the Ulster salient and inflicted horrendous casualties. In all, of the seventeen thousand men who went forward on D-Day, some five thousand were casualties, of which more than two thousand died.

Ulster's victories and defeats around the Schwaben Redoubt were rendered particularly poignant by the coincidence that the attack on the Somme took place on the anniversary of the Battle of the Boyne (1690), giving the Orangemen of Ulster added symbolic mysticism to carry with them over the top.[8] (Some, it is said, pinned orange pennants to their tunics.) Then there is the fact that the adjacent divisions (one of them British) "let down" the Ulstermen by failing to meet their objectives. In taking the Redoubt and suffering five thousand casualties, Ulster did "its bit" for the empire, and in the years to follow (including to the present day, if you judge by the sidewalk art in Belfast) repayment was expected in unwavering British commitment to Northern Ireland's inclusion in the United Kingdom. Beginning in July 1917 (before the war had even ended), marchers in Belfast began remembering on the same day the battles of the Boyne and Somme, until in the minds of many locals I am sure that it became difficult to sort out the historical differences between the two.

It was only during the later stages of the Troubles that leaders in the north and south of Ireland decided to use the suffering along the Western Front as a point of common ancestry. Hence the Messines memorial is not just dedicated to the 36th (Ulster) Division but to all Irish troops, Protestant and Catholic, who fought and died in the trenches. (Ulster lost 32,186 men in the war, and Ireland—the south—lost 37,761.) Ireland and Great Britain bridged their divide by erecting the memorial tower (on Belgian soil, and paid for with European Union, largely German, funds). For one day (November 11, 1998), the leaders of these dysfunctional countries could meet in Flanders and with their hands on their hearts pledge themselves to eternal peace and reconciliation. As the Irish foreign minister said on the occasion: "All those untold human stories that we lost in the first World War and more recently in the conflict in Northern Ireland, must be remembered. And, in remembering, they must not be told for nothing. They must not be told to deepen divisions. They must be told to inspire us to overcome them."

---

[8] In the battle, Protestant Britain defeated Catholic Ireland about an hour north of Dublin, settling the stage for two hundred years of British domination in Ireland.

The Somme's Thiepval Monument:
Site of mourning

JUST DOWN THE road from the Ulster Monument is the Thiepval Memorial, which is at the center of Somme remembrance, as it records the names of British soldiers whose bodies were never found. The memorial is a succession of triumphal arches, although such is the arrangement of the soaring vaults and the setting on the edge of gloomy woods that from some angles the memorial resembles a house of horror. I leaned my bicycle against one of the chain gates near the entrance (there was no point in locking it, as I was the only visitor on a cold winter day) and read the inscription, which states: "Here are recorded names of officers and men of the British Armies who fell on the Somme battlefields July 1915 to February 1918 but to whom the fortune of war denied the known and honoured burial given to their comrades in death." The memorial is the Somme's tomb of the unknown Newfoundland soldier, at least for the British and South African armies. Australia, New Zealand, India, and Canada—the other members of the disillusioned Commonwealth—erected memorials elsewhere to their missing.

    I was interested to learn that the imperial architect Sir Edward Lutyens designed the Thiepval Memorial, as I had come across his war memorial in Mells, when I went in search of Siegfried Sassoon's gravesite. Lutyens also designed the Cenotaph in London, perhaps the most famous World War I monument, and numerous memorials and manor houses around the British Empire. (An argument can be made that when we think of imperial Britain what we really are recalling is Lutyens' memorials and statues.) Jay Winter in his *Sites of Memory, Sites of Morning: The Great War in European Cultural History*, writes of Lutyens:

> It was not at all a mind closed to conventional imagery, especially when an individual was commemorated. Witness the mounted cavalry officer, by Alfred Munnings, on a plinth designed by Lutyens in commemoration of Edward Horner in the Church of St Andrew, Mells, Somerset. Lutyens also accompanied Horner's mother when the two of them placed a tablet

in the parish church for Raymond Asquith, the Prime Minister's son and her son-in-law. Here too the subject was the loss of one man. But so many individual had died that, for Lutyens, a different language was required to express the meaning of the 'lost generation'. While inspecting sites for the war memorial at Mells, Lutyens simply noted of the people accompanying him: 'All their young men are killed.' In this setting he went beyond Christian symbols of sacrifice, and explored what he called more 'elemental' (or universal) responses to the terrible loss of life in war.

From Thiepval, I followed signs toward Mouquet Farm and Pozières, two names that resonate in the minds of Australian families who lost many ancestors in the battles around these locations. Mouquet Farm is on a ridge line that extends several miles from Pozières (a crossroads town), and in August 1916 it fell to the Australian divisions (1st, 2nd, and 4th) in the Somme lines to take both positions. At Pozières the Germans had yet another hilltop redoubt and a vast network of trenches, and it cost the Australians some seventeen thousand casualties to take the town, which was on the road to Bapaume—ostensibly the objective of the Somme offensive. Then the Australians were sent up the sloping farmland to take Mouquet Farm (they called it Moo-cow Farm). That fighting claimed around six thousand casualties. Sir Edward Lutyens designed the Australian war memorial at Villers-Bretonneux near Corbie, although that wasn't enough, after the war, to maintain the affection Australia previously had for Great Britain.

Pozières has a number of Australian war memorials, and signposts around the church indicate a path to follow to understand the course of the fighting. I followed the *parcours*, as it is called in French, and found such landmarks as Dead Man's Road, Gibraltar Bunker, the 1st Division Memorial, and an area of restored trenches from which the Australians launched their fateful (and fatal, for both sides) attacks. By the time the Australians were ordered forward to their deaths or mutilation, in August 1916, the Somme had already claimed more than 158,000 casualties, and Allied troops had made little progress since D-Day. When the campaign ended in November 1916, the Australians would only be a few miles forward on the Bapaume road. In the battle as a whole, the British allies suffered more than five hundred thousand casualties, and in exchange, the forward lines advanced less than eight miles. For good reason did many later write that the British Empire ended on the banks of the Somme.

From Pozières I rode a secondary road along what in the battle was known as Bazentin Ridge. Here and there in the rolling landscape I passed through small forests. During the fighting, the Germans anchored their trench lines in these woods on the high ground, and often the only way for the British to clear them from the breastworks was in hand-to-hand fighting, which accounted for the horrendous casualties on both sides.

One of these casualties here was Robert Graves, who was severely wounded by shellfire in late July 1916, near what is now the Bazentin-le-Petit Military Cemetery. Initially Graves was reported as killed in action, which prompted Sassoon to write a poem, "To His Dead Body," about his lost friend:

> *When roaring gloom surged inward and you cried,*
> *Groping for friendly hands, and clutched, and died,*
> *Like racing smoke, swift from your lolling head*
> *Phantoms of thought and memory thinned and fled.*
>
> *Yet, though my dreams that throng the darkened stair*
> *Can bring me no report of how you fare,*
> *Safe quit of wars, I speed you on your way*
> *Up lonely, glimmering fields to find new day,*
> *Slow-rising, saintless, confident and kind—*
> *Dear, red-faced father God who lit your mind.*

Only two weeks later did Sassoon hear that Graves had survived the shell blast and was on his way to hospital in Britain. Of his return to the British isles, Graves wrote:

> England looked strange to us returned soldiers. We could not understand the war-madness that ran wild everywhere, looking for a pseudo-military outlet. The civilians talked a foreign language; and it was newspaper language. I found serious conversation with my parents all but impossible.

FRIENDS OF A KIND

Later, Graves and Sassoon met up in Harlech, where Graves' family had its summer house, and worked on each other's poems for publication, which gave Graves the chance—which few have—to make changes to his own obituary.

Graves and Sassoon:
Once more to Mametz Wood

CONTINUING MY RIDE across the battlefields of the Somme, I biked in a large circle from Delville Wood and Longueval toward Mametz. In particular, I was searching for Mametz Wood, where some of the worst fighting on the Somme took place, much of it involving both Graves and Sassoon. From Mametz, a tiny farming village, I followed signs for the Royal Welch Division memorial, which pointed me out of the center on a series of agricultural lanes that followed the contours of what were once the German front lines. After about a fifteen-minute ride from the village, I pulled the bicycle into a parking area and ascended a set of metal stairs, the kind you might find inside a warehouse. On a small promontory I stood in front of the Royal Welch's proud red dragon, which with its wings aloft looks ready to renew the battle.

In *Memoirs of an Infantry Officer*, Sassoon writes: "Mametz Wood was a menacing wall of gloom, and now an outburst of rapid thudding explosions began from that direction." And he adds this aside about one of his commanding officers: "I wondered whether he had ever allowed himself to find out that the Gommecourt show had been nothing but a massacre of good troops. Probably he kept a war map with little flags on it; when Mametz Wood was reported captured he moved a little flag an inch forward after breakfast. For him the Wood was a small green patch on a piece of paper. For the Welch Division it had been a bloody nightmare..."

After the battle, Robert Graves wrote: "It was full of dead Prussian Guards, big men, and dead Royal Welch Fusiliers and South Wales Borderers, little men. Not a single tree in the wood remained unbroken." It was in these woods that Sassoon won his Military Cross, the same one that he later threw into Liverpool's Mersey River.

A plaque beside the memorial notes that the attack on the Wood began a week after D-Day (July 1, 1916), when Mametz fell to the British. It reads:

> The Welch Division attacked from the east on 7th July 1916, and after advancing slowly and uncertainly, it occupied the wood almost completely by 11th July.

FRIENDS OF A KIND

> Exhausted, it [later] evacuated the sector after losing
> 4000 men, including 600 dead and 600 missing.

Sassoon's feat of arms, as might have been expected, was to rush some nearby German trenches and to show one of the ways into the forest, which otherwise was the green equivalent of the Schwaben Redoubt. His citation reads: "For conspicuous gallantry during a raid on the enemy's trenches. He remained for 1½ hours under rifle and bomb fire collecting and bringing in our wounded. Owing to his courage and determination all the killed and wounded were brought in." Not all of his contemporaries thought the medal was justified, as his antics might have delayed the opening of the British assault on the wood. In his biography of Sassoon, Max Egremont writers:

> He went over with bombs in daylight, under covering fire from a couple of rifles, and scared away the occupants. A pointless feat, since instead of signalling for reinforcements, he sat down in the German trench and began reading a book of poems which he had brought with him. When he went back he did not even report. Colonel Stockwell, then in command, raged at him. The attack on Mametz Wood had been delayed for two hours because British patrols were still reported to be out. "British patrols" were Siegfried and his book of poems. "I'd have got you a D.S.O., if you'd only shown more sense," stormed Stockwell.

Strangely, the citation, allegedly thrown into the Mersey, turned up in an attic trunk among Sassoon's possessions when his step-grandson went through some of the family's papers. (I suppose it's possible that later in his life the British Army replaced the medal that he had earlier thrown away.) In any case, Mametz Wood was a cauldron for the Royal Welch, which had no choice but to take the German lines head-on in the forest, after first crossing a broad field that the troops mordantly nicknamed "Happy Valley."

I stayed long enough at the memorial to acquaint myself with the order of the battle and to take pictures of the trees, which in winter were a brown barrier rising out of the fields. I read some of the inscriptions and later was sorry that the memorial did not include this passage from *Good-*

THE WESTERN FRONT

Bye to All That, which pays appropriate tribute to what the Royal Welch endured throughout the war:

> The regimental spirit persistently survived all catastrophes. Our First Battalion, for instance, was practically annihilated within two months of joining the British Expeditionary Force. Young Orme, who joined straight from Sandhurst, at the crisis of the first battle of Ypres, found himself commanding a battalion reduced to only about forty rifles. With these, and another small force, the remnants of the Second Battalion of the Queen's Regiment, reduced to thirty men and two officers, he helped to recapture three lines of lost trenches and was himself killed. The reconstituted battalion saw heavy fighting at Bois Grenier in December, but got smashed up at the Aubers Ridge and Festubert in the following May; and again at Loos in September, when only one combatant officer survived the attack—a machine-gun officer on loan from the South Staffordshire Regiment. The same sort of thing happened time after time in fighting at Fricourt [near Mametz], the Quadrangle, High Wood, Delville Wood, and Ginchy on the Somme in 1916; and again at Puisieux and Bulle-court in the spring fighting of 1917; and again, and again, until the Armistice. In the course of the war, at least fifteen or twenty thousand men must have passed through each of the two line battalions, whose fighting strength never stood at more than eight hundred. After each catastrophe the ranks were filled up with new drafts from home, with the lightly wounded from the disaster of three or four months before, and with the more seriously wounded of earlier ones.

From the memorial, I decided to make a long loop around Mametz Wood and to approach Fricourt downhill from Contalmaison, yet another battle village on the Somme. It meant biking along a dirt and paved road to Flatiron Copse Cemetery and joining the D20 at Bazentin (where Graves was later wounded).

FRIENDS OF A KIND

The ride warmed me up, as did the rolling hills between Bazentin and Contalmaison, where I came across a sad memorial dedicated to the 16th Royal Scots, led by Lieutenant Colonel Sir George McCrae, who on D-Day broke through the German lines and stormed the heights at Contalmaison. The action was similar to what the Ulster Division achieved around Thiepval. But as with the 36th Division, no British commander was on the spot to rush more men through the breach, and the Scots were forced to pull back to their starting point, squandering the lives of 256 men in the process.

Among the casualties in the regiment were a number of local professional football players, who had answered McCrae's call, which explains allusions to football on the plaques around the Contalmaison monument. One ditty, now in bronze, reads:

> *Come pack up your footballs and scarves of maroon,*
> *Leave all your sweethearts in Auld Reekie toon.*
> *Fall in wi' the lads for they're aff and away,*
> *To take on the bold Hun with old*
> *Geordie McCrae*

Sadly, the battle for Contalmaison broke McCrae, who was bitter that his men were not reinforced after their breakthrough on the first day. In turn, his commanders thought the Scotsman was a showboater and an amateur, and relieved him of his command. The fact remains that he was one of the few on D-Day on the Somme to achieve his objective, at the cost of much of his regiment. For that he was cashiered—by an army that otherwise chose to reinforce failure.

I was glad that the ride from Contalmaison was downhill, as I still had not eaten lunch and my legs were weary. The descent, along the western edge of Mametz Wood (past where Sassoon had rushed the German trench), renewed my admiration for Colonel McCrae and his men, who had to attack up steep slopes that were exposed to fire from both sides.

Fricourt was the only place on the Somme where I came across German cemeteries, which have stark, black crosses of Gothic darkness to mark their dead. I didn't stop to read the inscriptions, as I was searching for a number of British memorials, notably Fricourt Military Cemetery and what was called Wing Corner, where on D-Day British forces were annihilated in yet another senseless frontal attack against wire and machine guns.

THE WESTERN FRONT

Today a farming village with some larger businesses, Fricourt was at the hinge of the British lines in 1916, and between the two arms of the advancing armies the Germans fought tenaciously, holding back the advances on either side. If Germany won the Battle of the Somme (which I think it did), it did so on D-Day from the trenches around Wing Corner, which today is simply a stretch of road along D938, where backdrafts from speeding trucks make it hard to reimagine the fighting.

Up the hillside from Fricourt, on the other side of the busy road, is the Bois Français, where Sassoon watched the first day of the battle. (He described the sector as "a few hundred yards of waste ground—a jumble of derelict wire, meaningless ditches, and craters no longer formidable.") His battalion was in reserve, but he had a perfect view of the fighting. And it was there that he wrote the supremely ironic line: "I didn't want to die—not before I'd finished reading *The Return of the Native* anyhow."

FRIENDS OF A KIND

Albert and the Road to Corbie

LEAVING FRICOURT, I stopped at a farm in the center of the village, where one of the workers was power-washing the mud away from the courtyard. When I spoke to him in French, he did not respond. Nor did he understand English or my little German. After a while I made it clear to him that I was asking for him to give my bicycle a rinse, as mud was caked all over my brakes and tires. The farmhand loved the diversion from his courtyard washing, and he set about giving my bicycle a thorough cleaning, although I never did figure out his nationality.

The short bike ride from Fricourt into Albert—the regional center—was on another stretch of busy highway, with cars and trucks all passing me at high speeds. On a few stretches I waited in the roadside grass while a large truck went past, but in less than fifteen minutes I was clear of the traffic and into Albert, notable during the war for the "leaning virgin" that was on top of the cathedral and visible from many vantages across the Somme battlefields. The Germans shelled the cathedral repeatedly (it was used by Allied spotters), and the statue of the Virgin Mary atop the steeple dangled precariously. But it never fell. The myth grew up that the war would end when the virgin fell. But then French forces—perhaps wanting the war to continue?—wired the virgin to her base, which meant that for much of the war she was dangling on her back, maybe in the position that most appealed to wise-cracking troops in the field.

I knew about a war museum in Albert, but when I rolled up to the front door I wasn't surprised to find that it was closed. At least the museum was in the town center, where it was easy to find a bistro lunch. I went with the Hygge Café, across the street from the cathedral, and ordered the *plat du jour*, which consisted of veal, frites, salad, and dessert, all of which (after biking in the rain since 8 a.m.) disappeared in an instant. Over coffee, I wondered how I could catch my evening train to Paris from Amiens, from which I had a ticket.

Amiens is eighteen miles from Albert, but when I biked over to the Albert train station (just outside the town center in a lovely rebuilt station) I discovered that the next train wasn't until 4:45 that afternoon, which left me with about two hours and nothing to do. I was tempted to catch a series of regional buses from Albert to Amiens, as they might have taken me past the Château de Querrieu, where in the baroque headquarters of

General Sir Henry Rawlinson the British high command endured the worst of the fighting over nightly meals of foie gras, claret, and cigars. The château seemed like the perfect metaphor for everything that went wrong on the Somme, but when I checked the schedules at the train station there were no connections, metaphorical or otherwise.

In the end I got back on my bicycle (the charm was beginning to wear thin, although it helped me to stay warm) and started riding toward Corbie, a town on the Somme about ten miles from Albert. I knew that the Australian War Memorial that Sir Edward Luytens had designed was nearby in Villers-Bretonneux. And I remembered seeing the landscape around Corbie in the paintings of the Australian impressionist Arthur Streeton, whose work I much admire. During the later stages of the war—after Gallipoli and Pozières anyway—Streeton had followed the Australian Army in France and recorded its progress in a series of paintings that are part of the collection of the Gallery of New South Wales, Sydney's fine art museum. (And one of his paintings is the cover of this book.)

Despite more rain, I was lucky with my ride. I was able to follow what local signs referred to as *La Véloroute N°32 de la Mémoire*, a cycle path between Albert and Corbie that guided me across the valley of the Somme on a succession of small lanes and forgotten roads. I soon discovered that someone in the cycle path corporation had overstocked on signs indicating that Corbie was "20 kilometers away," and for the longest time, no matter how hard I pedaled, I was no closer to my destination than I had been fifteen minutes earlier. Eventually the numbers on the distance markers began to decrease, although never quite fast enough to bring comfort to my burning legs. I was riding through landscape that was fought over in summer 1918, after the German spring offensive pushed the Allies back to a line that ran from Corbie to just outside Amiens; the eight-mile gain around the earlier Somme offensive, just like the five hundred thousand lives that it cost to procure, was wiped out.

By the time the Australians made their stand outside Corbie, the war had ended for many of those mentioned in this book, although T. E. Lawrence was chasing the Turks out of Palestine well into autumn 1918. By that point Churchill was a cabinet member back in London, angling to play a role in the peace conference (that was denied) and soldiers such as Graves and Sassoon were recovering from their wounds, although still in uniform.

Sassoon was in London on Armistice Day, having dinner with the soldier whom he dismissed as someone "who spent the war supplying the liquor board," and within hours of the war's end, Sassoon—like so many of his contemporaries in uniform, including Hitler himself—had become intolerant of anyone who had not spent the war at the sharp end. Sassoon writes of his dinner companion: "In 1918…I had I no tolerance for those who fought their country's battles from arm-chairs." In the late 1920s, he wrote: "…the man who had really endured the War at its worst was everlastingly differentiated from everyone except his fellow soldiers," which might explain why men as different as Lawrence, Sassoon, Graves, and Churchill would find solace in each other's company after the war. They were trying to make sense of something that defied comprehension—a war that exchanged five hundred thousand lives for eight miles of northern France that, two years later, was ceded to the Germans. Even Erskine Childers, who traded his loyalties toward England for similar ties with Irish Republicanism, was trying to process some aspect of the war that made no sense to him.

FRIENDS OF A KIND

Had **Wilfred Owen** never been sent in 1916 to Craiglockhart hospital outside Edinburgh for his unsteady nerves (in World War II it was called "battle fatigue"), he never would have met Siegfried Sassoon, another patient, or Robert Graves, who came there to visit his friend Sassoon. (It was Sassoon who arranged for Owen's poetry to be published after the war.) Owen died just a few days before the 1918 armistice in a meaningless attack along the Sambre-Oise Canal in northeastern France.

Section X

WILFRED OWEN'S LONG ROAD

Coming of Age Near Liverpool

WITHOUT DETOURING TO Villers-Bretonneux and the Australian War Memorial, I caught a train to Paris and back home to Geneva, thinking that in a few months' time I would return with the bicycle to Amiens, so that I could continue the journey east in the general direction of Ors, on the Sambre-Oise Canal, where Wilfred Owen—friend to both Sassoon and Graves—was killed on almost the last day of the war. In fact, his mother received his death notice by telegram on November 11, 1918 and presumably had it at hand when the church bells pealed the armistice at 11 a.m.

Before I could repack my saddlebags, the Covid pandemic returned in force, and with it went my ability to search for the wartime footsteps of Wilfred Owen. Instead, I spent more of the lockdown contenting myself with armchair travels, which I confess I found satisfying. Many evenings in front of the fireplace I unfolded my piles of road maps and propped open my books, and, in the quiet of the living room, I would plot my Wilfred Owen wanderings, mostly the trail of his fateful last march across northern France to his rendezvous with death on the banks of the Sambre-Oise Canal (the same stretch of water on which Robert Louis Stevenson paddled to write his amusing narrative, *An Inland Voyage*, about a continental canoe trip).

The pandemic lull did, however, give me time to order from Abe Books an out-of-print Wilfred Owen biography by Jon Stallworthy, which seemed to take months to reach me. With the book, *Wilfred Owen*, which was published in 1974 when some members of Owen's immediate family were still alive, I was able to trace his childhood across the English

Midlands. His father worked as a station master for the railways, and for a while, when Owen was young, the family lived in Birkenhead (a section of Liverpool). Later they moved to Shrewsbury in the West Midlands, and online it is possible to download a walking tour of the landmarks in Owen's young life ("Now you can walk in the footsteps of the Shropshire war poet…"). But I had to wait for the all-clear whistle before I could return to Britain.

WILFRED OWEN

Owen's Childhood: *Woodside, Birkenhead, Shrewsbury*

WITH MY BICYCLE in tow, I finally made it to Birkenhead and Shrewsbury and saw where Owen spent his formative years. The station in Woodside, on the River Mersey across from Liverpool, is long gone, replaced by a parking lot and what looked like on-ramps for the ferry. When Wilfred's father Tom was working at the Woodside train station, the family lived in the residential section of Birkenhead, which is several miles southwest of the ferry landing.

I got there on my bicycle to find a section of terrace houses—some well tended, others less so—that formed a grid along the side of a hill. The house at 7 Elm Grove had a round, blue historic plaque indicating that Owen had lived there from 1900 to 1903. Then on Whitestone Lane I found what was once called the Birkenhead Institute—Owen's grammar school—where he got his early education, although his training as a poet came from his mother and from his own determination to be a writer.

I felt more at home with the Owens when I took the train down the line across a corner of Wales and arrived in Shrewsbury, where Owen's father managed the imposing train station, the façade of which was bathed in illuminated, colored lights. I had no idea that Shrewsbury was so elegant, as some of the nearby cities and towns are remnants of the coal-mining era.

The GPS navigation system on my phone, however, was less amendable to tracing some of Owen's footsteps around the town. I plugged in some of his waypoints, notably the family house they called "Mahim," and all I got back was a series of officious instructions to "do a u-turn" and to "head southwest." Eventually I tired of online officialdom and pulled out a printed copy of the walking tour, and with that propped on my bicycle handlebars I rode off in the direction of the Shrewsbury Abbey, where Owen is mentioned inside on a roll-of-honor plaque and remembered outside with a sculpture that represents a fragment of a World War I pontoon bridge.

It was dark by the time I rolled up to the beautiful abbey, and the front doors were locked. I did find "Symmetry"—the Owen memorial sculpture in the abbey's gardens—and by turning on my phone's flashlight I could read the dedication, which is a line from Owen's poem "Strange Meeting," which reads: "I am the enemy you killed."

Continuing in the darkness, I managed to find "Mahim" (the name comes from India, where Owen's father was stationed before he had a family). The house is located on what is now a busy road, and the current owners stared at me through a front window when I stopped on my bicycle to take a picture. Around the corner I found the house where Owen's grandfather had encouraged young Wilfred to plant a garden. Then I headed back to the station along the River Severn, which, dappled with nearby streetlights, had the elegance of a Venetian canal.

WILFRED OWEN

The Making of the Modern Poet

IT WAS IN his teens, as Owen worked his way through secondary school (he never went to university; his family could not afford it for him), that he found himself more and more drawn to poetry, particularly the Romantics (Wordsworth, Shelley, and Keats). On one trip, he went in search of a house where Keats had briefly lived, which prompted him to write (only a fragment remains):

> *There is a set of men today who deal*
> *– Or think they deal – with spirits of the past.*

On another excursion, he rode his bicycle to a cottage where Shelley had lived, writing to a friend:

> …that Shelley lived at a cottage within easy cycling distance from here. And I was very surprised (tho 'really I don't know why) to find that he used to 'visit the sick in their beds; kept a regular list of the industrious poor whom he assisted to make up their accounts;' and for a time walked the hospitals in order to be more useful to the poor he visited! I knew the lives of men who produced such marvellous verse could not be otherwise than lovely, and I am being confirmed in this continually.

The influences, however, that most shaped his poetry were his mother and a succession of teachers and vicars who encouraged the boy to express his intense feelings in verse. Stallworthy writes of one encounter during his schooling:

> It is significant that, no matter what the subject of his letters, he cannot keep his mind off poetry for more than a few lines at a time. In June, his botany lecturer at University College discovered his literary interests and sent him on to the Head of the English Department, Miss Edith Morley, who found him an 'unhappy

adolescent, suffering badly from lack of understanding… and in need of encouragement and praise'. These she gave him, together with some useful advice about the technicalities of poetry, and at her recommendation he read Ruskin and Milton on his free afternoons and evenings in the gloomy vicarage.

Reading Owen's poetry today, I find a lot of it to be Victorian in tone and language, a cathedral of images and ideas that evoke the soaring ideology and sentimentality of England in the prewar years. Later on, when he's describing the desperation and horrors of trench warfare, his poems lose their Romantic superstructure and become, as it were, more spare and modern. His famous poem, "Dulce et Decorum Est," is about a gas attack on the Western Front, far from the church yards and glades of his idyllic childhood in the West Country. It reads:

> *If in some smothering dreams, you too could pace*
> *Behind the wagon that we flung him in,*
> *And watch the white eyes writhing in his face,*
> *His hanging face, like a devil's sick of sin;*
> *If you could hear, at every jolt, the blood*
> *Come gargling from the froth-corrupted lungs,*
> *Obscene as cancer, bitter as the cud*
> *Of vile, incurable sores on innocent tongues,—*
> *My friend, you would not tell with such high zest*
> *To children ardent for some desperate glory,*
> *The old Lie:* Dulce et decorum est
> Pro patria mori.

Owen Enlists

FOR WILFRED OWEN, the interlude between his childhood and the war was a series of trips he made to France and Bordeaux, where he studied, worked as a tutor, acquired the French language, stayed with local families, and heard the news out of a "clear blue sky" in summer 1914 that Europe was on the precipice of war. Owen might have passed a tranquil life as a schoolteacher or church warden, writing poetry on the side and making the occasional trip to France. Instead he was swept into the war fever, even in a remote corner of France. As he wrote to a friend:

> I feel shamefully 'out of it' here, passing my time reading the Newspapers in an armchair in a shady garden. Numbers of Bordeaux ladies are going to the Armies as Nurses. The only thing I could do, so Madame Léger says, would be to serve as a stretcher-bearer, on the battlefield. After all my years of playing soldiers, and then reading History, I have almost a mania to be in the East, to see fighting, to serve. For I like to think this is the last War of the World.

Despite his impatience for action, Owen only enlisted in October 1915, when he enrolled in the Artists' Rifles Officers' Training Corps. Once he earned his commission he was assigned as a subaltern in the Manchester Regiment. In John Lewis-Stempel's *Six Weeks: The Short and Gallant Life of the British Officer in the First World War*, there is a passage quoting Owen on his duties in the unit:

> The sub. has a stiffish day's work: has to do the 'Third' Physical Training (i.e. most strenuous) at 6.15, carries pack on parade & march, and has a good deal of responsibility, writing, and ceremonial to fetter him. I had the misfortune to walk down the road to some Camp Shops when the men were 'at large': and had to take millions of salutes… My most irksome duty is acting Taskmaster while the tired fellows dig: the most pleasant is marching home over the wild country at the

head of my platoon, with a flourish of trumpets, and an everlasting roll of drums.

Owen was commissioned an officer in June 1916 and sent to France toward the end of the year. He missed the first day of the Somme offensive, but his Manchester regiment saw action up and down the British lines, often outside the town of Saint-Quentin, with its soaring cathedral often visible on the horizon, as if a vision of eternity. Sometimes his unit was engaged in heavy fighting; at others it was away from the front, but between the weather (often miserable) and the endless killing, Owen saw war at the sharp end. In winter 1917 he wrote home:

> We stuck to our line 4 days (and 4 nights) without relief, in the open, and in the snow. Not an hour passed without a shell amongst us. I never went off to sleep for those days, because the others were far more fagged after several days of fighting than I fresh from bed. We lay in wet snow. I kept alive on brandy, the fear of death, and the glorious prospect of the cathedral Town [Saint-Quentin] just below us, glittering with the morning. With glasses I could easily make out the general architecture of the cathedral: so I have told you how near we have got.

In spring 1917, having spent about four months in and out of the front lines, Owen began to suffer from the strain of combat. Falling into a well, he suffered a concussion, and later, according to one of his senior officers, was "acting strangely." By then he had exceeded the six weeks that were, according to Lewis-Stempel and others, the useful expectancy of a junior officer's service on the Western Front. (Of going on the attack Owen wrote: "The sensations of going over the top are about as exhilarating as those dreams of falling over a precipice, when you see the rocks at the bottom surging up to you. I woke up without being squashed. Some didn't. There was an extraordinary exultation in the act of slowly walking forward, showing ourselves openly.") Owen was pulled from the lines and later sent to Craiglockhart, where Siegfried Sassoon was already a patient so that the doctors could treat his anti-war sentiments and prose as a variation on shell shock.

When Britons spoke of the Lost Generation that vanished into the fiery mists of the Somme battlefields in summer 1916, they might well have had in mind the death there of **Raymond Asquith**, an officer who was killed leading his men along the road from Ginchy to Lesbœfs. Asquith was known publicly as the son of the British prime minister, Herbert Asquith, but on his own he had many accomplishments and admirers in the worlds of law, letters, and politics. The marker on Guillemont Road in France for Lieutenant Asquith reads: "Small time but in that small most greatly lived this Star of England."

Section XI

RAYMOND ASQUITH: FRIEND TO MANY

Echoes of War in Amiens Cathedral

BY THE TIME I returned with my bicycle to Amiens, France, I had thoroughly rehearsed my route in Wilfred Owen's last footsteps. The endpaper map in Stallworthy's *Owen* biography shows the villages through which the Manchester Regiment advanced in 1918 toward the Sambre-Oise Canal, but I decided on a slightly more circuitous route toward Ors, so I could ride through the Somme valley and see some things that I had missed on my earlier trips.

For starters, I wanted to go into the Amiens cathedral and find the plaque inside erected in memory of Raymond Asquith. I also wanted to get another look at the Bois Français above Fricourt and Mametz Wood, and find the exact spot where Sassoon watched "the first day on the Somme." Then I would spend my first night in the war town of Péronne, which was fought over for four years from 1914 to 1918 and which in its old castle ramparts has an important World War I museum. After that I would continue the Owen march—in my case it was a bike ride—to the northeast and his destiny.

The problem with my best-laid plans was that I had not counted on my train arriving in Amiens four hours late. If I wanted to see all the little places that I had highlighted on my Picardie map (during all the months of the shutdown), I had no choice but to ride with some determination for the thirty-five miles to Péronne (where I had booked a hotel). I kept measuring distances on the map with my thumb and forefinger, trying to will myself there in daylight. In the end I decided to stick to my designed route, knowing that it would probably get dark around 8:00 p.m. After that, I decided to ride either on roads that had wide shoulders or on narrow lanes. I didn't want to come this far and yet again feel I was missing out; the pandemic had gone on too long.

I had explicit directions from Raymond Asquith's grandson and namesake (my friend) for locating the plaque in the Amiens Cathedral, and I found it easily. The interior of the soaring and beautiful cathedral has a number of war memorials and plaques, and after inspecting one for a regiment of American engineers and another for a New Zealand division (both of which defended Amiens in its many hours of darkness), I found the Asquith plaque right where his grandson said I would. It is beautifully carved and mounted, and has inscriptions in French and Latin, which is fitting as Raymond Asquith was heavily immersed in the classical world. In Latin, the inscription reads:

> O ORIENS SPLENDOR LUCIS ÆTERNI ET
> SOL JUSTITIAE VENI ET ILLUMINA
> SEDENTES IN TENEBRIS ET UMBRA MORTIS.

With the help of my high school Latin teacher and lifelong friend, Peggy Brucia, I read it to mean:

> O dawn of the east, brightness of light eternal, and sun
> of justice: come, and enlighten those who sit in darkness
> and in the shadow of death.

The plaque notes that Asquith was killed on September 15, 1916 outside the village of Guinchy (now spelled Ginchy) but not that, after being fatally wounded in the chest, he lit a cigarette to give a signal to the men of his company that he would be fine and was, in any case, insouciant "in the shadow of death."

In a *Six Weeks* chapter on the boundless courage of young British officers in the Great War, Lewis-Stempel uses Asquith as just one example to describe the many ways that platoon and company commanders inspired their troops, even in death. He writes:

> Rankers in the Army machine frequently felt
> themselves to be automata, or cogs, to be moved by the
> dictat of an unseen and careless hand on high. Robert
> Graves wrote that he and Sassoon believed that 'being
> commanded by someone whom they [rankers] could

count as a friend—someone who protected them…
from the grosser indignities of the military system…
made all the difference in the world'. It did. And there
were thousands of thoughtful, brave, and compassionate
junior officers like Graves and Sassoon…

Before pedaling away from Amiens, I tracked down the Belfort Hotel, now the Carlton, which is near the railway station and is where Robert Graves and Siegfried Sassoon would sometimes, when on leave, go for a drink or a meal. Not far from the hotel, I stopped in front of the Comedie de Picardie, which was another restaurant, the Godbert, during the war years. Now it looks like an elegant supper club, with music, dance, and theater on the program. I was a little sorry that my delayed train ruled out the option of passing an evening or two in the audience.

My tight schedule also eliminated the chance of a stop at the Maison de Jules Vernes, another museum in Amiens. I love Verne's books, especially *Around the World in Eighty Days*, and would have taken great pleasure in seeing the writing table where he imagined the existence of my cultural hero, Mr. Phileas Fogg ("It's really useful to travel, if you want to see new things…"). My only consolation is that Fogg himself, on a schedule as fixed as mine, would not have hesitated to pass up the house of his creator ("…Mr Fogg had no time to lose…").

FRIENDS OF A KIND

The British High Command at Château Querrieu

FROM AMIENS I was headed toward Château Querrieu, where the British commanders leading the attack on the Somme had their headquarters. As I was stressed about being so far behind schedule, I switched on my phone's cellular data and pointed the navigation system in the direction of Querrieu. For the first kilometer or two, everything went according to the satellite plan. I was off the main highway to Albert, with its trucks and speeding cars, and I was riding through some of the small villages on the outskirts of Amiens.

The problems developed when after a stretch on D1, the navigational gods instructed me to turn left on an agricultural road. I obeyed and after three hundred meters or so I was on a path strewn with rocks and potholes. Maybe if I had been riding a mountain bike with suspension I would not have minded, but here I was on a Brompton folding bike with small wheels and saddlebags, closer to being a circus performer than a rider setting out to shred some single-track.

Fearing a flat tire among the sharp stones, I pushed the bicycle for about a mile through the fields until I found another agricultural road with fewer death traps. That led nowhere, although it prompted an outpouring of "head northeast…head northeast" from the GPS's disembodied voice. Finally I came out of the fields, only to find myself back among the trucks. It was unnerving, but in a short while the trucks went left to an autoroute and I continued straight into Querrieu, where I found the château at the bottom of the village. I had anticipated turrets and drawbridges, but the château resembled an English manor house at the end of a long, circular, stone drive shaded with trees.

I was hoping for a tour of the rooms used by the British high command. In particular, I was interested in a dinner of general officers that preceded the July 1, 1916 offensive, as in my reading it epitomized the ignorance of "the donkeys" (i.e., the British command under Douglas Haig) regarding the conditions in the trenches and what tactics might break the German lines.

I leaned my bicycle against a hedge and approached two women sitting at a small table by the front door, asking if I could visit the drawing rooms used by General Rawlinson (he was the immediate Somme commander under Haig). Unfortunately, the women explained, this week the château was having an exhibition of Indonesian marionettes and there were no public tours. "Can I buy a ticket for the puppet show?" I asked. Yes, that was possible, they said. Even better, when I parted with €8, one then went inside to summon "the comtesse d'Alcantara de Querrieu" to show me around the marionette exhibition.

The comtesse—Madame Yola d'Alcantara—greeted me kindly at the front door, showed me around the marionette collection (those of a local doctor who traveled often in the East), and explained that her family had owned the château for many centuries. According to the comtesse, Rawlinson's office was in the salon on the ground floor, and dinners would have been served in an adjoining dining room. She was unfamiliar with the dinner that preceded the attack on the Somme but showed me what looked like family pictures of Haig, Rawlinson, and others standing in front of the château in their riding habits and hats.

Prior to World War I, generals maintained a physical attachment to their troops and a presence on the battlefields. After industrial warfare broke out in 1914, commanders-in-chief, such as Sir Douglas Haig, became chief executive officers of killing and directed the fighting from corporate suites, such as the ground floor salon at Château Querrieu, which was about twelve miles behind the front lines on the Somme. (During World War II, the distance between generals and their troops became that much wider, so that for much of the Pacific war Douglas MacArthur was in his command post in Melbourne, Australia, while his men were fighting thousands of miles away, in places like New Britain.) Even the relatively short distance between Querrieu and the Somme meant that the high command had no clue what they were ordering their men to endure.

The German defense lines on the Somme had vast subterranean roots that allowed the defenders to survive the artillery bombardments on the first day and emerge from their holes in time to shoot down the attacking Allied troops in waves. In his history *To End All Wars: A Story of Loyalty and Rebellion, 1914-1918*, Adam Hochschild writes: "Of the 120,000 British troops who went into battle on July 1, 1916, more than 57,000 were dead or wounded before the day was over—nearly two casualties for every yard of the front. Nineteen thousand were killed, most of them within the attack's first disastrous hour, and some 2,000 more who were badly wounded would die in hospitals later." He continues: "On the second day of the battle, Haig was told that the casualties had been over 40,000 so far—a gross underestimate but still an appalling figure. 'This cannot be considered severe,' he wrote in his diary, 'in view of the numbers engaged, and the length of front attacked.'" Hochschild notes that, "in his dispatches, Haig began to redefine success: 'breakthrough' was gone; taking a toll on the Germans in a 'wearing out fight' became the new catch phrase." He concludes: "…when autumn rains and mud brought combat to a halt, troops under British command had suffered almost 500,000 casualties on the Somme front, including at least 125,000 deaths. French soldiers, who also took part in the battle, had lost 200,000 dead and wounded. The Allies had gained roughly seven square miles of ground."

RAYMOND ASQUITH

The Red Baron Falls to Earth

IT WAS GETTING close to 5:00 p.m. when I biked away from the grounds of Château Querrieu and headed up and down some long hills in the direction of Corbie, aiming for Bray-sur-Somme. I chose this route as I would ride past the field where the Red Baron (the German ace Manfred von Richthofen) died when his plane was shot down, and I would see another Australian war memorial—that of its Third Division, which defended Amiens from attacking Germans and later forced them back across the Hindenburg Line.

Manfred von Richthofen, aka the Red Baron, was a larger-than-life figure in the Great War. He was a German aristocrat from Breslau and began the war as a cavalry officer. He had a profound grasp of aerial tactics and formations, as well as for showmanship. (Richthofen painted his aircraft a bright red. His colorful squadron was the first to be known as "The Flying Circus.") He is credited with shooting down eighty enemy planes, and his fame drew attention to the aerial war, even if its contribution to the outcome was negligible. Haig, the British commander, never flew during the war, and the American commander General John Pershing didn't understand the connection between ground forces and air power. In *Over There: The United States in the Great War, 1917-1918*, Byron Farwell writes:

> At its peak, just before the Armistice, the United States had only forty-five squadrons at the front, and of its 740 flyable planes—ten percent of the Allied air strength—only twelve were American made.

Most likely it was an Australian anti-aircraft gun that brought down the Red Baron, by shooting him through the chest, after which his plane crashed along the Corbie-Bray road. (Souvenir hunters, even then, carried off the fragments.) The spot, where now there is a roadside marker, draws a number of visitors each year, as Richthofen's wartime record has created a cult following that gathers on the ground in France and at conferences in Germany.

Down the road I found the memorial to the Third Australian Division, which in spring 1918 held off the Germans on this expansive, sloping ridge line near the village of Sailly-le-Sec. On the obelisk was a list of the major battles fought by the division during its two years in Europe:

> Messines 1917 - The Windmill - 3rd Battle of Ypres - Broodseinde - Passchendaele - Morlancourt - Treux Hamel - 8th August - Proyant - Suzanne - Bray-sur-Somme - Curlu - Clery-sur-Somme - Bouchavesnes - Roisel - Hindenburg Line

Another plaque nearby stated that after 1917 the Third Division "took part in all major Australian operations on the Western Front." On the day I stopped and walked around the memorial, the news was dominated by Australia's cancellation of a multibillion-dollar submarine contract signed with the French government and corporations. The gist of the newscasts and talk shows on French television was that Australia was a faithless, ungrateful nation that had never done anything for France.

RAYMOND ASQUITH

Sassoon's War Opera Box: *Bois Français above the Somme*

IT WAS CLOSE to 6:30 p.m. by the time I rolled into Bray-sur-Somme. Mercifully the last long hill was a descent. I was running low on food and water. For a moment I thought of bailing on the ride, given the approaching darkness, and hiring a taxi or an Uber (were they even out here?) to drive me the last twenty kilometers to Péronne. But I revived myself with a beer from an estaminet and my last sandwich. Then I set off in the direction of the Bois Français, Ginchy, and Péronne, persuading myself that I would make it.

For fifteen minutes or so I rode steadily up a long incline on the road that I am sure Sassoon and Graves took when they marched into their lines for the jump-off on July 1, 1916. In his 1917 book, *The Old Front Line*, the future poet laureate John Masefield described the landscape of the Somme and this particular route: "Those roads then were indeed paths of glory leading to the grave."

As it was close to dinnertime in France, there was almost no traffic, but halfway up the hill there was a barrier blocking cars from going any farther. I stood by the traffic gate for a while but then went around it with my bicycle and continued pedaling up the road. Generally, cyclists can go where banned drivers cannot. Here the blockage was for work being done on a roundabout and it was easy to navigate on two wheels.

On my last visit to Fricourt I had looked up at the woods and guessed about where Sassoon had watched the attacks on July 1, 1916. This time, I was coming up from behind the Bois Français and along the way passing several cemeteries where close friends of both Sassoon and Graves were buried.

It was near Bois Français that a fellow officer and good friend to both Graves and Sassoon, David Thomas, was killed (although it was before the July 1, 1916 offensive). Graves wrote of its effect on Sassoon: "I felt David's death worse than any other since I had been in France, but it did not anger me as it did Siegfried. He was acting transport-officer and every evening now, when he came up with the rations, went out on patrol looking for Germans to kill. I just felt empty and lost." As Sassoon himself wrote of this period: "My courage was of the cock-fighting kind. Cock-fighting is illegal in England, but in July, 1916 the man could boast that he'd killed a German in the Battle of the Somme would have been patted on the back by a bishop in a hospital ward."

In *The Man Who Shot Siegfried Sassoon*, John Hollands suggests a possible romantic attachment that Sassoon developed for the young lieutenant, "a remarkably handsome son of a Welch vicar who he had first met at Cambridge." (He writes of another of Siegfried's infatuations: "Unrequited love was no stranger to Sassoon. He had had similar experiences with David Thomas and Bobbie Hanmer…") As do other Sassoon biographers, Hollands links Thomas' death to Sassoon's thirst for revenge against the Germans. He says:

> Then tragedy struck. David Thomas was killed. A sniper's bullet hit him in the throat and he died a few hours later. Statistically, it was just another death; the sort of thing which was happening to hundreds every day, but to Sassoon and Graves the loss of their dear friend had a devastating impact. For Sassoon it was the first time the horror of war had struck home personally; far more than with his brother's death, which had been cushioned by its remoteness. He swore revenge and straight away arranged an interview with Buffalo Bill at which he pleaded to be put back in command of Seven Platoon. Buffalo Bill was so impressed by his persistence that he agreed. As battalion commander he was reluctant to hold back anyone so desperate to see action and the truth was that Sassoon's replacement had been a disaster. He had such cold feet that he was in danger of frost-bite.

Thomas was buried in Point 110 New Military Cemetery, which in 1916 was placed behind the British lines in the Bois Français. About his burial, Sassoon wrote: "Tonight I saw his shrouded form laid in the earth—Robert Graves beside me with his white whimsical face twisted and grieving. Once we could not hear the solemn words for the noise of a machine-gun along the line; and when all was finished a canister fell a hundred yards away and burst with a crash. So Tommy left us, a gentle soldier, perfect and without stain. And so he will remain in my heart, fresh and happy and brave."

Now the cemetery is a stone rectangle seemingly adrift in the expansive field that ascends the plain to the woods. Actually there are two cemeteries with the coordinates of Point 110, one "new" and the other "old," although I suspect they date to the same period of the fighting (March 1916).

I could have parked my bicycle in the fields and walked up the stone and dirt path to the Point 110 Cemetery, but by my calculations it might have taken me almost forty-five minutes to walk up the hillside. Instead I took distant pictures of the cemeteries—they might have been afloat in the neatly cropped fields—and continued down this road to the corner of the Bois Français where Sassoon sat in horror on the first day of the Somme.

From his biographer Max Egremont, we know that on July 1, 1916 Sassoon, whose battalion was in reserve, was sitting on what was called Crawley Point, now just open field to the west of the road on which I was riding. Egremont says Sassoon was "eating oranges...saw a lark...heard the cry of birds as the explosions died out" and that Sassoon imagined he was seeing "a sunlit picture of hell."

Online, it's possible to view a facsimile of Sassoon's diary for that morning, in which he writes:

> We had breakfast at 6—the morning is brilliantly fine—after a mist early. Since 6:30 there has been hell let loose. The air vibrates with the incessant din—the whole earth shakes and rocks and throbs. It is one continuous roar—machine guns tap and rattle—bullets whistling over our head—small fry quite outdone by the gangs of hooligan-shells that dash over to reach the German lines with their demolition parties....
>
> Inferno—inferno—bang smash!!

The handwritten diary entry looks like the text of a postcard—as perhaps it was, addressed to future generations.

FRIENDS OF A KIND

The Death of Raymond Asquith

THE ROADWORK BEING done around Fricourt might well have obliterated—I could not really judge—what Graves and Sassoon would have called Wing Corner, a fatal intersection in the offensive on the first day, in which British troops attacked down the slopes from the Bois Français and took the nearby villages of Fricourt and Mametz. There were no markers along the widened D highway, and I didn't pause in the fading daylight to survey the location.

And somewhere in this vicinity, Prime Minister Herbert Asquith, out from London on a field inspection, stopped long enough to greet his son Raymond, then in the lines near Ginchy. Raymond's *Life and Letters* contains an excellent description of the meeting—the last with his father, as he would be killed eight days later. To his wife Katharine, Raymond wrote on September 7, 1916:

> ...I was called up by the Brigadier and thought at first that I must have committed some ghastly military blunder (I was commanding the Company in Sloper's absence) but was relieved to find that it was only a telegram from the corps saying "Lieut. Asquith will meet his father at cross roads K.6d at 10:45 a.m." So I vaulted into the saddle and bumped off to Fricourt where I arrived exactly at the appointed time. I waited for an hour on a very muddy road congested with troops and lorries and surrounded by barking guns. Then 2 handsome motors from G.H.Q. arrived, the P.M in one of them with 2 staff officers, and in the other Bongie, Hankey, and one or two of those moth-eaten nondescripts who hang about the corridors of Downing Street in the twilight region between the civil and domestic service.
>
> We went up to see some of the captured German dug-outs [in Fricourt I believe] and just as we were arriving at our first objective the Boches began putting over a few 4.2 shells from their field howitzer. The P.M. was not discomposed by this, but the G.H.Q. chauffeur

to whom I had handed over my horse to hold, flung the reins into the air and himself flat on his belly in the mud. It was funny enough.

The shells fell about 200 yards behind us I should think. Luckily the dug-out we were approaching was one of the best and deepest I have ever seen—as safe as the bottom of the sea, wood-lined, 3 storeys and electric light, and perfect ventilation. We were shown around by several generals who kept us there for 1/2 an hour or so to let the shelling die down, and the P.M. drove off to luncheon with the G.O.C. 4th Army [General Sir Henry Rawlinson] and I rode back to my billets.

It took me about a half hour on quieter roads to ride from Fricourt to the Guillemont Road Cemetery, where Raymond Asquith is buried. I looked up Asquith in the cemetery registry and found the following entry:

Asquith, Lieutenant, RAYMOND. 3rd Bn., Grenadier Guards. 15 September 1916. Age 37. Son of the Rt. Hon. (and former M.P.) H.H. Asquith, P.C., Prime Minister of the United Kingdom 1908-1916 (now 1st Earl of Oxford and Asquith, K.G.), and Helen his wife; husband of Katharine Asquith, of 17, Oxford Square, London, W.2. Grave Reference: I.B.3.

On his headstone, I found this often-quoted epitaph: "Small time but in that small most greatly lived this star of England." There were also some flowers around the headstone, perhaps left there on Armistice Day.

The words are from Shakespeare's *Henry V*, and they refer to the 1415 Battle of Agincourt (that took place not all that far away from the Somme). The remainder of the passage reads:

But we in it shall be remembered;
We few, we happy few, we band of brothers;
For he to-day that sheds his blood with me
Shall be my brother

Asquith was killed a few miles to the northeast, between the villages of Ginchy and Lesbœufs. He was leading an attack during the mid-September 1916 "push" that claimed another thirty thousand British lives—and accomplished little in terms of captured land. His sister, Violet Bonham Carter, wrote to a friend a week later: "He was shot through the chest and carried back to a shell-hole where there was an improvised dressing station. There they gave him morphia and he died an hour later. God bless him. How he has vindicated himself—before all those who thought him merely a scoffer—by the modest heroism with which he chose the simplest and most dangerous form of service—and having so much to keep for England gave it all to her with his life.

Where he fell was just outside Ginchy, in what is now a broad field of wind turbines. Just before jumping off, he wrote to his wife: "We move either tomorrow or the day after. Probably tomorrow. We are only allowed 50 lbs. of kit, which is a bore. It would be awful to arrive in Berlin looking a perfect scarecrow." No doubt when his father went to lunch with General Rawlinson, he heard all about how the next "push" might break the back of the German Army. Actually, the first casualty was the prime minister himself, who never recovered from his son's death and soon was out of office, replaced by David Lloyd George.

Back home, I retrieved my copy of Raymond Asquith's *Life and Letters*, which a relative, John Jolliffe, published in 1980. In his book Jolliffe includes the letter that Winston Churchill wrote to Raymond's father, the prime minister, when he learned of his son's death. Winston writes:

> He was so brave and true that nothing less than the most dangerous and intensely personal service would content him.... His was a character of singular charm and distinction—so gifted and yet so devoid of personal ambition, so critically detached from ordinary affairs yet capable of utmost will sacrifice. Altogether he seemed to above the wordy sum of things, yet so full of enjoyment of them and purpose in them... I mourn with you the cruel cutting off of this rare and precious life so dearly beloved.

What is remarkable about Churchill's letter is that he was writing to the man whose generals, directly below him in the chain of command, were issuing the orders in such blunders as the Battle of the Somme.

In 1928, Winston Churchill wrote more about the loss of his friend Raymond, although the tone is that he was claimed as if by the fate of Greek gods (not the incompetence of British generals). He wrote:

> It seemed quite easy for Raymond Asquith, when the time came, to face death and to die. When I saw him at the Front he seemed to move through the cold, squalor and peril of the winter trenches as if were above and immune from the common ills of the flesh, a being clad in polished armor, entirely undisturbed, presumably invulnerable. The War which found the measure of so many, never got to the bottom of him, and when the Grenadiers strode into the crash and thunder of the Somme, he went to his fate cool, poised, resolute, matter of fact, debonair. And well we know that his father, then bearing the supreme burden of the State, would proudly have marched at his side.

To hear Churchill recount his death is to hear that no one in the British aristocracy that ran the country ever conceived of a tactic other than "going over the bags."

A Dark Ride Toward the Hindenburg Line

BY THE TIME I had biked from the fields outside Ginchy to Lesbœufs it was dark. The narrow lane between the two villages was lined with memorials and a cemetery, but mostly what struck me was the open expanse of the land, the reason it was so fatal to advancing infantry. In Lesbœufs, just to read my maps, I had to huddle under a streetlamp, which became slightly unnerving when a watchdog on duty, behind a nearby gate, seemed to take exception to my presence.

To get me to Péronne, GPS wanted me to ride back to Ginchy, but as I hate backtracking, especially on a bicycle, I decided instead to go forward to Combles, where there was a small road that either went under or over the autoroute, one of the complications of my night ride. Then from the village of Rancourt, I figured I could thread my way south to Péronne on secondary roads, although I was getting to the point in the ride when I just wanted to get there.

I had been to Combles years before, in a car, but I remembered nothing about it. I was able to bypass Rancourt on a road cutting around to the south. That put me on D1017, which on one of my maps was suspiciously red, meaning a *route nationale*, roads I had avoided at all costs in my bicycle travel. From the turn I figured I was about nine kilometers outside Péronne, but I decided to stick to the main road, as it had streetlights and wide shoulders. And it even afforded me some night sightseeing, as in Bouchavesnes I knew there was an imposing statue of the French commander-in-chief (late in the war), Ferdinand Foch.

After a few kilometers of riding in the darkness, I found the marshal standing at attention out by the main road. What I remembered about Foch were his sour relations with the American commander, John "Black Jack" Pershing. Foch was resentful when the Americans in 1917-18 refused to divvy up their arriving troops into existing British and French formations, preferring instead to keep their men in a stand-alone army under American command. Foch had contempt for the raw Americans and soon developed the same feelings for their commander, whom he tried to have relieved, replaced, or recalled on any number of occasions.

In the Meuse-Argonne campaign at the end of the war, Foch belittled Pershing for the confused nature of his command (he could well have been right) and the slow progress of the American advance (they were up against twenty-six German divisions along a narrow front), adding coldly: "I myself only consider results." When the Armistice was signed on November 11, 1918, Foch declined to invite the Americans to the ceremony at Compiègne. Foch seemed to overlook the fact that the Americans sent several million troops to a fight that wasn't their own. Without them Foch himself might well have been on trial in Berlin as a war criminal, not guarding the road entrance to Bouchavesnes.

Section XII

WILFRED OWEN: THE LAST FOOTSTEPS

The American Cut Grass at Bellicourt

FROM PÉRONNE MY plan was to ride about forty miles to Ors, where Wilfred Owen was killed at war's end. I decided to give myself two days to see the places in between, including the American cemetery on the Somme (near Bony) and an American war memorial nearby at Bellicourt (once a strongpoint in the Hindenburg Line). According to GPS, I should have ridden from Péronne to Bony in one hour and twenty-four minutes, but in the end I needed three hours to get there. Along the way I bought a picnic lunch, and here and there—in villages such as Roisel—I stopped to read inscriptions on roadside monuments. (During the war troops from France, Britain, Germany, Canada, and Australia all came and went through Roisel.) Off a dirt road in a field near the American cemetery—GPS was back to its old tricks—I found a plaque to a New York regiment (the 107th, part of the 27th Division) that at this farm helped to crack open the Hindenburg Line on September 29-30, 1918.

Approaching the American Somme Cemetery on dirt lanes, I could see the American flag snapping in the wind from a distance of several kilometers. Although I was the only visitor present, the French guard on duty in a little hut didn't like it that I had arrived on a bicycle. Rather than let me lean it against a tree, she made me stow it in the parking lot, and then admonished me against having a picnic on the grounds. Then she stalked me as I walked among the 1,844 headstones, as if she thought I might try to sneak in a sandwich (she wasn't wrong).

The grass was immaculately cut, and all the marble was in perfect order, with soaring inscriptions and even a Purple Heart awarded to the cemetery by President Lyndon Johnson on October 10, 1965 (just as he was sending thousands of troops to Vietnam). But the cemetery offers little information on the battles fought on nearby ridges or about the larger experience of America in World War I (during which the country continued its march from republic to national security state). It felt like a ghost town.

A short ride about two miles brought me to the Bellicourt American Monument, where I had planned to eat my lunch overlooking the section of the Hindenburg Line that was attacked by two American divisions in late September 1918. But there was a sign at the entrance to the monument saying that picnics were forbidden. I tried to ignore my hunger by studying a map engraved in the stone of the memorial, which for my purposes was more useful than GPS. It showed the outline of the Hindenburg Line and the location of landmarks that interested me, such as the villages of Riqueval and Nauroy. Robert Graves wrote of similar places: "We would never break the German line by hammering at it. So far our losses were heavier than the Germans'."

Only in the Bellicourt British Cemetery 1917-1919 did I find a bench that was sheltered from the wind and on which I could spread out my picnic, which was, by bicycle standards, a lavish buffet of cold salmon, tomatoes, bread, cheese, wine, and dessert. Unlike the Americans, the British rarely centralized their graveyards. Their war dead are buried in hundreds of small plots that are scattered across northern France, as if part of an earthly constellation of headstones and roses. Nor do the British cemeteries have guards or posted rules. They feel like English parks. While eating, I was reminded of the landscapes around Oxford and Cambridge, which must have been a comfort to the families of the English war dead who made the pilgrimage to the Western Front after the war to see where their sons, brothers, or fathers were buried.

Just to the south of Bellicourt, I found Riqueval and the bridge over the Saint-Quentin Canal, which a company from the 1/6th North Staffordshire Regiment managed to capture intact. The Napoleonic-era canal had been wired into the Hindenburg Line by the Germans, with tunnels leading to the surrounding hillside woods, and it was a miracle that one company was able to capture and hold such an important bridge, allowing the British to funnel men and materiel across an otherwise impregnable strongpoint of the Hindenburg line.

I rode further south to Bellenglise, where I had read there was a monument for the 4th Australian Division. Riding to Bellenglise was easy, but getting to the monument proved harder, as it was located up a long dirt track in fields out of town, and the only way I could get up to what is called Les Chaudriès was to push the bicycle through mud. Trudging along, I kept thinking I would give up and take a picture of the obelisk from the surrounding fields. But I have a friend in Australia whose grandfather fought in one these divisions, and I didn't want him to think I had given up. When I got to the top, I found its roll call from 1916-18 inscribed on the monument. It read:

> Somme - Pozières - Bullecourt - Messines - Ypres - Menin Road - Polygon Wood - Passechendaele - Arras - Ancre - Villers-Bretonneux - Hamel- Amiens - Albert - Hindenburg Line - Epehy

In other words, some of the worst battles of the war, or in history.

 I had booked a room for the night in a Gîtes de France (a farmhouse room) located near Beaurevoir, and decided, yet again, to dodge main roads to get there. I wanted to ride through some of the villages through which Owen had marched and fought in October 1918, on his way to the Sambre-Oise Canal. As best as I could figure, from the endpaper map in John Stallworthy's biography, he would have passed close to the Australian monument in Bellenglise and then fought his way through Nauroy, Joncourt, Bohain-en-Vermandois, and Busigny before coming to Le Cateau and the canal. Mercifully, this part of the ride, once I was up and over the ridges of the Hindenburg Line, was largely absent of cars and relatively flat, and I had a breeze at my back.

WILFRED OWEN

Joncourt: *Owen's Military Cross*

IT WAS IN early October 1918, near the village of Joncourt that Wilfred Owen won his Military Cross and where, had there been some kind of cosmic justice, his war should have ended.

Having come across the Saint-Quentin Canal and through the village of Bellenglise, Owen's company was thrown into the lines between Magny-la-Fosse and Joncourt, along the road on which I was riding. When the company captain was wounded, Owen assumed command, and during the fighting he captured a German machine gun and made prisoners of its crew. That night he wrote to his mother:

> I lost all of my earthly faculties, and fought like an angel.
> If I started into detail of our engagement I should disturb the censor and my own Rest.
> You will guess what has happened when I say I am now Commanding the Company, and in the line had a boy lance-corporal as my Sergeant-Major.
> With this corporal who stuck to me and shadowed me like your prayers I captured a German Machine Gun and scores of prisoners.
> I'll tell you exactly how another time. I only shot one man with my revolver (at about 30 yards!); The rest I took with a smile. The same thing happened with our parties all along the line we entered.
> I have been recommended for the Military Cross; and have recommended every single N.C.O. who was with me!
> My nerves are in perfect order.
> I came out in order to help these boys—directly by leading them as an officer can; indirectly, by watching their sufferings that I may speak of them as well as a pleader can. I have done the first.
> Of whose blood yet crimson on my shoulder where his head was—and where so lately yours was—I must not write now.

FRIENDS OF A KIND

He was given the award, and the citation reads:

> For conspicuous gallantry and devotion to duty in the attack on the Fonsomme Line on 1st/2nd October 1918. On the Company Commander becoming a casualty, he assumed command and showed fine leadership and resisted a heavy counter-attack. He personally manipulated a captured enemy machine gun in an isolated position and inflicted considerable losses on the enemy. Throughout he behaved most gallantly.

After the battle he wrote in a letter to Siegfried Sassoon:

> It is a strange truth: that your *Counter-Attack* [the poem] frightened me much more than the real one: though the boy by my side, shot through the head, lay on top of me, soaking my shoulder, for half an hour.

Joncourt today is a prim and proper French village. I turned left at the intersection and shortly found myself in front of the town hall, where I was surprised to find a plaque in Owen's honor on the façade, put up eighty years after the fighting. It reads:

> En Homage à
> Wilfred Owen et aux
> 2eme Manchester 15eme et
> 16eme Lancashire
> 1er Octobre 1918 - 4 Octobre 1998

After Owen and his cohorts cleared the town of Germans, it became the headquarters of the advancing American 27th Division. One can still see, painted on the town hall's bricks, the words:

> Rear Echelon
> Amer. Div.
> Headquarters

Owen's unit was briefly pulled from the lines and returned to Hancourt, to the west of Bellenglise, and it was from there that he wrote more to his mother about his Military Cross and to Sassoon. And it was in reserve in Hancourt that he would have had the last chance to look over some of his poems about the fighting.

Ironically, in his lifetime Owen published only four poems. His fame as one of the great war poets is posthumous. It was only because of Sassoon and others that his great works, including "Spring Offensive" and "Dulce et Decorum Est," came to light. In *Six Weeks*, Lewis-Stempel writes about the composition of so much prose and poetry on the front lines:

> Tempting though the picture is of a subaltern composing poetry by the light of a guttering candle in a dug-out, most of the soldier poets composed their verse in billets or on leave. The reason was obvious: 'One cannot be a good soldier and a good poet at the same time', wrote Lieutenant Sassoon in his diary in 1918. 'Soldiery depends on a multitude of small details; one must not miss any of the details.' Tolkien was more blunt still: 'You might scribble something on the back of an envelope and shove it in your back pocket, but that's all. You couldn't write… You'd be crouching down among flies and filth.'

Nevertheless, Owen's biographer, Stallworthy, writes: "He came to the War with his imagination in large measure conditioned and prepared to receive and record the experience of the trenches." Or as Owen wrote to his mother from Joncourt: "that I may speak of them as well as a pleader can…"

FRIENDS OF A KIND

Beaurevoir to the Maison Forestière Owen

MY FARMHOUSE ROOM in Beaurevoir turned out to be an elegant self-contained apartment in one of the outbuildings, although there was neither food nor an ample kitchen on the premises. I roused my tired legs and biked about two miles to a small supermarket, and bought what felt like an airline dinner that I could cook in the microwave. It was good, as was the supermarket's house wine.

Over dinner I plotted my course for the next day. Ors was about thirty-five kilometers away from where I was staying. I wanted to see more of the villages through which Owen had marched, so I decided to head for Montbrehain (I knew the name from an Australian war memorial) and from there ride along a succession of smaller roads to Bohain, Busigny, and St. Souplet, all of which I had highlighted on my Owen endpaper map.

Montbrehain is one of those battles in World War I that few have ever heard about but which still cost some four hundred casualties, and among the dead were a number of officers who were leading the attacks. The British and Australians were involved in the assault, storming a well-fortified trench network that wove inside and out of the village. No traces remain of the fighting. I found a few war memorials in the town center, but they were for French World War I dead rather than the 2nd Australian Division that took Montbrehain, although outside the village are several Commonwealth cemeteries. It was one of the last actions that the Australians fought on the Western Front. An official Australian history notes how unnecessary the action was: "It is difficult to feel that it was wisely undertaken; it seemed, rather, devised to make some use of these troops before withdrawing them in accordance with the Prime Minister's demand." The same might be said of Owen's fatal advance on the Sambre-Oise Canal.

Signs and a statue in Bohain-en-Vermandois informed me that the French painter Henri Matisse was born and grew up nearby. Owen passed through the town and through Busigny, which is just up the road, on October 18. He then "went into the line" at St. Souplet, a village that is on a secondary road to Le Cateau. Nearly all the towns I rode through had memorials or military cemeteries.

Le Cateau has a substantial town centre (and a Matisse museum), and the tourist office, with which I had been corresponding, is located in the main square. Leaning my bicycle inside the entrance, I went in to see if Madame Angélique Labiouse (*conseillère en séjour*, aka "vacation advisor") might by chance be on duty that morning. I walked in the office and there she was, seated behind a desk, as if waiting for my arrival. We chatted about Owen, and his "last night" at what is now called the Maison Forestière Owen, a memorial to the poet. Again, as she had in her emails, Madame Labiouse explained to me (adding in a lot of "*désolés*") that the house was closed to visitors because of renovations. As a consolation she gave me a brochure, "In the footsteps of Wilfred Owen: A walking guide," and wished me well as I headed toward the canal.

It was about a five-mile ride to the Owen house, so before setting out I went to a *traiteur* in town and stocked up on items for my picnic lunch. The woman behind the counter of the elegant shop loved the story of my ride from Beaurevoir and Péronne, and she insisted I try this and that from her prepared foods (including some Mexican chicken legs), all of which she had prepared that morning (and now reheated). Now I began to wonder if the "Bois l'Evêque" Forest would have any picnic tables.

Between Le Cateau and the Maison Forestière Owen there were several daunting hills, but I made it to the top each time, and finally found the memorial house on the edge of a thick *domaniale* forest. When the forester's house was transformed from a farmhouse into a "commemorative space," it was painted white and surrounded with swirling ramps (a bit like New York's Guggenheim Museum, although on a much smaller scale), so it's impossible to miss from the road. The English artist Simon Patterson oversaw the transfiguration. One review of the finished work noted:

> Working with French architect Jean-Christophe Denise, he gutted the decrepit house to create one double height room and rendered the whole building white. A white circular walkway, engraved with extracts from Owen's final letter, connects the house to the cellar. From the road, the house looks like an artwork, its form loaded with symbolism. 'The roof resembles an open book; the white echoes the bleached bones of a skeleton,' says Patterson.

In the nearby parking lot were three men who were setting up for a road race the next day. As I watched, one of the men carried a box and headed into the cellar, which I knew was where Owen had spent his last night. I followed along.

Unlike the rest of the house, the cellar is a sacred space and unchanged from 1918, although I did notice that the race committee was using it to store some of their sound system. I explained that I was on an Owen pilgrimage, and the cellar man said that his colleague had the key to the upstairs museum. Seemingly in no time I was being let into the memorial room. As my new friend turned the key to the front door, he joked: "You know, it's empty. There's nothing in here."

In a way he was right. Except for one bench, there was no furniture in the Maison Forestière, but it was dramatic space, open to the roof, and the walls were lined with tinted glass panels that showed, in Owen's handwriting, the manuscript for "Dulce et Decorum Est," which in part might well describe Owen's own last march through Bohain and Busigny:

> *Bent double, like old beggars under sacks,*
> *Knock-kneed, coughing like hags, we cursed through sludge,*
> *Till on the haunting flares we turned our backs,*
> *And towards our distant rest began to trudge.*

The only other words at the memorial are on the walls of the circular walkway down to Owen's cellar, which is where Patterson engraved much of Owen's last letter, written to his mother. Here is the letter in full:

> I will call the place from which I'm now writing "The Smoky Cellar of the Forester's House". I write on the first sheet of the writing pad which came in the parcel yesterday. Luckily the parcel was small, as it reached me just before we moved off to the line. Thus only the paraffin was unwelcome in my pack. My servant & I ate the chocolate in the cold middle of last night, crouched under a draughty Tamboo, roofed with planks. I husband the Malted Milk for tonight, & tomorrow night. The handkerchief & socks are most opportune, as the ground is marshy, & I have a slight cold!

So thick is the smoke in this cellar that I can hardly see by a candle 12 ins. away, and so thick are the inmates that I can hardly write for pokes, nudges & jolts. On my left the Coy. Commander snores on a bench: other officers repose on wire beds behind me. At my right hand, Kellett, a delightful servant of A Coy in The Old Days radiates joy & contentment from pink cheeks and baby eyes. He laughs with a signaller, to whose left ear is glued the Receiver; but whose eyes rolling with gaiety show that he is listening with his right ear to a merry corporal, who appears at this distance away (some three feet) nothing [but] a gleam of white teeth & a wheeze of jokes.

Splashing my hand, an old soldier with a walrus moustache peels & drops potatoes into the pot. By him, Keyes, my cook, chops wood; another feeds the smoke with the damp wood.

It is a great life. I am more oblivious than alas! yourself, dear Mother, of the ghastly glimmering of the guns outside, & the hollow crashing of the shells.

There is no danger down here, or if any, it will be well over before you read these lines.

I hope you are as warm as I am; as serene in your room as I am here; and that you think of me never in bed as resignedly as I think of you always in bed. Of this I am certain you could not be visited by a band of friends half so fine as surround me here.

The next morning Owen and his band saddled up and set out to cross the canal.

FRIENDS OF A KIND

The Long Shadows Over the Sambre-Oise Canal

OUTSIDE THE MAISON FORESTIÈRE, my new race-committee friends gave me directions to the canal, pointing on my map to the spot where Owen had been killed. Then they went back to their race organizing, and I disappeared into the woods on my bicycle. In his Owen biography Stallworthy writes:

> The night of 3/4 November had been chosen for the crossing of the Sambre Canal. Rain fell until midnight and, when it stopped, a thick mist settled into the valley. Zero for the 32nd Division was set for 5:45 a.m. and, as it ticked closer, the assault troops moved into position in little irregular fields about 300 yards from the Canal. With them were men of the Royal Engineers carrying the bridges that were to cross, first, a 3 ft. deep ditch running parallel with the Canal and then, 15 yards beyond it, the Canal itself.

Amazingly, I found that the landscape between the woods and the canal felt like a corner of a foreign field that is forever England. Pushing and carrying the bicycle, I crossed over stiles, slipped down narrow paths, and walked along paddocks filled with cows and wildflowers, as if I had entered a John Constable painting. In a November rain at 5:30 a.m. it surely looked like a variation on the Underworld, but as I approached the canal the sun was finally shining on my travels and the fog had congealed into droplets that shimmered on the tall grass.

In front of the ditch and canal is the Ors British Cemetery, and logically it is where Owen should be buried, although his grave is in the Ors Communal Cemetery, back in the town. This small, hollow square, edged with a stone wall, is set beside an orchard, as Rupert Brooke wrote, "washed by the rivers, blest by suns of home." I crossed the ditch on a small metal bridge guarded by cows, and immediately I was standing on the banks of the canal, looking left or right to imagine where Owen had fallen.

WILFRED OWEN

According to several accounts that I read about the mission, the Manchesters and some other units were to support the Royal Engineers in fording the canal with pontoon bridges, and then they were to clear the Germans from the east bank of the canal where they were dug in with mortars and machine guns.

The pontoon bridges (I thought of the memorial in the garden of the Shrewsbury Abbey) never got across the water, however, as the Germans were pouring fire across the canal. Stallworthy writes:

> Through this hurricane the small figure of Wilfred Owen walked backwards and forwards between his men, patting them on the shoulder, saying 'Well done' and 'You're doing very well, my boy'. He was at the water's edge, giving a hand with some duckboards, when he was hit and killed.

A week later the Germans surrendered, and on the same day his mother received the telegram informing her of his death. What she could not have known is that he had died on a stretch of water as evocative as any in France of Shrewsbury's River Severn, along which Owen had walked and played as a boy.

An Owen Farewell

TO GET BACK into Ors I walked and pushed the bicycle along the narrow towpath for about a kilometer. Two or three times, I went past fishermen who were seated in chairs, surrounded by poles, gear, beer, and wine. Back on terra firma in the town of Ors, I ate my gourmet picnic (which included a cheese course and wine) at the canal lock under the one bridge in town. Then I set off to find the Communal Cemetery where Owen is buried.

The Communal or town cemetery is near the railroad station, behind gates and high walls. I walked among the headstones. Only at the back of the cemetery did I find a small enclosure behind a low hedge containing British headstones, including Owen's. His mother chose the inscription for his headstone:

Lieutenant
W.E.S. Owen, M.C.
Manchester Regiment
4th November 1918 Age 25

Below a simple cross is this quotation from one of Owen's poems, entitled "The End":

> *Shall life renew*
> *These bodies*
> *Of a truth*
> *All death will he annul?*

Stallworthy says that Owen's mother, with her excerpt, misunderstood his poem completely. He could have added American Civil War General William T. Sherman's remark: "I think I understand what military fame is; to be killed on the field of battle and have your name misspelled in the newspapers." (I can imagine Owen and his band of brothers, after their last supper in the gloomy Maison Forestière, chuckling over that observation in their snippets of conversation before the canal battle.)

For a memorial Owen might have preferred what Sassoon wrote in memory of David Thomas, in one of his finest poems, "To Any Dead

WILFRED OWEN

Officer," which reads:

Well, how are things in Heaven? I wish you'd say,
Because I'd like to know that you're all right.
Tell me, have you found everlasting day,
Or been sucked in by everlasting night?
For when I shut my eyes your face shows plain;
I hear you make some cheery old remark—
I can rebuild you in my brain,
Though you've gone out patrolling in the dark.

You hated tours of trenches; you were proud
Of nothing more than having good years to spend;
Longed to get home and join the careless crowd
Of chaps who work in peace with Time for friend.
That's all washed out now. You're beyond the wire:
No earthly chance can send you crawling back;
You've finished with machine-gun fire—
Knocked over in a hopeless dud-attack.

Somehow I always thought you'd get done in,
Because you were so desperate keen to live:
You were all out to try and save your skin,
Well knowing how much the world had got to give.
You joked at shells and talked the usual "shop,"
Stuck to your dirty job and did it fine:
With "Jesus Christ! when will it stop?
Three years... It's hell unless we break their line."

So when they told me you'd been left for dead
I wouldn't believe them, feeling it must be true.
Next week the bloody Roll of Honour said
"Wounded and missing"—(That's the thing to do
When lads are left in shell-holes dying slow,
With nothing but blank sky and wounds that ache,
Moaning for water till they know
It's night, and then it's not worth while to wake!)

FRIENDS OF A KIND

Good-bye, old lad! Remember me to God,
And tell Him that our politicians swear
They won't give in till Prussian Rule's been trod
Under the Heel of England... Are you there?...
Yes...and the war won't end for at least two years;
But we've got stacks of men... I'm blind with tears,
Staring into the dark. Cheero!
I wish they'd killed you in a decent show.

Rupert Brooke might well be considered the first of the Great War poets, although he only knew the likes of Siegfried Sassoon in passing, thanks to an introduction from Sir Edward Marsh, his benefactor and friend. Brooke died relatively early in the war—in April 1915—before the works of Robert Graves and T. E. Lawrence, not to mention Sassoon, were published. His influence on the later poets was profound, if only because his 1915 poem "The Soldier" defined so much of the idealism of the early war years.

Section XIII

RUPERT BROOKE, LADY OTTOLINE MORRELL, AND SIR EDWARD MARSH

Defining the War

WHEN I GOT to the end of my roads, at least with this group of poets, writers, and friends, I felt there was something missing. On one hand I did not mind ending the story on the Sambre-Oise Canal in northeastern France at the place where Owen was killed on what felt like the last day of the war. It seemed, as Abraham Lincoln wrote in his *Gettysburg Address*, "altogether fitting and proper." On the other hand I suspected that I had left something out of the story, and I decided to add material about three figures that I had touched upon, but never in sufficient detail: Rupert Brooke, Ottoline Morrell, and Sir Edward Marsh.

Brooke is best remembered for these lines in his poem "The Soldier:"

> *If I should die, think only this of me:*
> *That there's some corner of a foreign field*
> *That is for ever England.*

In fact, Brooke did die in the early stages of the war, as his battalion was heading toward the 1915 campaign at Gallipoli in the Dardanelles Strait, and he was buried "in the corner of a foreign field" on the Greek island of Skyros, which was along the route of the naval and amphibious troops heading for what was once the Greek city of Troy.

While Brooke did not know many of the figures in this story, he did know some, in particular Sir Edward Marsh. Moreover, Brooke's death early in the war and the publication of his poetry thereafter inspired other soldiers to remember the war in verse and in prose, which allows us today to recall the fighting better than if they had recorded the fighting on their cell phones.

I also wanted to take a longer, last look at Lady Ottoline Morrell, as I had found her name cropping up in the footnotes of many stories, in particular those involving Siegfried Sassoon, who in 1917 had taken a draft of his war denunciation letter to her country house near Oxford, Garsington Manor, and worked on it with the likes of philosopher Bertrand Russell, who was Lady Ottoline's lover for many years.

Finally, I did not think that I could end this story without digging into more detail about the voluminous life of Edward Marsh, whom I figured was the one person who would have known everyone I write about in this book. Professionally, Marsh worked for Winston Churchill as his private secretary for many years, but notably in the Admiralty at the beginning of the World War. Emotionally, however, Marsh was a patron of young poets, writers, and artists. When not drafting speeches and letters for Churchill or accompanying him to political rallies, Marsh befriended the likes of Rupert Brooke, Robert Graves, Siegfried Sassoon, and T. E. Lawrence. At the same time, he knew Erskine Childers while at Cambridge, came across John Buchan in his government service, had contact with Lady Ottoline and Joseph Conrad, and was a close friend of the Asquith family, including Raymond and his wife Katharine. It was Marsh who introduced Sassoon to Lawrence, and it was Marsh who tried to intercede with Churchill on behalf of Childers to save his life. Marsh also encouraged Robert Graves, when still at Charterhouse School, to carry on with his poetry, and, notably, it was Marsh who published the first full-length biography of Rupert Brooke after he died. So before closing this book, I decided to look more closely into these three lives.

On the Road to Birmingham and Coventry

I BEGAN THIS final turn on a flight from Geneva to Birmingham, in the English Midlands, where I had figured out that I could rent a Brompton bicycle from a "hire scheme" box located outside the Birmingham Airport railway station. By that point my membership in the scheme had expired, and no amount of coaxing from the website allowed me to re-input my credit card information. I finally called a Brompton hotline, and gave the information over the phone, and soon I was back in Brompton's good favors.

With my membership renewed, I had no trouble retrieving a Brompton from one of the Birmingham station lockboxes, although I found it less well equipped for the hills than my own Brompton (which has six gears and a rack for carrying clothes). I attached my front bag to the Brompton mounting device and in no time I was off on the train to Rugby, where Rupert Brooke was born and grew up on the grounds of the famous boarding school of the same name.

I needed to change trains in Coventry, the medieval city destroyed in World War II by German bombers, and I decided to spend an hour riding around the city center, visiting the hulking remains of the bombed-out cathedral. On the morning that I arrived, it was chilly and spitting with rain, but I managed to get a cycle map from a tourist office and ride along what is called the Coventry Peace Trail, taking in such sites as the Reconciliation Sculpture, a Cross of Nails, a Memorial to Civilians Killed in War, and a Charred Cross.

Almost eighty years after the bombs fell on Coventry, the scars of war remain. At the core of the old town is the roofless cathedral and numerous war memorials, and around the edges are the buildings of postwar Coventry that have none of the grace or beauty of the old city, even in its shell form. I rode past cheap clothing shops, betting parlours, and numerous kebab houses before I found the Peace Pole or the Stalingrad Madonna. Despite all of the pictures showing Coventry "then and now," I found it hard to imagine the city that was lost.

I associate the Coventry bombing, which took place on the night of November 14-15, 1940, with the escalation of the fighting to what might be called total war. Before that both sides in the fighting might have felt some constraints about attacking cities or civilization populations. After the destruction of Coventry, in the minds of Allied war leaders—notably Churchill—everything on the other side became a military target. In many ways there is a straight line from the Coventry Blitz to the later destruction of Dresden, Tokyo, Hiroshima, and Nagasaki—just as the German assault on Coventry (which had no military significance) presaged the V-2 rockets fired at London.

The Rugby rail station is on the northern edge of the town (I would not quite call it a city). To find the center I had to pick my way through a nondescript residential neighborhood of terrace houses, always, it seemed, finding myself on the wrong end of a one-way street. I finally emerged from the maze in the town center, and there I hunted around on the bicycle until I located a bronze statue of Rupert Brooke on the edge of a central square park. The plinth has the famous "forever England" lines from "The Soldier," but the bronze figure does not show a crusader on his way to liberate the Holy Land from the dreaded Turks but an undergraduate in rumpled clothing, using his hand to prop up his chin, as if in poetic contemplation.

I had timed my arrival in Rugby to coincide with a weekly tour given by the school to anyone who signs up, although I sense that mostly it is for the parents and families of prospective students. As I was early for the tour, I first went in search of the house where the Brookes were living when Rupert was born and then to Field House, where Brooke grew up on the grounds of the school, where his father was one of the masters. The birth house at 5 Hillmorton Road is located on what is now a busy, narrow road, and it took me several tries in speeding traffic to navigate into the driveway and take a picture of the plaque that has been hung over the front door.

Field House is more impressive, as—to use an American expression—it's a school dormitory with an elegant basketweave brick design on its façade. It was there that Brooke spent his most formative years, first as a child in his parents' apartment, and then as a student himself attending Rugby School. When his father died in 1910, he even came back to Field House and served briefly himself as its master, teaching at the school until a more permanent replacement could be found for his father. After both her husband and famous son were dead, Mrs. Brooke lived on in Rugby, where she fought a rear-guard action with Edward Marsh (both in a way were Rupert's literary executors) to establish whose version of Brooke would be his most lasting legacy.

Remembering Rupert Brooke

BY THE TIME I rolled up to the impressive grounds of Rugby School—it's one of the prestigious British boarding schools, on a par with Eton and Harrow—I had read several biographies of Rupert Brooke, all of which I found slightly unsatisfying. Marsh's biography, *Rupert Brooke: A Memoir*, was published in 1918, after a nearly endless correspondence between Marsh and Brooke's mother, who didn't think much of his recollections. Marsh based much of his book on Rupert's correspondence, poetry, and prose, and therefore it is long on literary appreciation and short on capturing Brooke's essence, which was that he was a delightful friend and had a way of brightening any room or life that he entered.

Another book that I read was Christopher Hassall's *Rupert Brooke: A Biography*, which came out in 1964 and drew on Hassall's earlier biography of Marsh and on conversations with some who had known Brooke personally. Hassall's biography is well written and, I am sure, definitive. It runs to almost six hundred pages of tiny typeface, providing context for Brooke's poetry and quoting endlessly from his letters (he sent off many daily). I also read a shorter biography, John Lehmann's *Rupert Brooke: His Life and His Legend*, which was published in the 1980s by which time Brooke's legend, while still vibrant, no longer warranted six hundred pages. Lehmann's book is aimed at an audience curious to learn about Brooke's life and works, without needing to take two weeks off from work. Lastly, I read Brooke's own *Letters from America*, which is a collection of newspaper stories that he wrote while on a grand tour of the United States, Canada, and the South Pacific. The only thing that makes the book notable is that Henry James (a friend of Marsh's) wrote the preface.

As Brooke died at age twenty-seven in 1915, most of his life took place at school (from Rugby he went to Cambridge) and then in his work and travels after his undergraduate graduation in 1909. In short form, Brooke returned to Cambridge for postgraduate studies, lived for a while in Berlin, had numerous friends in and around London, set off for the New World in May 1913, and enlisted in the British Navy (thanks to Churchill's intervention via Marsh) in 1914. All the while Brooke was working on his poetry—some of which was good, some of which was not—and corresponding with his wide circle of friends (his letters capture his many wry observations and abiding humanity).

Brooke's interest in poetry and literature went back to his days at Rugby, where he also played many sports, including the game that was invented on its grounds (it started out as an all-school scrum that involved chasing a ball up and down the central grounds). What set Brooke apart in his generation were his striking good looks (he's often compared to one of the Greek gods) and the good humor that in his short lifetime brought him friendship with all sorts of notables, including Marsh, Churchill, and the family of Prime Minister Herbert Asquith. In Marsh's biography, there's this description of Brooke in his early years, written by a classmate:

> Rupert had an extraordinary vitality at school, which showed itself in a glorious enthusiasm and an almost boisterous sense of fun—qualities that are only too rare in combination. Of his enthusiasm it is hard to speak; we know less about it, although we felt it. We know much more of his glorious fooling—in his letters, in his inimitable and always kind burlesques of masters or boys, in his parodies of himself. He seems almost always ready for laughter.... I see him tearing across the grass so as not to be late for Chapel. I generally think of him with a book... But whatever he was doing or wherever he was, he was always the same incomparable friend.

It is no doubt thanks to Marsh that we remember Brooke at all, as he published some of his poems and introduced him to his influential circle, and after his death curated his literary reputation, beginning with his memoir. Marsh was fifteen years older than Brooke, but he had also attended Cambridge (Trinity, while Rupert went to King's), and when visiting the university while Brooke was an undergraduate, Marsh saw him acting in a school play. Afterward, they were introduced, and the older Marsh took the undergraduate Brooke under his wing—letting him use his London flat as a base, publishing his poems in anthologies and magazines, introducing him around literary London. Here's a description in Hassall's biography of Marsh on his first encounter with Brooke:

> One item of news which might have been mentioned [in Marsh's letter to Edward Horner] seemed at the

time too trivial to report. In mid-November he had been to stay with his father at Cambridge to hear his old friend Dr. Verrail lecture on the Eumenides and to watch a performance of the play given by the Amateur Dramatic Club. A young man [Rupert Brooke] had entered upon the scene, tall, slim, with a long neck, a pallid, almost girlishly good-looking face, and a bright red wig. He wore *papier-mâché* armour with a short cloak of red, blue, and gold. Striding to centre he put a property trumpet to his lips and someone in the wings blew a fanfare as Eddie Marsh, seated between Dr. and Mrs. Verrall, for the first time set eyes on Rupert Brooke. After the show he was taken on stage and introduced to the cast. Brooke was nineteen, a freshman at King's who had just come up from Rugby. Only a few words were exchanged.

Perhaps more modern biographies about Marsh and Brooke might ask whether there was a romantic infatuation on Marsh's part with the younger, handsome Brooke. It strikes me as a fair question, as Marsh was a "confirmed" bachelor who almost obsessively "collected" young poets and writers as if for one of his galleries. On his side, Brooke had a fluid sexual identity and at different times in his life was attracted to men and women, although with neither sex did he form a lasting romantic bond. That said, there is nothing in the correspondence or elsewhere to suggest that the relationship between Marsh and Brooke went beyond that of friendship based on a shared love of poetry and the arts.

FRIENDS OF A KIND

At Rugby School

JUST BEFORE 2 P.M. I presented myself in the Rugby School store, from which the organized tour was to depart. There I met Ms. Julie Morton, who was on duty behind the desk, and she warmed to my story. She even rummaged through a box and found a discarded paperback book that had Brooke's collected poems, and gave it to me. When I learned to my disappointment that the tour would focus on the campus more than Brooke's time there, Julie suggested that she take me to the chapel, where there is a plaque honoring Brooke. We walked along the perimeter of two massive rugby fields, which dominate the school grounds, and Julie recounted the history of the 1797 school riot that took place on a small island located behind a campus moat. It seems some of the boys then at the school thought the administration was being heavy-handed in asking them to pay for damages they had caused on a student spree. As a local constabulary read the boys the Riot Act, the boys retreated to the island and there set fire to some collected furniture and wood, which flamed away as local soldiers took the island from behind and captured the rebellious boys.

In the 18th and 19th centuries, according to Julie, schoolboy riots happened more often than one might think, as the sons of the ruling class often didn't appreciate being told that the rules applied to them (a timely anecdote as in the news that day were the reports that UK Prime Minister Boris Johnson had attended several raucous staff parties in the garden at 10 Downing Street during the Covid lockdowns).

The word *chapel* hardly does justice to the impressive and historic Rugby School church, with its soaring arches and stained glass windows. Julie showed me the Brooke plaque: below his profile is the full text of "The Soldier" (the only one of his poems that survives in modern sensibility). She also pointed out memorials of other famous Rugby graduates, including Charles Dodgson, who wrote *Alice's Adventures in Wonderland* under the pen name Lewis Carroll. Neither Julie nor I, however, could find any mention of British Prime Minister Neville Chamberlain, another famous alumnus, who bequeathed to history the signed 1938 Munich Agreement giving Adolf Hitler permission to annex the Sudetenland in Czechoslovakia.

Back to Oxford and Garsington Manor

OUTSIDE THE RUGBY chapel I looked at the wooden cross that was originally placed over Brooke's grave on the Greek island of Skyros. Then I was back on the bicycle and heading to catch an afternoon train to Oxford by way of Coventry. I refilled my tea caddy with hot water when I changed trains (the coffee shop charged 50 pence for the transaction). On a crowded Saturday afternoon train I tried to work out the best way to go from Oxford out to Lady Ottoline's Garsington Manor, which is about six miles from the railroad station. According to information on my phone, there was a bus running from somewhere in Oxford out to Garsington village, but it only ran once an hour. To catch it, I would have to wait about forty-five minutes, in which time I figured I could simply ride my bicycle to Garsington.

It turned out to be one of the more unpleasant bicycle rides in this book, as the GPS on my phone directed me to a cycle path alongside a busy thoroughfare. Where there was a segregated bike path, I was fine, but occasionally it crossed through chaotic roundabouts or ended abruptly. Toward the end of the ride I was on the edge of a road that buzzed with fast cars and swaying trucks, none of which I fancied. Plus it was starting to rain, although that description could be applied to just about any day in England.

I entered the village of Garsington by riding up a hill, which would have been fine on my own Brompton (with its low gears) but was a challenge on this rental model. I had printed out directions to the manor house, but when I got there I discovered that the new owners had put up a solid gate, perhaps to keep literary gawkers like me from peering into their lives. I rode farther along into the Garsington fields, so as to get a better view of the hilltop house. But even out there all I could see was the roofline of the manor house and its many chimneys. For more about Lady Ottoline's hectic life at Garsington manor, I would have to turn to Sarah Jobson Darroch's biography, *Ottoline: The Life of Lady Ottoline Morrell*, and to *Ottoline at Garsington: Memoirs of Lady Ottoline Morrell*, edited by Robert Gathorn-Hardy from her diaries and letters.

FRIENDS OF A KIND

Like her friend Sir Edward Marsh, **Lady Ottoline Morrell** figures in these stories as a patron of the arts. She had residences on Bedford Square in London and on the outskirts of Oxford in the village of Garsington. In both places she drew together circles of friends and acquaintances that helped her to define the literary age. There's a pub in London called the Lady Ottoline Morrell, and on the walls are reprints of her portrait. She's often shown wearing swirling colors and provocative hats, but what comes through most in the prints is the fiery passion that she brought to her many friendships.

BROOKE, MORRELL, AND MARSH

Lady Ottoline Morrell's Drawing Rooms

IN EVERY WAY, Lady Ottoline was larger than life. She was six feet tall, wore elaborate hats and flowing dresses, knew everyone, had Bertrand Russell and others as lovers, and thought it was her life's calling to bring together "interesting people" in her living rooms. Before she instituted her salons in Garsington Manor she gathered people at her townhouse in London, at 44 Bedford Square, in what was Bloomsbury—both the neighborhood and the smart set. Her world of wonder included, in no particular order, the aforementioned Russell, Prime Minister Herbert Asquith, D. H. Lawrence, Aldous Huxley, Gertrude Stein, Henry Lamb, Nijinsky, Maynard Keynes, Lytton Strachey, Siegfried Sassoon, Edward Marsh, George Bernard Shaw, Virginia Woolf, George Santayana, Clive Bell, Roger Fry, Vanessa Bell, Joseph Conrad, and Robert Graves—although this list would not fill a side parlor at any of her sprawling soirees in either London or Garsington. Some of her friends excited her sexually, others socially, and some politically. When she wasn't entertaining, she was being entertained. In her prime—the first two decades of the twentieth century—everyone who was anybody in London fetched up at one of her parties.

One of her biographers, Sandra Jobson Darroch, came across a trove of seven thousand letters in the archives at the University of Texas in Austin that she wrote or received. Hundreds came from Bertrand Russell during their long and tempestuous relationship, and it is these letters, as well as Lady Ottoline's diaries, that allow us to form a picture of her life.

It would be wrong to think of Lady Ottoline simply as a London courtesan, despite a succession of prominent lovers whose affections occasionally overlapped. Bertrand Russell was one of the great intellects of the twentieth century, and he found her captivating, as did Prime Minister Herbert Asquith and many others. The prescient Virginia Woolf wrote in 1909: "We have just got to know a wonderful Lady Ottoline Morrell, who has the head of a Medusa; but she is very simple & innocent in spite of it, & worships the arts."

Ottoline came of age in the late nineteenth century, the daughter of wealth and privilege, but not warmth or happiness. Darroch writes: "...her life was strange and lonely: she had no playmates and her only companions were servants." She took pleasure in some early grand tours on the continent, especially to Italy, then settled down in London, wedded to Philip Morrell, in what might best be described as a marriage of convenience. She admired his kindness to others, and he tolerated her flights of fantasy, and together they found common ground in opening their houses to an endless procession of friends and strangers, some of whom found their way into Ottoline's boudoir (where Philip was not often in residence). With her help, Morrell won a seat for Parliament from a district around Oxford that included Garsington, which explains why they ended up there in the manor house. A member of the Liberal Party, Philip was a champion of conscientious objectors, which perhaps explains why he was so tolerant of his wife's lover, Bertrand Russell, who also strongly opposed war.

In many accounts of Sassoon's anti-war statement published in summer 1917, it is suggested that he brought a draft of it to Garsington during one of the endless party weekends there, and that he received encouragement from Lady Ottoline and Bertrand Russell to release it. But Darroch's biography differs from the standard accounts of Russell's influence over Sassoon. She writes:

> Lytton [Strachey] was another visitor in May.... He sat out on the terrace in a deck chair...observing in a bemused fashion Ottoline's "new love," Siegfried, who had returned from France. Ottoline was overjoyed to have him back—the more so because he was now totally opposed to the war: his months in the trenches had shattered his nerves and he had written no more poetry. Siegfried felt he should make some public statement protesting the slaughter and was encouraged in this by Ottoline. Philip was less keen, pointing out the absurdity of a solitary second lieutenant raising his voice. Siegfried thought Philip's attitude was weak-kneed. He remembered one talk he had had with Philip: "Staring at the sunset he leant on a farm gate, he himself—in his wide-brimmed hat—had looked somehow defeated and ineffective, a compromising

pacifist who had lost hope of dissuading mankind from its madness." But Philip had been fighting for his beliefs far longer than Siegfried. Soon the poet had to return to his camp near Liverpool and a constant stream of gifts followed him there, including a large rug Ottoline had crocheted and doused with scent, the smell of which caused much ribaldry among his fellow officers. Finally in July he sent to a newspaper his "Soldier's Declaration" against the war and waited for the storm to burst. When nothing happened he flung his MC ribbon into the Mersey. Two of his friends, Robert Graves and Eddie Marsh, fearing Siegfried might do something to get himself into even deeper trouble, mounted a campaign to have him declared mentally overwrought, and soon afterwards Siegfried was sent to a convalescent hospital near Edinburgh.

This account would indicate that Ottoline herself was more invested in Sassoon's anti-war protest than either her husband Philip or her lover Russell, who only rarely came out to Garsington Manor, the preserve of Ottoline's husband. In her own memoirs, she wrote: "Siegfried is terribly self-centered, and it seems almost as if when he does a valiant action, such as this protest, that he watches himself doing it, as he would look into a mirror." She also described meeting with him in London: "I had to go to London on the Tuesday to see a doctor; so I arranged that Siegfried should come and meet Bertie [Russell] and [John Middleton] Murry at luncheon at a restaurant, and Bertie took Siegfried to his rooms afterwards to have more talk, but said he never listened to what was said to him."

If I were to guess, I would think that Sassoon had the mindset of a front-line officer, to whom the opinions of non-combatants, on questions of war, meant little. He sought their opinions but then acted on his own, willfully, as he did in battle.

FRIENDS OF A KIND

Sir Edward Marsh was at the centre of this loosely defined literary circle. Another title for this book could be: *The Friends of Sir Edward Marsh*. He worked for Winston Churchill, discovered Robert Graves at Charterhouse, made it his business to meet and publish the poetry of Siegfried Sassoon and many others, mixed socially and politically with John Buchan, Raymond Asquith, and Erskine Childers, introduced T.E. Lawrence to his literary friends, and—most of all—promoted the literary career of Rupert Brooke (to the point of writing his biography and serving as one of his literary executors). Like his friend Lady Ottoline Morrell, Marsh embraced the cause of mentoring young writers and artists, and he was a relentless entertainer and matchmaker. Most unusual of all, Marsh managed to have a life of his own while serving perhaps the most difficult taskmaster in British politics, Winston Churchill. It speaks volumes about both men that their working relationship coincided with extremely productive periods in their lives.

Sir Edward Marsh's Many Degrees of Connection

I SPENT THE night at a hotel near Oxford, and the next day took a train and rode my bicycle into London, detouring to see Eton School (it's across the Thames from Windsor Castle) and the spot where the Magna Carta was signed at Runnymede in 1215. In the same glade—it could well be a setting for a John Buchan adventure story—is Britain's only memorial to assassinated American President John F. Kennedy. From there I followed the Thames on my bicycle toward London (until a friend in Surbiton decided I was crazy and gave me a lift in his car into the city).

I spent a few days in London, and found several of Sir Edward Marsh's flats, one in an apartment complex at Grey's Inn Place and another around the corner at Five Raymond Buildings, and then a last apartment in Belgravia at 86 Walton Street, where he lived toward the end of his life. It was at Five Raymond Buildings (now law offices, as best as I could tell) where Marsh spent most of his adult life, amassing his modern art collection and providing a spare bedroom and meals to wandering poets such as Rupert Brooke.

Not unlike Lady Ottoline, Marsh grew up in an austere upper-class family, one that could trace its roots to Prime Minister Spencer Perceval (1809-1812), who was assassinated while in office by a lone gunman who nursed a grievance against the British government for time he had served in a Russian prison. Although it took a while, the British government eventually awarded the Perceval family compensation for their loss, and some of those funds—Marsh called it his "death money"—survived into his generation, sufficient for him to begin buying modest pieces of modern art and to subsidize the odd starving artist.

Marsh grew up with his nose in a book, but he also had a wide circle of friends (many were the so-called Apostles, a distinguished discussion group at Cambridge). In the class a year ahead of him at Trinity College, Cambridge, was Bertrand Russell. It was while at a Cambridge "reading party" (a group gathering at some country estate to catch up with their homework) that Marsh became acquainted with Erskine Childers, who taught him the rudiments of fly fishing.

Marsh's education was in the classics, but he expanded those interests to include art, drama, literature, poetry, and music. In the late Victorian era, he was a man for all seasons, and not long after his Cambridge years he joined the Civil Service, that branch of the British government that supplies highly qualified staffers to politicians in high office. At first he was the private secretary for Joseph Chamberlain, the colonial secretary during the Boer War, which is when he became acquainted with John Buchan. But Marsh's professional break came when he was hired to serve as the private secretary to an up-and-coming, ambitious politician by the name of Winston Churchill.

Marsh served as Churchill's private secretary from 1905 to 1915, when Churchill left government to serve in the Ploegsteert trenches. In between, Marsh was at Churchill's side—drafting his letters, attending to the details of office—at such posts as the Board of Trade, the Home Office, and the Admiralty. The two men proved to be a perfect match: if Churchill was loud and voluble, Marsh was precise and discreet. Miraculously, I do not think that either got on the other's nerves, and before long they were not just colleagues but friends who mixed in the same social circles. Both men had deep ties to the Asquith family. Marsh's biographer, Christopher Hassall (who would later write Brooke's biography), describes the job interview that led to Marsh getting the job with Churchill:

> Not only was he older than his new Chief by nearly three years, but so different from him in character as almost to be his very antithesis; moreover…Churchill had seemed, for all his obvious brilliance, rather truculent in manner. On Marsh's making this last point Lady Lytton put in a remark which he never forgot. 'The first time you meet Winston you see all his faults, and the rest of your life you spend in discovering his virtues.' She did not tell him, or perhaps she did not know, that it was largely on the recommendation of her own daughter-in-law, Pamela Lytton, one of Churchill's oldest friends who was also at the party, that the new Undersecretary for the Colonies had made his choice of a right-hand man.

Professionally, wherever Churchill went—and he liked to go everywhere—Marsh went with him, which included over the years a safari in Africa and a tour of the Franco-Prussian battlefields in France. Marsh even went with him on the celebrated 1912 Mediterranean cruise of *Enchantress*, the yacht assigned to the prime minister. (Hassall writes: "They saw the Parthenon, and Mr. Churchill, indignant at the sight of so many fragments of tumbled columns lying around which still looked serviceable, came out with the idea that a posse of blue-jackets from the *Enchantress* might be detailed to set them up.") On the surface it was just a summer cruise among well-connected friends, but historians have written about it as giving Churchill firsthand familiarity with numerous Mediterranean naval installations, which stood him in good stead during the World War II naval battles to control that sea.

Churchill and Marsh campaigned together in places such as Manchester and Glasgow, and very often, late at night on a train, Marsh would proofread or rewrite one of Churchill's campaign speeches. Churchill was a man of action mostly interested in military affairs and strategic matters while Marsh was an aesthete who loved art, and artists, for their own sake. But Marsh could make himself useful to Churchill in almost any setting, and in turn Churchill was broad-minded enough over the years to befriend many of the poets, such as Siegfried Sassoon, who were the pet projects of his private secretary. Because Marsh had introduced Sassoon to Churchill (who later could recite from memory a number of his poems from the trenches), Sassoon was spared a firing squad after publishing his 1917 denunciation of the war.

Marsh's devotion to his boss was exceeded only by his attachment to Rupert Brooke, whom he first saw in that Cambridge play in 1906—about the same time that March started working for Churchill. Marsh and his housekeeper, Mrs. Elgy, put themselves out to welcome Brooke into the world of Five Raymond Buildings, and in almost no time Rupert had access to the front door key and could come and go as he pleased, knowing there would always be a hot meal or attention given to his laundry. When Marsh and Brooke were together in London, they very often attended recitals or poetry readings, or went to the opera or a play. Marsh generously introduced Brooke into his politically prominent social world, which included many members of the Asquith family and the woman, Katharine Horner, who would eventually marry Raymond. In fact, when Raymond and Katharine were married in 1907, their first address in London was that of Marsh's flat. And thanks to the influences of Marsh and Churchill, when Brooke eventually got his commission in the Royal Navy (in a special Churchill battalion of marines), he would serve alongside Raymond's brother, Oc, who was with him when he died.

Marsh's great gift to Brooke was encouragement. He believed in him, and in his poetry, and he provided a showcase for Brooke and other young poets when he published, largely at his own expense (with some of the "death money"), a book of *Georgian Poetry*, which turned out to be a bestseller, at least for a collection of poems. Not only did Marsh champion Brooke's poetry but he also was there for Rupert as an emotional sea anchor, someone who delighted in his letters and escapades as Brooke made the transition from spirited undergraduate to a serious poet and man of letters. Marsh was sad but supportive when Brooke departed in 1913 for the New World and South Pacific, but it was in his letters home to Marsh that Brooke experimented with ideas and styles of writing, all of which later found a home and voice in his poetry and essays.

Grantchester: Byronic summer days

DURING ONE OF these days in London, I headed out on the train to Cambridge to see where Brooke had spent some of his most idyllic days, living in the nearby village of Grantchester. When I first went to Cambridge in the 1970s, the trains leaving from either Liverpool Street or King's Cross took forever to meander toward the Fens, but in recent years service has improved so that the journey can now be done in about forty-five minutes. So it perplexed me when the train I was on stopped at every town and village between London and Cambridge, until I reflected on my ticket purchase and recalled that I had bought passage on the cheapest train (a Liverpool Street local).

From Cambridge I biked down to Grantchester on a path that ran alongside the River Cam. Later I heard from numerous friends that a popular summer excursion in Cambridge is to "punt" (in those long boats with poles) down the river to Grantchester and there to take tea in the Old Orchard, which is where Brooke first lived when he moved to the village. Later he took rooms in what is called The Old Vicarage, a sprawling mansion that was then suitable for university housing but which is now the summer house of the Conservative politician, thriller writer, and convicted felon, Jeffrey Archer. (His wife, Mary, wrote *Rupert Brooke and The Old Vicarage, Grantchester*, to tell the history of the house.)

Even though I was traveling down to Cambridge out of season (meaning it was winter), I still thought I could have lunch at the Orchard Tea Garden, and sit under the same trees that Brooke had described so passionately in his celebrated poem, "The Old Vicarage, Grantchester." He actually wrote the poem in the Westens café in Berlin, during one of trips abroad, and he originally proposed using the title "The Sentimental Exile," until Marsh persuaded him to use the now more familiar title when he published it in *Georgian Poetry*. From Berlin Brooke wrote:

> *I only know that you may lie*
> *Day long and watch the Cambridge sky,*
> *And, flower-lulled in sleepy grass,*
> *Hear the cool lapse of hours pass,*
> *Until the centuries blend and blur*
> *In Grantchester, in Grantchester....*

FRIENDS OF A KIND

Still in the dawnlit waters cool
His ghostly Lordship swims his pool,
And tries the strokes, essays the tricks,
Long learnt on Hellespont, or Styx.

When I arrived at the Orchard Tea Garden, it was shut tight. The only people there were a group of local women out with their dogs, and they said cheerfully, "Come back in June when you can sit outside."

From the walking ladies, I got directions to the Old Vicarage, which was literally next door to the orchard garden. When he moved in, Brooke described the house to a friend, writing: "This is a deserted, lonely, dank, ruined, overgrown, gloomy, lovely house: with a garden to match. It is all five hundred years old, and fusty with the ghosts of generations of mouldering clergymen. It is a fit place to write my kind of poetry in…" Brooke moved into the Old Vicarage in 1910, on his return from Berlin. Hassall writes in his biography of Marsh:

> His [Brooke's] experiences in Munich had revolutionized his politics. He now felt that German culture 'must never, never prevail! The Germans are nice and well-meaning and they try, but they are soft.' He was homesick for Grantchester, and on his return was going to move into the house almost next door, which was called The Old Vicarage. There, at the end of July, Marsh paid his first visit to the new home, having followed Brooke's instructions to come in 'primitive' clothes. 'One talks eight hours, reads eight, and sleeps eight,' he wrote. 'The food is simple and extremely unwholesome.'

Needless to say, Brooke's "lonely, dank, ruined, overgrown, gloomy, lovely house" is long gone. When I rode my bicycle (it took about thirty seconds) to the house, I discovered that the driveway gates were open, and inside there was a late-model car parked near the front door. The house itself was well cared for, testimony to Archer's millions from his bestselling books (which presumably pay better than perjury and perverting the course of justice, which earned him a year in another big house). In the center of the circular drive stands a bronze statue of Rupert Brooke, as you might find at a five-star hotel of the same name. (It's a little too new and polished.) Unlike the Rupert Brooke statue in Rugby, this Brooke wears an officer's uniform, complete with jodhpurs and leggings. Instead of a sidearm in his right hand, he is holding a book, as if he is going to war for the cause of literature—as perhaps he did.

From the Old Vicarage I rode across the River Cam and down a muddy lane in search of what locally is called Byron's Pool, an eddy in the river that is popular among swimmers in summer. It explains the verse in his poem that connects Grantchester to Byron and his swim across the Hellespont at Gallipoli:

> *His ghostly Lordship swims his pool,*
> *And tries the strokes, essays the tricks,*
> *Long learnt on Hellespont, or Styx.*

I went down that dirt path as it speaks to much in Brooke's soul. He would often go there at midnight, and go skinny dipping, as he did once with his childhood friend, Virginia Stephen, who was later better known as Virginia Woolf. Brooke said, before plunging in: "Let's go swimming quite naked."

It was while clogging my bicycle wheels with mud on the way to the swimming hole that I thought about the long and enduring friendship between Brooke and Woolf, and how she wrote some of the most perceptive remarks about his life. For example, she wrote anonymously in the *Times Literary Supplement* in 1916, a year after he died:

> I thought perhaps I was arrogant and scratchy in the way I talked of Rupert the other day. I never think his poetry is good enough for him, but I did admire him very much indeed, and he always seemed to me a fully grown person among mummies and starvelings (which refers to the people I lived among).

And she wrote this to Rupert's mother, after Marsh's memoir was published, and later her review of the book:

> Also I am afraid that I gave the impression that I disliked Mr. Marsh's memoir much more than I meant

to. If I was at all disappointed it was that he gave of course rather his impression of Rupert than the impression which one had always had of him partly from the Stracheys and other friends of his own age. But then Mr. Marsh could not have done otherwise, and one is very glad to have the *Memoir* as it is. Rupert was so great a figure in his friends eyes that no memoir could possibly be good enough. Indeed I felt it to be useless to try to write about him. One couldn't get near to his extraordinary charm and goodness.

BROOKE, MORRELL, AND MARSH

Gallipoli and the Distant Echoes of Troy

LIKE MANY HIS age in England at the outbreak of war in 1914, Brooke wanted to serve in some capacity, but he didn't quite relish the prospect of joining the ranks as cannon fodder. Enter Marsh, who had a word with Churchill about several young men in his circle, and soon they were commissioned as sub-lieutenants in the Royal Naval Volunteer Reserve, a battalion that was under Churchill's direct command. With almost no training, the battalion was sent to Antwerp in late September 1914, as Churchill sought to prevent that strategic English Channel port from falling into German hands. Brooke and the men in his company marched through the smoldering ruins of the city and took up a position on the outskirts, only to find that the Germans would soon have them cut off, and quickly they withdrew to Dover, although not before Brooke experienced a small taste of combat (his only one of the war). Antwerp fell to the Germans in early October. In its last days Churchill himself (without Marsh this time) crossed over to the Belgian city and personally rallied some of the defense forces. As a literary footnote to these battles, it seems likely that Brooke wrote the first draft of "The Soldier" while waiting for his evacuation from Dover. Hassall writes:

> While in camp Brooke had drafted two more sonnets. These may have included the first draft of 'If I should die, think only this of me', but he was rash enough to take over with him these and other manuscripts in his kitbag, which was subsequently jettisoned in the retreat and never heard of again.

Lehmann adds in his Brooke biography: "It was the war sonnets that changed him into the almost sacred, supreme poet-figure of his generation, the mellifluous mouthpiece of the sentiments that had before been half incoherently felt by all those English people who were struggling to make sense of the war into which they had so suddenly been plunged, and who clung to the hope that the trials and sufferings, still only mistily revealed, that lay before them could be considered as part of a crusade of right against wrong, as a testing ground of courage and belief in their own country and its cause." Brooke's poems were in no way similar to the war prose or poetry of Sassoon, Robert Graves, Wilfred Owen, or even T. E. Lawrence. They might later have scoffed at his patriotic sentimentality, but at the same time they would have known from their mutual friend Edward Marsh that Brooke was regarded with reverence in his—and thus their—circle.

Brooke, a platoon leader with no military experience in a hastily formed battalion, was not an ordinary soldier in wartime, as can be seen by this passage in Hassall's biography, describing Antwerp's aftermath:

> Brooke and 'Oc' (Arthur) Asquith, the Prime Minister's son, who was also a subaltern in the battalion, went straight from Dover to Whitehall, where they called on Marsh, who admitted them to the First Lord. Mr. Churchill listened to their accounts of the Antwerp expedition. They had been granted a week's leave before rejoining their unit at Chatham, so Brooke went back to Raymond Buildings, where during a bath which lasted over an hour he gave Eddie Marsh a fuller account of his adventure.

After their leave, Brooke and the men in his battalion were transferred to the Mediterranean command. From January 1915 Churchill had the notion that he could shorten the stalemated war in the trenches on the Western Front with a naval attack on the Dardanelles and the capture of Constantinople. His hope was to knock Turkey out of the war and come at the Axis Powers from the east. The Allied (British and French) naval assault on the straits took place on March 18, 1915, but failed for want of minesweepers to carry the Dardanelles. It was then decided that land forces would be needed to occupy the Gallipoli peninsula overlooking the straits where the Turkish Army had placed artillery that was sinking Allied warships. It was as part of that land and sea armada that Brooke entered his last campaign, sailing to war on a converted Union-Castle Line steamer, *Grantully Castle*.

At first Brooke and his men thought they would immediately deploy at Gallipoli in March 1915, just after the failed naval encounter, but then they withdrew to the island of Lemnos (a staging area for the subsequent amphibious landing) and then back to Egypt, where Brooke wrote letters to Marsh and numerous friends—more about poetry and pyramids than the impending action. At some point while in Egypt, Brooke began to suffer from dysentery and the feverish effects of an infected mosquito bite on his lip, which would eventually turn septic and kill him.

FRIENDS OF A KIND

Section XIV

THE LAST POST

War's End on Skyros

I HAD HOPED that I might be able to find a ferry into the Aegean Sea, at least for part of the journey to the island of Skyros, off which Brooke died and on which he was buried, but the only boat that runs off-season to Skyros leaves once a day from the small town of Kymi, on the east coast of Euboea, which is itself about a three-hour bus ride from Athens. I decided simply to keep going in the air and changed from my Geneva flight at Athens International Airport to an island-hopping plane for the last leg to Skyros.

No sooner had we taken off and crossed Euboea—a dark, mountainous island—than we were approaching Skyros, which is the southernmost island of the Sporades chain that hugs the Aegean coast between Athens and Thessaloniki. I studied the contours of the island's west coast and could identify Tris Boukes Bay in southern Skyros, where Brooke's burial party went ashore.

When I walked out of the Skyros terminal (it's on an air force base) with my small bag into the parking lot, I saw one taxi driver, and this being Greece he charged me the oligopoly rate for the short ride into Skyros town. Even for that fee, I wasn't taken to my Airbnb but instead dropped on the main street, where I played hide-and-seek to find my accommodation, which was, as Churchill might have said, an enigma wrapped inside a riddle.

Once I was checked in, I followed a sign on my back alley street for something called Rupert Brooke Square. I only saw one sign for it, and so it took me almost an hour of wandering (I went up to the Byzantine fortress and came back down) to find the sculpture at the center of a stone circle overlooking the sea. This sculpted Brooke is a Greek god, capable of love or war on the shores of the Aegean. He's naked, as if ready for that swim in Bryon's Pool with Virginia Stephen, buffed up, and well-endowed, but not very warlike, as he's holding a book in his right hand. His golden locks are shorn and his muscles are firm. I cannot be sure of the angle, but I sense he's gazing in the general direction of Gallipoli, if not Troy. This would make sense, as Brooke's correspondence with Marsh is full of allusions to Homer and the underworld.

After lunch, I asked around about rental cars, but then came across a cab driver friendlier than my airport hack, and she agreed to drive me down and back to Brooke's gravesite. She warned me that it would take a while, as it was about where the road ended in southern Skyros. I didn't mind, and settled into the back seat with my maps and sheaf of papers, many of which recounted Brooke's last days, when he was on his battalion's ship, drifting in and out of consciousness as the blood infection from the mosquito bite took control of his fate.

During his brief, final illness, Brooke was able to write enough letters, to Marsh and others, that we have a good sense of what was on his mind in his last days. He divided his literary estate between Marsh and his mother—which led to their endless wrangling over the publication of Marsh's *Memoir* and the disposition of Brooke's poetry (Marsh got the poems and eventually published most of them). He wrote also to Cathleen Nesbitt, an actress with whom he had an on-again, off-again romance, and tried to make amends for his diffidence. It was during this time—Brooke would improve and then relapse—that Marsh wrote to Brooke telling him that in the Easter sermon at St. Paul's Cathedral in London, a Dean Inge had quoted from Brooke's "The Soldier" (in particular the phrase, "If I should die…"), ensuring Brooke's immortality just as he was succumbing to blood poisoning in the Aegean.

At one point, as Brooke's ship was maneuvering in anticipation of action at Gallipoli, his battalion was put ashore at Tris Boukes Bay for training exercises, and during the course of that long, hot day in the near lunar landscape of southern Skyros, Brooke and his men paused for a break in a shaded olive grove that overlooked the Aegean. It was there, several days later, that Brooke's fellow officers buried him when he died on the afternoon of April 23, 1915. Hassall describes the scene:

> The day after Brooke and Browne had got their mail there was a battalion field-day during which Browne, who was parted from the others, made a small discovery. About a mile from the shore in a dried-up river bed,

overlooked by the highest point of the island, he came upon a secluded olive-grove bare of scrub and sheltered by about a dozen olive-trees. On the following day, April 20, during a lull in an exhausting divisional field-exercise in which they had all done a great deal of clambering among loose rocks and torn their boots, he conducted his friends Lister, Shaw-Stewart, and Brooke to this place. There they rested, and Brooke remarked on the pleasantness of the shade.

I am glad now that I didn't rent a car, as I am not sure I would have found the gravesite. There might only be one road in that part of Skyros, but it's little better than a goat trail, and I didn't see any signs or markers indicating the way toward Brooke. There is a Greek naval station of sorts at Tris Boukes Bay, and most directions to the Brooke gravesite indicate that if you come to the base barrier you've gone too far, and that he's buried back up the hillside by about two hundred meters. I am not sure that on my own I could even have found the naval station, and the only living creatures in southern Skyros are grazing sheep and goats.

The taxi parked near a footpath, and I walked back through the olive grove to where Brooke was buried under a pile of rocks and the cross that now hangs outside the chapel at Rugby School. Now there is a fenced marble sarcophagus—worthy of some departed pope—over his grave. In the grove around the tomb someone more recently scattered a semicircle of square concrete blocks, perhaps so that pilgrims could sit in contemplation in front of what felt like Brooke's altar. On the base of the sarcophagus there was a plaque with yet another text of "The Soldier," which spoke to the idealism of the war's early days, when the fight was more of a crusade or an update on *The Iliad*. Only in time would Sassoon write about "suicide in the trenches" and "the hell where youth and laughter go," and only in time would the path in the Skyros olive grove lead to that corner of a foreign field along the Sambre-Oise Canal.

The End

ACKNOWLEDGEMENTS

WHEN I CAME to the end of my roads on this journey, I kept wishing that I might find an excuse to make one more ride across the battlefields of northern France or another reason to make a side trip to Greece or Saudi Arabia. This book had got me across the great divide of the pandemic shutdown, as most nights during the long blockade I poured over timetables and road maps, wondering how I could ride, say, from Soissons to Rheims. Even during the worst of the shutdown, I always managed to slip my bicycle across the Swiss border (where I live) into France and visit one or two sites that later became chapters. The book was my answer to enforced confinement.

Even if I no longer have a professional reason to visit Mametz Wood on the Somme or Matfield in Kent, I remain grateful to all of the helping hands that reached out to me along the way. In many cases, the help came from friendly Airbnb owners or hotel desk clerks who kindly let me store a folding bicycle in my room, probably not aware that I would be using the shower nozzle to clear the dirt from the drive train. And often in my rides across England, I was lucky to find beds for a night from a constellation of friends, some of whom I met when I was a student in London in the 1970s.

No doubt the idea for this book germinated with Paul Fussell's *The Great War and Modern Memory*, published in 1975, which is an academic treatment of the World War I poets, although written in an accessible style. When I began dating my wife in the fall of 1977, it was among the first books she prodded me to read—the message being that if I wanted to spend more time with her romantically I might need to keep up with the required reading. Not only did I read and admire Fussell's book (despite some weighty passages of literary criticism), I upped the ante at the great relationship poker table and invited Fussell to lunch, as in those days I was a magazine editor at *Harper's Magazine* in New York and always hunting for contributors. For the next few years, while that job lasted, Fussell and I were friends, and he often wrote essays for the magazine. Whenever we met he would give me brochures and maps from his own travels along the Western Front, and some of those I carried with me on these explorations.

Another godfather, so to speak, for this book was my English friend

ACKNOWLEDGEMENTS

Edward Mortimer, who sadly died before it was published. Edward was well known for his journalism and columns with the London *Times* and the *Financial Times*, and later he wrote speeches for the United Nations Secretary General, Kofi Annan. Edward and I met at a dinner in January 1980 in New York City, when he had a fellowship at the Carnegie Endowment for International Peace to finish a book about the politics of the Islamic world, published as *Faith and Power*. Our meeting was just one of many professional dinners, but the friendship held, even though Edward was working in New York and I was in Europe. He would visit us in Geneva when he came here for his UN work, and when I embarked on the roads of the war poets and writers, Edward (brilliant in so many fields) warmed to the overlapping connections of these many writers. He invited me to the T.E. Lawrence exhibition in Oxford at the library of Magdalen College, and the next day he introduced me to his friend, David Buchan, the grandson of John Buchan who still lives in the writer's Oxford house, Elsfield Manor. In turn, David introduced me to his cousin, Ursula Buchan, who was then finishing her impressive biography, *A Life of John Buchan: Beyond the Thirty-Nine Steps*.

The third guiding star for this book was another English friend, who when I met him was named Raymond Asquith, the namesake and grandson of the Raymond Asquith mentioned so often in these pages. My friend Raymond (it all gets confusing) spoke to me often about his grandfather's death on the battlefield of the Somme in 1916, and when I was thinking about this project I went to his grave at Guillemont Road Cemetery, near Albert, France. But it took me two more trips to France to find the Asquith memorial plaque in Amiens Cathedral and the place where he was killed, while attacking from the village of Ginchy towards Lesbœufs. Each time I went to the Somme, I wrote to Raymond asking for more details, and finally when we met for dinner in London, he explained the precise coordinates of both his grandfather's last battle and where I could find the Amiens plaque (itself worth a visit to that lofty cathedral). At the dinner Raymond explained that upon the death of his father he had succeeded to the title of 3rd Earl of Oxford and Asquith, and now uses the name Raymond Oxford. It was Raymond who described the connections that his grandfather had with John Buchan and Winston Churchill, among others in this story, which got my mind wondering about other similar ties in this overlapping literary circle. Over our dinner he told me about being a young boy and going with his parents to

Heytesbury, and there on the grounds of the manor house playing cricket with Siegfried Sassoon.

When I went to Rugby in search of more details about the life there of Rupert Brooke, I had read some of his biographies, but otherwise showed up without an introduction. All that I could think to do was sign up for the school tour for prospective students and parents, and hope that along the way the guide would speak about the school's most famous graduate. The tour left from the school store (scarves, notebooks, jackets, etc.), and as I had arrived early, I chatted up one of the clerks on duty, Julie Morton, who immediately understood what I was looking for (notably the cross under which Brooke was buried on Skyros). Not only did Julie find for me some books of Brooke's poetry, but when the store closed in the middle of the afternoon she took me on my own walking tour around Rugby School, and showed me many Brooke artefacts, especially in the school's chapel, which also has a plaque for another famous school graduate, Neville Chamberlain. In turn, to thank Julie and the school for their warm hospitality, I mailed them a homemade mounting of a stone that I took from the island of Skyros, not far from Brooke's grave.

Another English school official who helped me was Mrs. Catherine Smith, who is the Charterhouse archivist. When—also unannounced—I took my bicycle to Charterhouse (where Robert Graves had studied), I was told that no one was then free to walk me around the campus. Nor were they then conducting any tours from the admissions office. But later on, as promised, Mrs. Smith wrote me the most helpful email that, as attachments, had many of the poems that Robert Graves wrote while he was a student there—the same poems that would have been shown to Sir Edward Marsh, who first "discovered" Graves when he made his own visit to Charterhouse.

I first heard of Erskine Childers back in the 1980s from my friend, the writer Simon Winchester, who said that *The Riddle of the Sands* was one of his favourite novels. Occasionally as I was biking in northern Europe, I thought about a side trip to the Frisian Islands, that stretch along the North Sea coast from The Netherlands to Germany and Denmark, as much of that novel is set along those estuaries. Simon is a more intrepid traveler than I am, and he would have gone, but when I got close, I detoured to Heligoland, another island pawn in the great games between England and Germany. And then I could never fit Heligoland into this story.

By great good luck, my high school friend Kevin Glynn was in Ireland

ACKNOWLEDGEMENTS

on exactly the same weekend I was landing in Dublin to search for T.E. Lawrence's Anglo-Irish roots. Even better, Kevin came with a rental car (I had planned to take buses and trains). He immediately warmed to my book project, and in less than an hour from the airport we found the Lawrence homestead at South Hill. The manor house is now a public works office, but seeing it allowed me to tell Kevin the story, from Lawrence's Clouds Hill, of how a descendant from one of his half-sisters had taken me through the cottage after the staff on duty had punched their time clock and left the onerous job.

It's hard for me to reconstruct how the books of Joseph Conrad came into my life. I remember reading *Heart of Darkness* in Harry Shaw's high school English class, but I cannot say that that alone would have moved me to search for his house near Canterbury. From the library of my friend Robert Koch I inherited his anthology of Conrad novels, which I treasure, but mostly as a connection to Bob, whom I much admired. After graduate school at Columbia University, I interviewed the Columbia professor Edward Said, whom I had known slightly while I was a student. Ostensibly the interview was about Palestine and the Hundred Years' War in the Middle East, but Said used the occasion to speak to me at length about Conrad, especially his writing about identity, and urged me to read widely among his novels. In any case, while I was searching around Canterbury for Conrad's home and gravesite, I thought of all three influences, while, of course, "sailing toward Poland."

I am grateful to the literary agent, editor, and publisher Christopher Sinclair-Stevenson (no family relation), who much enjoyed working on this manuscript with me. It was Christopher who shaped the conclusion, especially the sections about Sir Edward Marsh. And it was Christopher who encouraged me to end the story on the Greek island of Skyros at Brooke's grave. Sadly, Christopher's health was declining, and his literary affairs were passed to Andrew Lownie, whom I had met and interviewed early in this journey, when I read his biography *John Buchan: The Presbyterian Cavalier*, an excellent account of his active life. But while his health was stable, Christopher introduced me to his close friend Francis Bennett, the publisher of Marble Hill Books, who has patiently steered this somewhat unwieldy manuscript (in its early stages) into what I hope is a more compact story. Francis has often pushed me—quite rightly—to define whether this is a book about World War I, certain war poets, or a series of bicycle rides. It has aspects of all three, obviously, but what was great about the bicycle on these many stops is that it gave me time to think about what I had seen—be it in Arras or Loos—and compare what I was seeing to what I had read in books. To me it is exciting to match literary texts to places in the world, and I feel lucky that I was able to make those connections on a Brompton bicycle. And it is Francis who came up with the idea of the Cycling Historian, which captures all of these overlapping worlds.

Foremost, I want to thank my wife, Constance Fogler, for everything she does for me and our children. Connie keeps the cats fed and the home fires burning in my absence, just as she is a genius, each and every day, at reaching out to our now far-flung children and emotionally letting them know that they remain at the center of our family universe and her affections. I think it speaks volumes for our marriage that 47 years after we met and she showed me her copy of *The Great War and Modern Memory*, the mystic chords of that early romance are still in the air.

Matthew Stevenson
Laconnex, Switzerland
October 22, 2024

COPYRIGHT PERMISSIONS

For the photographs that appear on pages xx, 32, 56, 100, 120, 136, 150, 208, 218, 252, 262, and on the front cover, Alamy Limited (U.K.) has granted permission to reproduce the images used in this publication, for which the author is grateful.

For the poetry and prose of Siegfried Sassoon, the copyright is in the name of Siegfried Sassoon, and the quotations are reprinted here by kind permission of the Estate of George Sassoon.

To include the portrait of Sir Edward Marsh that appears on page 266, permission is granted by the Kirklees Collection at Huddersfield Art Gallery, located in Huddersfield, U.K.

Ms. Cherie Northon of Mapping Solutions (www.mapmakers.com), Anchorage, Alaska, designed the maps that appear on pages viii, xi, and xiii.

The image on the front cover is from Arthur Streeton's painting, "Boulogne: 1918", which is on display in the Gallery of New South Wales, located in Sydney, Australia, on Gadigal land within The Domain.

THE CYCLING HISTORIAN

"I USUALLY GO in search of history—I have found the bicycle to be a passport to distant worlds every bit as delightful as a magic carpet." (Matthew Mills Stevenson)

Beginning with *Biking with Bismarck*, in which he rides trains and his bicycle across France, Matthew Stevenson decided to marry his love of writing and trains with his love for cycling. He says, "I never learned very much belted up in a car, and there's no such thing as a bad bike ride."

After discovering that European trains require endless paperwork to transport a bicycle, Stevenson acquired a six-speed "touring Brompton" together with several saddlebags, and he has never looked back. He has taken the Brompton across the United States, to Crimea just before the war, up and down Vietnam, and, most recently, to Romania, Turkey, Georgia, and Armenia. He says:

"Traveling with trains and a folding bicycle has given me back the pleasures of travel, which I was beginning to loathe when on a discount airline or stuffed in a car. I am freed from taking taxis or hiring guides, and I can go wherever I want, especially after dinner in foreign cities when I wander on the bicycle through places I might not want to walk.

"I go in search of history—to this battlefield or that author's house—and I have found the bicycle to be a passport to distant worlds every bit as delightful as a magic carpet. To write about the Vietnam War, I rode (and took trains and buses) across Indochina. Yes, learning to ride in Saigon traffic was a nightmare, but I mastered the skill (which is never to turn sharply or abruptly), and I have since made endless bicycle-and-train journeys across Europe, where I have used the Brompton to track down aspects of the two world wars.

"To be sure, I get flat tires in inconvenient places (Crimea was notable in that regard), and I get caught out in the rain, but I patch the tires and my clothes dry, and I come back to my writing desk with the feeling that I am still a young boy, discovering neighbourhoods on my bike after school, and that's a thrill."

Stevenson is married to Constance Fogler, and together they have four children, all of whom have incorporated bicycles into their lives. His forthcoming books in this "Cycling Historian" series will cover the

THE CYCLING HISTORIAN

Vietnam War, Dag Hammarskjöld, Crimea on the edge of war and peace, and history in Eastern Europe. On his coffee table at home there are road maps about Cuba and histories of the 1848 Mexican-American war.

ABOUT THE BICYCLE

This Brompton was made in 2014, and it has six speeds, a classic Brooks saddle, and touring butterfly handlebars. Ortlieb made the front bag, and it carries papers, tools, a book, maps, and a computer; the Dutch-made rear pannier has three days' worth of clothes and some food. I wish I did not have to ride with a bulky lock, but not every museum wants visitors to drag in a folding bicycle.

MY ADULT FASCINATION with bicycles began with a long-ago transit strike in New York City. (For some reason the city's mayor, Ed Koch, used the subway-less occasion to greet commuters trudging over the Brooklyn Bridge with a gleeful: "So how am I doin'?") To get around the shutdown city, I brought my childhood Raleigh ten-speed bike (made in Nottingham) into New York and pedaled around the mean streets, delighted to discover that cities and bicycles can be a great match.

After moving to Europe and getting around on trains, I often wanted to bring along a bicycle on my travels, and did, but quickly discovered that most European rail networks have more regulations for bicycles than does the New York City Department of Transportation. In Germany, for example, on the crack Intercity and Eurocity express trains, bicycles need both a ticket and a reservation; in France, you cannot buy a ticket for a bicycle after you buy your rail ticket.

I persisted with my bicycle travels (even using a bike to write a book about the 1870 Franco-Prussian war), but moaned about the ordeal whenever I returned home, assuming my family was interested to hear endless details about how hard it is to travel with a full touring bicycle from Krakow to Prague. They eventually tired of my whinging and in 2014 presented me with a touring Brompton bicycle, complete with six speeds, an Ortlieb front bag and a pannier, a Brooks saddle, and butterfly handlebars. In its folded state, it can ride free on any train in the world (although the fastidious Swiss and Amtrak in the USA demand it go into a bag).

Since then, the Brommie and I have been across the American Midwest, Vietnam, Russia, the Caucasus, and most countries in Europe, including to the Polish-Ukrainian border. At the same time I am not one to set off on a multi-day, cross-country ride. On the bike I am more a flâneur, happy to ride more modest kilometers to the places that interest me. Nothing pleases me more than to meander on the Brompton around unfamiliar cities, especially at night in summer, when even the most banal outpost can take on the magic of Venice, and I am pedaling a gondola.

Usually I pair the Brompton with trains and ferries, although I have taken it on the occasional flight, on which it weighs less than the normal baggage allotment. For me the pleasure of the Brompton is that I am freed from taxis, buses, subways, tour guides, and long walks in unfamiliar surroundings, and come the end of a day I feel in my legs the pleasure of miles ridden. On the Brompton, I am an immortal ten-year-old boy, wandering the (world) neighborhood after school.

In Search of the Great War and its Writers

ON THE CHANCE that this book inspires some readers to make their own search of the writers and poets of the Great War, let me offer a few thoughts for those roads.

For starters, I would suggest that you look for writers or war veterans who inspire you—for whatever reason. I picked these because I had read some of their books and wanted to learn more about their lives on the front lines, but there are many others—Vera Brittain (*Testament of Youth*) and Edmund Blunden (*Undertones of War*) come to mind—who deserve their own quests.

Not everyone will want to travel around Europe on a folding bicycle, but one still merits consideration because a Brompton (what I ride) makes it much easier to cross the Channel on Eurostar or to glide across France on a TGV. With a full-sized bicycle, you will find yourself having to endure endless bureaucratic hassles just to buy bicycle train tickets and reservations, and you will worry about locking it up on the streets of London, Paris, or Lille. With a folding bicycle, it's a breeze to take trains around France, England, Ireland, and Scotland, and you will sleep well at night after poking around Verdun or Normandy.

I realize that paper road maps, even ones dedicated to history or cycling, are things of the past, but if you do decide to embark on your own crusade, make an early stop in the basement of Stanfords, the travel map and bookstore located in London's Covent Garden. Phone apps can be great for navigating the last mile, but there's nothing like paper to allow you to dream about the places where you are going.

Don't think that you need to see everything on one long ride or excursion. To write this book, I made almost a dozen journeys to corners of northern Europe—and then to Saudi Arabia—and I always came home annoyed with myself that I had missed some key element of the story. (It took about three tries until I found the Bois Français near Fricourt). Don't regret your misses; just go again.

France and rural England have an endless supply of hostels, inns, auberges, hotels, and Airbnbs, and many can be booked at lunchtime,

EPILOGUE

if you are leaving things to the last minute. Keep in mind that not every hotel desk manager will admire your bicycle as much as you do, but I have found that most of them become tolerant when you explain that "it folds up." I try to book places that I imagine will act kindly to cycling historians, and often that means taking a single room in an upmarket hostel or booking stand-alone quarters on Airbnb.com at some French farmhouse.

Finally, when it comes to your reading and research, don't think that you need to have read a certain number of books before setting forth. Having read a few books will, of course, make it easier to get started, but really any book on the subject that you have chosen will be that key first step. After that, you will find books, as I did, in small shops, at Waterstones, on Amazon, and in your own library (books you bought but never read). Books slide easily into your saddlebags or onto your Kindle.

For books that might be a good introduction to the vast, endless subject of the Great War, I suggest starting with Robert Graves' *Good-bye to All That* or any of the Siegfried Sassoon memoirs (I love the *Sherston* trilogy, but he has others). Written almost a hundred years ago, their language remains fresh and modern, and the books are laced with trench wit and humor. (At Gallipoli, Anzac soldiers, aka "diggers," used to say to those who were complaining: "The next thing you'll want is flowers on your grave.")

In the end, what will most spark your reading is seeing places like Mametz Wood or the Somme valley for yourself. After even one visit, you will find yourself wanting to know more about this battle or that author, and pretty soon, if you stick with it long enough, you will have your own book in hand. I hope so.

M.M.S 2025

INDEX

Asquith, Raymond
  burial in Guillemont Road Cemetery, France, x, 218, 231, 283
  death near Ginchy, France, 101, 220, 230-233
  early years at Oxford University, 100
  father, Prime Minister Herbert Asquith, x, 34, 101, 116, 153, 218, 230-231, 263
  friendship with John Buchan, x, xvi, 34, 100-101, 102
  friendship with Sir Edward Marsh, xviii, 266, 268-269, 276
  later influence on John F. Kennedy, 34, 116-118
  links to Rupert Brooke, 258
  marriage to Katharine Horner, 231, 254
  meets prime minister/father in 1916 near front lines, 230-231
  namesake of Raymond Asquith, 3rd Earl of Oxford and Asquith, x, 34, 283
  plaque in Amiens Cathedral, 219-221
  political potential of, 116-118
  ties with Lady Ottoline Morrell, 163
  visits with Winston Churchill near WW I trenches, 154-155

Brooke, Rupert
  association with Robert Graves, 62
  biography of, by Sir Edward Marsh, 266-270
  book about America, 257
  briefly meets Sassoon, xvii
  burial on Greek island of Skyros, xvi, 253, 261, 278-280
  at Cambridge University, xvii, 257-258, 269, 271
  cross over Skyros grave, 260 261, 280, 284
  debriefs Winston Churchill on the battle Antwerp, 257, 276
  early years at Rugby School, xvii, 255-257, 260
  famous poem, "The Soldier," 252-253, 256, 260, 275, 279, 280
  friendship with Raymond Asquith's sister, Violet Bonham Carter, xviii, 232
  friendship with Sir Edward Marsh, xviii, 254-259
  friendship with Virginia Woolf, 273-274
  house in Grantchester, near Cambridge, 271-274
  poetry, 271-274, 279
  serves in Battle of Antwerp, 275 277

INDEX

Buchan, John
  acquainted with T. E. Lawrence, 97-98, 101
  connection to Sir Edward Marsh, 142
  contemporary of Winston Churchill, xvi, 102, 106-107, 110-111
  during the Great War, 103-105
  early life in Glasgow, 102-103, 110
  friendship with Raymond Asquith, 14, 100-103, 116-118
  Greenmantle, x, 100-101, 104, 107, 110
  home in Elsfield, near Oxford, xv, 101-102, 109-112, 283
  influence on John F. Kennedy, 116-118
  memoir, *Pilgrim's Way*, x, 34, 101, 103, 116-118
  postwar years, 106-108
  service in Boer War, 103, 268
  The Thirty-Nine Steps, ix, 100, 103, 110, 112
  walks in Peebles, 112-115

Childers, Erskine
  author, *The Riddle of the Sands*, ix, 136-137, 140-141, 144, 284
  civil service in British government, 142-146
  dealings with Winston Churchill, x, 136-138, 140, 142, 144, 146, 148, 152
  death by execution in 1922 in Ireland, 137, 144-146
  drawn to the cause of Irish home rule, x, 137-139, 206
  friendship with Sir Edward Marsh, xviii, 146, 266-267
  influence on John Buchan, 101, 107, 114
  love of sailing, 136-139, 142-143
  running guns to Irish rebellion, 138, 143-144
  service in Boer War, 142-145
  similarities to T. E. Lawrence, 141-149
  yacht *Asgard* in Dublin, xii, 136 139, 143

Churchill, Winston S.
  1921 Cairo Conference 1921, x, 11, 16, 26
  association with Erskine Childers, x, 136-138, 140, 142, 144, 146, 148, 152
  association with Rupert Brooke, 258
  attends funeral of T. E. Lawrence, 7
  contemporary of John Buchan, 106
  creation of Iraq, 6, 11, 16, 26, 67, 94
  friendship with Lawrence, x, xv, 10-11, 16, 26, 94-99, 110-111, 150, 152
  Gallipoli campaign, 144, 150, 153, 155, 157, 205, 275
  intervention in Battle of Antwerp, 275-276
  meets with Raymond Asquith in WW I, 154-155
  saves Siegfried Sassoon from

firing squad, x, xvii, 44, 184, 269
serving officer in the trenches of Belgium, 151-159
takes T. E. Lawrence to Cairo, x, 11, 16, 94-99
works with Sir Edward Marsh, xvii-xviii, 44, 63, 97, 150, 254, 268-269
writes about death of Raymond to Herbert Asquith, others, 232-233

Conrad, Joseph
becomes a novelist, 128-130
burial, Canterbury, xv, 128-130, 285
descriptions of the Congo, 98, 126-127
early life in Poland, 120-127
friendship with Lady Ottoline Morrell, 125, 129
friendship with Sir Edward Marsh, 254
Heart of Darkness, novel, 98, 121 122, 127, 285
house outside Canterbury in Bishopsbourne, xv, 120, 128-129
influence on T. E. Lawrence, xv, 98, 121
Professor Edward Said on Conrad, 64, 12, 285
sailing as a career, 124-127

Graves, Robert
action with Royal Welch Fusiliers on Western Front, 165-167
in Battle of Loos, 174-176
as a British officer, 220-221
connection with John Buchan, 101
death of fellow officer David Thomas, 227
describes T. E. Lawrence in Middle East, 75-76, 77-78
description of 1921 Cairo Conference, 95-96
on first day of Battle of the Somme, 227-229
friendship with mountaineer George Mallory, 62-63
Good-bye to All That, ix, 21, 56-59, 61, 71, 172
Graves' *Lawrence and the Arabs*, 20, 69, 71-74
intervenes in the matter of Siegfried Sassoon's letter, 184-188, 264-265
at Mametz Wood in 1916, with Siegfried Sassoon, 43, 199-203, 219, 282
meets Wilfred Owen at Craiglockhart, 187
meets Siegfried Sassoon, 57-60, 171-172
meets Sir Edward Marsh, 63, 254, 266
postwar meeting with T. E. Lawrence, in Oxford, 64-68, 71
school days at Charterhouse, 61-63
summers in Wales, 61-63, 138, 198
wounded at the Somme, 197 198, 201-202

INDEX

Lawrence, Thomas Edward
at 1921 Cairo Conference, x, 11, 16, 26, 94-99
biography of Michael Korda, 84-88
Bovington and fatal motorcycle crash, 1-2, 7-8
conflicted over Sykes-Picot Agreement, 15, 25, 66-67, 76, 90, 95
cottage at Clouds Hills, 2-7, 11, 16, 18, 20, 25, 29
early years in Oxford, 11-14
father's family in Ireland, 138 141, 142, 146-149, 285
film *Lawrence of Arabia*, 2, 15, 20, 25, 72, 77-78, 97
friendship with Sir Edward Marsh, 254
friendship with Thomas Hardy, 2, 9-10, 28-30
friendship with Winston Churchill, x, xv, 10-11, 16, 26, 94-99, 110-111, 150, 152
guerrilla in Arabian desert, ix, xx, 4, 6, 8, 15-19, 20-21
Hejaz Railway during World War I, 69-74, 82-83
incident at Dera'a (now southern Syria), 17-19, 68, 85, 131-134
influence of Conrad upon, 121, 131-134
legend "of Arabia," ix, xii, xiii, 1-2, 11, 15, 20-27, 65, 69, 78, 85, 92, 97
meeting Siegfried Sassoon, 48 50, 152, 189
postwar years, enlistment under assumed names, 4-6, 16, 111, 148
relationship with Thomas Hardy, 28-30
Robert Graves, 56, 64-68, 69-74
Seven Pillars of Wisdom, ix, xii, 2, 4, 6, 8, 15, 17, 19, 20-27, 64-66, 71, 99, 131-134
sexuality of, 17-19, 68, 85, 131 134
walks across Syria as a university student, 14
in Yenbo, 91-93
as a young man, cycling in France, 14

Marsh, Sir Edward
biography of Rupert Brooke, 257-259
classmate of Erskine Childers at Cambridge, 142
correspondence with John Buchan, xviii
friendship with Raymond Asquith and family, 254, 258
helps Siegfried Sassoon over anti-war letter, 265
home life and art collection, 267 270
influences on many writers and artists, xvi-xviii, 253-254
introduces Siegfried Sassoon to T. E. Lawrence, xviii, 48, 66, 189
knows Joseph Conrad, 254

meets Robert Graves at
  Charterhouse, xviii, 63, 254,
  266, 284
mentor to Rupert Brooke, xvii,
  252-254, 258-259, 279
with Rupert Brooke, in aftermath
  of Battle of Antwerp, 276
ties to T. E. Lawrence, 97, 98
ties with Lady Ottoline Morrell,
  253, 262-263
Winston Churchill's private
  secretary, xvii-xviii, 44, 63, 97,
  150, 254, 268-269

Morrell, Lady Ottoline
home, Garsington Manor, near
  Oxford, xvii, 254, 261-265
infatuation with Siegfried
  Sassoon and his 1917 anti-
  war letter, xv, 129, 185, 254,
  264-265
knows Sir Edward Marsh, 253
love affair with writer and
  philosopher Bertrand Russell,
  43, 120, 125, 263-265
marriage to Philip Morrell, 264
salon life in London and Oxford,
  262-265

Owen, Wilfred
burial site in Ors Communal
  Cemetery, 248-250
at Craiglockhart with Sassoon,
  183-188
death along Sambre-Oise canal
  near Ors, 246-250
develops as a poet, 213-214

early days near Liverpool and
  Shrewsbury, xvi, 209-212,
  247
enlistment in British Army,
  Manchester Regiment, 215-
  216
La Maison forestière à Ors
  (Wilfred Owen House),
  France, 242-247
last letter to his mother, 244-245
meets Robert Graves, 187
mentioned unfavorably in
  Graves, 57
route of last 1918 march across
  France, 219, 236-245
wins Military Cross in northern
  France, 239-241

Sassoon, Siegfried
on 1918 Armistice Day in
  London, 205-206
at Battle of Arras, 54, 152, 177
  182, 189-191
conversion to Catholicism and
  burial at Mells, 33, 35-36,
  116
critical of Robert Graves' war
  memoirs, 57-60
death of T. E. Lawrence, 2, 10
fighting at Mametz Wood, on
  the Somme, 199-203
fighting in the trenches of
  Western Front, 42-45
friendship with Lady Ottoline
  Morrell, 185, 263-265
friendship with T. E. Lawrence,
  48-50

INDEX

letter statement denouncing the war, x, 36, 43-44, 59, 129, 185, 264-265
letters from Wilfred Owen, 240 241
meets Wilfred Owen while at Craiglockhart Hospital, xviii, 44, 183-188, 208-209, 216
memoirs of, 32, 37-41, 51-55
military service with Robert Graves, 57-60, 165-167, 171-173
poem on death of fellow officer David Thomas, 155, 227-228, 248-250
postwar life, 46-50
postwar marriage, 46-47
sexuality, 46-50
Somme battles, 219, 227-229
spared firing squad by Winston Churchill, x, xvii, 44, 184, 269
visits at Craiglockhart by Robert Graves, 183-188

www.ingramcontent.com/pod-product-compliance
Lightning Source LLC
Chambersburg PA
CBHW020517080526
44583CB00013B/636